Phonics for P
Special Educational Needs

Book 1: Building Basics

Phonics for Pupils with Special Educational Needs is a complete, structured, multisensory programme for teaching reading and spelling, making it fun and accessible for all. This fantastic seven-part resource offers a refreshingly simple approach to the teaching of phonics, alongside activities to develop auditory and visual perceptual skills. Specifically designed to meet the needs of pupils of any age with special educational needs, the books break down phonics into manageable core elements and provide a huge wealth of resources to support teachers in teaching reading and spelling.

Book 1: Building Basics introduces basic sounds and explores their relationship with letters. It focuses on sounds and letters where there is a simple 1:1 correspondence between the two, and explores the sounds in simple words that follow the pattern of vowel-consonant or consonant-vowel-consonant. Sounds are grouped into seven sets, with each set containing more than 50 engaging activities, including: sound story, dynamic blending, reading race, spot the word and spelling challenge. Thorough guidance is provided on how to deliver each activity, as well as a lesson planner template, handy word lists and posters for teachers and teaching assistants to use to support learning.

Each book in the series gradually builds on children's understanding of sounds and letters and provides scaffolded support for children to learn about every sound in the English language. Offering tried and tested material which can be photocopied for each use, this is an invaluable resource to simplify phonics teaching for teachers and teaching assistants and provide fun new ways of learning phonics for all children.

Ann Sullivan is an educational consultant and trainer. Having gained experience of teaching in mainstream primary classrooms and in secondary learning support departments, she went on to become a high school SENCO. The move to specialist education seemed natural and for nine years she worked as an outreach/advisory teacher based at a specialist support school, providing advice, support and training to staff in mainstream schools to enable them to meet the needs of their pupils with SEND. She became a Specialist Leader in Education in 2017. Ann has made it her career's work to explore the best ways of teaching young people to read, spell and write effectively, leading her to develop these resources, which she has tested in a variety of mainstream and special schools.

Phonics for Pupils with Special Educational Needs

This fantastic seven-part resource offers an innovative and refreshingly simple approach to the teaching of phonics that is specifically designed to meet the needs of pupils with special educational needs. The books strip phonics down into manageable core elements and provide a wealth of resources to support teachers in teaching reading and spelling. They systematically take the pupil through incremental steps and help them to learn about and thoroughly understand all of the sounds in the English language.

Other resources in *Phonics for Pupils with Special Educational Needs*

Book 1: Building Basics	**Introducing Sounds and Letters**	
Book 2: Building Words	**Working on Word Structure with Basic Sounds**	
Book 3: Sound by Sound Part 1	**Discovering the Sounds**	
Book 4: Sound by Sound Part 2	**Investigating the Sounds**	
Book 5: Sound by Sound Part 3	**Exploring the Sounds**	
Book 6: Sound by Sound Part 4	**Surveying the Sounds**	
Book 7: Multisyllable Magic	**Revising the Main Sounds and Working on 2, 3 and 4 Syllable Words**	

Phonics for Pupils with Special Educational Needs

Book 1: Building Basics

Introducing Sounds and Letters

Ann Sullivan

Routledge
Taylor & Francis Group
LONDON AND NEW YORK

First published 2019
by Routledge
2 Park Square, Milton Park, Abingdon, Oxon OX14 4RN

and by Routledge
711 Third Avenue, New York, NY 10017

Routledge is an imprint of the Taylor & Francis Group, an informa business

British Library Cataloguing-in-Publication Data
A catalogue record for this book is available from the British Library

Library of Congress Cataloging-in-Publication Data
Names: Sullivan, Ann (Educational consultant) author.
Title: Phonics for pupils with special educational needs / Ann Sullivan.
Description: Abingdon, Oxon ; New York, NY : Routledge, 2019–
Identifiers: LCCN 2018015561 (print) | LCCN 2018033657 (ebook) | ISBN 9781351040303 (ebook) | ISBN 9781138488373 (book 1) | ISBN 9781351040303 (book 1 : ebk) | ISBN 9781138488434 (book 3) | ISBN 9781351040181 (book 3 : ebk) | ISBN 9781138313583 (book 5) | ISBN 9780429457555 (book 5 : ebk) | ISBN 9781138313637 (book 6) | ISBN 9780429457517 (book 6 : ebk) | ISBN 9781138313682 (book 7) | ISBN 9780429457487 (book 7 : ebk)
Subjects: LCSH: Reading—Phonetic method. | Reading disability. | Special education.
Classification: LCC LB1573.3 (ebook) | LCC LB1573.3 .S85 2019 (print) | DDC 372.46/5—dc23
LC record available at https://lccn.loc.gov/2018015561

ISBN: 978-1-138-48837-3 (pbk)
ISBN: 978-1-351-04030-3 (ebk)

Typeset in VAG Rounded
by Apex CoVantage, LLC

To Matthew, Ruth and Tom

Contents

Introduction

Phonics is the established method for teaching reading and spelling in schools, but many pupils with special educational needs find conventional phonics programmes and schemes difficult to access and so struggle to find success.

Pupils with special educational needs require a clear and consistent, multisensory approach to phonics and the teaching of reading and spelling. A programme should give them the opportunity to systematically and thoroughly explore all sounds and letters, gradually building up their understanding and knowledge of how the written English language works so that they are able to apply these when reading and spelling words. They also require specific instructional techniques to develop and master key reading and spelling skills and be given the opportunity to work at a pace appropriate to their individual needs.

Phonics for Pupils with Special Educational Needs is a complete programme, made up of seven books, which simplifies the way written language is presented to the child, demystifying phonics to make it accessible and fun. The programme is multisensory, systematic, logical, thorough and cumulative in its approach, taking the child from their first encounter with sounds and letters through to managing and using multisyllable words.

Many pupils with special educational needs have underlying difficulties with auditory and visual perception and processing, which often goes unrecognised. Difficulties processing auditory and visual information will have a direct impact on reading and spelling acquisition, as written English is essentially a cipher or code that converts speech sounds into visual figures for spelling and vice versa for reading. The cipher is dependent on an individual being able to work with and interpret sounds and symbols; yet processing auditory and visual information may be the very things that a pupil finds difficult to do. Pupils with perceptual difficulties require access to materials that work to develop and improve these auditory and visual skills in the context of the sounds and letters they are learning. Built into the *Phonics for Pupils with Special Educational Needs* programme are worksheets, resources and activities which support the development of underlying auditory and visual skills.

Difficulties with visual perception and processing will also impact on the child's ability to easily access teaching materials presented to them. For this reason, the worksheets, resources and activities in *Phonics for Pupils with Special Educational Needs* are simple in format, uncluttered and with a simple to follow linear progression.

Book 1 Building Basics: Introducing Sounds and Letters

This book focuses on simple **sounds** (speech sounds or phonemes) in words and explores the relationship between each sound and, in most cases, a single **letter**.

In Book 1, the pupil:

- learns an important concept or idea about the English language; that letters are ***symbols*** or ***pictures*** that ***represent*** speech sounds in spoken words;
- is gradually introduced to the basic sounds and the single letters that represent them;
- learns to manage these sounds in simple VC and CVC words (V = vowel, C = consonant);
- is taught the key reading and spelling skills of blending, segmenting and phoneme manipulation;
- learns a dynamic blending strategy for reading words;
- learns a sequential segmenting strategy for spelling words;
- develops auditory perceptual and processing skills in relation to the sounds introduced;
- develops visual perceptual and processing skills in relation to the letters introduced;
- experiences reading and spelling words at single word and sentence level and
- experiences reading at text level.

Book 2 develops the pupil's ability to work with these sounds in words with a more complex structure: VCC, CVCC, CCVC and CCVCC+ words. Books 3–6 introduce and systematically explore the more complex sounds in the English language and Book 7 revises and explores all the sounds in the context of 2, 3 and 4 syllable words and works on suffixes.

Working through the programme

It is strongly recommended that anyone delivering the programme reads through the teaching notes in the 'Working through the programme' section of this book, where the programme is explained in detail and specific techniques are described and explained.

Teaching materials

Most of the resources in the programme have instructions on delivery of the activity or worksheet on the sheet itself to provide a helpful prompt for teachers and teaching assistants. A few activities only have instructions written in the 'Working through the programme' section of this book and teachers and teaching assistants should make themselves familiar with the details of these.

All the resources in the programme are designed to have a simple format and presentation to support access for pupils with visual perceptual difficulties. As a result, they are age neutral and so are suitable for pupils of a wide age range; primary, secondary and post 16.

Phonics for Pupils with Special Educational Needs is suitable for pupils in mainstream and specialist school settings.

Planning and delivery

A simple to use planning sheet enables teachers and teaching assistants to plan teaching sessions by selecting from the menu of available programme activities, ensuring an overall even and complete coverage of skills, concepts and knowledge. The planning sheet also enables staff to track pupil progression thorough the programme.

A child or group of children can work through the programme at a pace that is appropriate for them or their peer group.

Working through the programme

Starting out

Before beginning to work through the programme with a child or a group of children, it is important for teachers and teaching assistants to read through this introductory section to familiarise themselves with the programme's structure and how it works, as well as the specific instructional techniques, resources and activities.

This section covers **the things you need to know about and understand before you start**:

- the ideas or concepts which underpin the structure of written English;
- the skills that children need to master to be able to work with sounds and letters / letter combinations: blending, segmenting and phoneme manipulation;
- the body of knowledge children need to know, remember and recall and
- visual and auditory perception and processing related to working with sounds and letters.

It covers **how to teach the programme** at Book 1 level:

- the teaching order of sounds,
- introducing sounds and letters,
- supporting auditory processing of sounds (hearing and accessing sounds),
- supporting visual processing of letters (seeing and accessing letters),
- teaching the concepts to the child,
- teaching the skills to the child and
- building up the child's knowledge of sounds and letters.

It also covers **how to organise delivery of the programme**:

- structuring a teaching session and
- planning and progression.

Note that in the explanations which follow, sounds are written in speech marks, e.g. 's' 'l' 'ch' and letters / letter combinations are written in bold, e.g. ***s l ch tch*** *etc.*

The written English language – an overview

Written language developed many years ago because people realised they needed to fix information in a form that remained constant over time. In this way information could be passed on easily, without people having to always speak directly to each other. Writing developed as a way of storing information, carrying messages and sharing news and stories.

Experiments in drawing pictures to represent information proved ineffective as pictures can be interpreted in so many ways and are open to an individual's interpretation. However, people soon realised that there is one characteristic of the spoken word that could be exploited to create a permanent, fixed visual representation of the information.

The spoken word is made up of speech sounds (or phonemes). When we say any word, we must be consistent with the sounds we use and the order we say them for us to convey the intended meaning.

If I say the sounds 'c' 'a' 't' together to make a word, then you think of a furry pet. If I change the first sound to 'h' then the meaning changes and you think of something quite different. Written English capitalises on this consistency and uses letters as ***symbols*** to, one by one, represent ***individual speech sounds***. In other words, letters are a written form of spoken sounds.

This is the first idea or concept that children need to understand to be able to read and spell but there are three more: all are explained below.

The concepts – how the written word is put together

1. **Letters represent sounds**

   In the written word the letters represent the speech sounds of the spoken word.

   For example, the word dog has three sounds in it, 'd' 'o' 'g' which are represented by the three letters:

   d o g.

   This concept is introduced in Book 1 of the programme.

   In *Phonics for Pupils with Special Educational Needs*, letters are referred to as '***sound spellings***'. This label describes letters in terms of their function. In other words, a ***sound*** is represented in a written form when we ***spell*** / write words. It gives the teacher a simple term that describes single letters and, more importantly, also describes combinations of letters, which appear later in the programme. This term also reinforces the sound to symbol relationship, '***sound > spelling***' and the term is easy for children to understand and remember.

2. Sound spellings can be one letter or more

Some of the sound spellings we use are made up of just one letter, like those in dog, but many are made up of several letters which, in combination, act as a single unit within the word, together representing one sound.

For example, **sh** is the sound spelling for the sound 'sh' in the word **sh**op and **th** is the sound spelling for the sound 'th' in the word mo**th**. **sh** and **th** are sound spellings that are made up of two letters, but some sound spellings are made up of three or even four letters e.g. **igh** representing 'i-e' in the word n**igh**t and **ough** representing 'o-e' in the word d**ough**.

This concept is introduced in Book 3 of the programme.

3. Sounds can be represented by more than just one sound spelling

Many sounds can be represented in more than just one way i.e. by more than one sound spelling.

For example: b**oa**t t**oe** s**o** gr**ow** c**o**d**e** th**ough**

These all have an 'o-e' sound in but it is written differently in each word, using the sound spellings:

oa, oe, o, ow, o-e and **ough**, respectively.

This concept is introduced in Book 3 where the focus is working on only **one sound at a time** and enabling the child to discover ***all*** the ways of representing that sound. Time is given to experience and explore all the sound spellings at word and sentence level before moving on to the next sound in the book.

4. Some sound spellings can represent more than one sound

Certain sound spellings can be used to represent one sound in one word but a different sound in another word.

For example: gr**ow** br**ow**n

The sound spelling **ow** is in both words but in the first it represents an 'o-e' sound and in the second it represents an 'ow' sound.

This concept is introduced in Book 4 of the programme.

Phonics for Pupils with Special Educational Needs addresses this at appropriate points in the programme for key sound spellings, giving the child the opportunity to explore all the sounds that these sound spellings can represent.

To be able to read and spell effectively, children need to understand these four concepts. *Phonics for Pupils with Special Educational Needs* presents children with the opportunity to explore them for each sound in English over the seven books in the programme.

At this point it is important to be aware that the child's understanding of these concepts will be implicit rather than explicit. This means that they will have processed their experiences of sounds, sound spellings and words and reached an unconscious understanding about the concepts. The programme does not demand that the child talks about or explains the concepts but instead they demonstrate their understanding by the way they respond to sounds, sound spellings and words during teaching sessions and whenever they are reading or writing.

This book, Book 1 of the series, primarily deals with the first concept but touches on the third when working on the sound 'k' and two of the sound spellings that represent it: **c** and **k**. Since the sound spellings **c** and **k** are very common in basic CVC words, it is not possible to avoid them and so dealing with the third concept is necessary at this stage. However, introduction of the third way of representing 'k', **ck**, is delayed until Book 3, when the sound 'k' is revisited, so as to minimise the cognitive load on the child. Concepts 2, 3 and 4 are studied in greater depth in Book 3 onwards.

The skills – what we do with the sounds and sound spellings

As well as understanding these four concepts, children also need to be able to ***work with*** the sounds and sound spellings to read or spell words. Like all skills, these need to be taught and practised to achieve mastery. The skills needed to be able to read and spell are:

1. **Blending** – to be able to push speech sounds together to make a meaningful word. This skill relates directly to reading.
2. **Segmenting** – to be able to break up words into all the separate speech sounds that make up that word, in the right order. This skill relates directly to spelling.
3. **Phoneme manipulation** – to be able to slide speech sounds in and out of words. This skill relates to both reading and spelling.

Developing an understanding of how the English language is put together and practising these important skills starts on day one of the programme and continues right the way through to mastery.

The knowledge – what we need to know, remember and recall

Skills and concepts are not the only things children need to learn to be able to read and spell effectively. They also need a good working knowledge of the sounds and sound spellings. Specifically, they need to know the relationship between the two and this is something that is gradually and cumulatively built up as the child works through this programme.

There are around 140 sound spellings representing the 40 *or so* sounds we use (*regional differences influence exactly how many sounds we perceive in words with variation from 40–42*).

At the end of this section there are two posters that show all the sounds and their main sound spellings which you may find helpful.

Step by step and sound by sound, *Phonics for Pupils with Special Educational Needs* works through all the sounds and all their sound spellings, guides the child to understand how written language is put together and supports them to master the skills needed to become fluent readers and spellers.

Automaticity

At first reading may be a slow process of working through a word, sound spelling by sound spelling, but with experience, repetition and practice the child achieves 'automaticity'. Automaticity happens when all the things the child has experienced and learned come together to enable them to look at a written word, process it rapidly and without apparent effort simply say the word. As competent adult readers we have achieved this automaticity and can no longer remember just how we learned to read.

The activities and techniques in *Phonics for Pupils with Special Educational Needs* are designed to provide the child with this experience, repetition and practice with the aim of children achieving reading and spelling automaticity.

Book 1 Building Basics: Introducing Sounds and Letters

In Book 1 the basic sound by sound spelling relationship is introduced for simple sounds, mostly represented by a single sound spelling made up of one letter. Sounds are grouped into seven sets, focusing on VC words (vowel consonant words such as **at, in, up** etc) and CVC words (consonant vowel consonant words such as **sat, him, tin** etc), as follows:

V = vowel   C = consonant

Set 1:	s a t p
Set 2:	i n m d
Set 3:	g o c k
Set 4:	e u r
Set 5:	h b f l
Set 6:	j v w x
Set 7:	y z

The teaching order of sounds and progression of the programme is shown in Table 1.

Table 1 The teaching order of sounds in *Phonics for Pupils with Special Educational Needs*

***Phonics for Pupils with Special Educational Needs* teaching order**			
Book	**Sounds**	**Word structure**	**Skills**
1 Building Basics: Introducing Sounds and Letters Focus: Basic sounds and their relationship with letters	s a t p	VC and CVC words	Blending, Segmenting & Phoneme Manipulation Teaching to Mastery
	i n m d		
	g o c k		
	e u r		
	h b f l		
	j v w x		
	y z		
2 Building Words: Working on Word Structure with Basic Sounds Focus: Increasingly complex word structure	All the sounds from Book 1	VCC words	
		CVCC words	
		CCVC words	
		CCVCC+ words	
		CAPITALS	
3 Sound by Sound Part 1: Discovering the Sounds Focus: Complex sounds and their relationship with letters and letter combinations	sh	Mixed VC CVC VCC CVCC CCVC CCVCC+ words	
	th		
	ch		
	k		
	qu		
	ng		
	f		
	l		
	s		
4 Sound by Sound Part 2: Investigating the Sounds Focus: Complex sounds and their relationship with letters and letter combinations	o-e		
	z		
	ee		
	a-e		
	er		
	e		
	ow		
5 Sound by Sound Part 3: Exploring the Sounds Focus: Complex sounds and their relationship with letters and letter combinations	oy		
	oo		
	u		
	i-e		
	aw		
	air		
	ar		
6 Sound by Sound Part 4: Surveying the Sounds Focus: Complex sounds and their relationship with letters and letter combinations	s (advanced)		
	l (advanced)		
	b and d (advanced)		
	o		
	i		
	u-e		
	Miscellaneous Consonants		

Phonics for Pupils with Special Educational Needs teaching order			
Book	**Sounds**	**Word structure**	**Skills**
7 Multisyllable Magic: Revising the Main Sounds and Working on 2, 3 and 4 Syllable Words Focus: Reading and spelling 2 syllable words and revising the main sounds. Reading and spelling 3 and 4 syllable words and words with key suffixes.	Revision of o-e	2 syllable words	
	Revision of ee		
	Revision of a-e		
	Revision of er		
	Revision of e		
	Revision of ow		
	Revision of oy		
	Revision of oo		
	Revision of u		
	Revision of i-e		
	Revision of aw		
	Revision of air		
	Revision of ar		
	Revision of o	3 and 4 syllable words	
	Revision of i		
	Revision of u-e		
	Suffixes		

Working with sounds

When working with a child on any reading and spelling activity it is important to be aware of the need to be careful about our personal articulation of the sounds as we are modelling our pronunciation for the child to copy and learn. When we say individual sounds to children it is easy to fall into the trap of saying them inaccurately or 'untidily'. Indeed, many of us were taught to say the sound that way when we were at school; but things have changed.

For example, the sound 'm' is often mispronounced as a 'muh' sound rather than a pure 'mmm'. This is unhelpful for the child who needs to hear the precise sound in order to be able to deal with it when reading and spelling words. The apparent addition of an 'uh' sound after the 'm' can easily result in confusion and lead to reading and spelling errors. So, we must make a conscious effort to say the sounds clearly and accurately. We also need to support the child to always say 'tidy' sounds themselves and gently correct them if necessary.

Be aware that we are not trying to change the way pupils speak. We are giving them as good a chance as possible to hear and access sounds in words (whatever their natural regional variations are) to increase their success with reading and spelling.

Table 2 goes some way to explain some of the pitfalls encountered when working with sounds but it may be helpful to access an audio or video file of correct 'phonics' pronunciation, many of which are readily available on the internet.

Table 2 Simple speech sounds and strategies for accurate articulation

Sounds	Strategy	Difficulties
b c/k d g j t ch	Be aware of the need to *gently* 'clip' these sounds when speaking and avoid the 'uh' on the end. When reading a word, it is more difficult to blend from these sounds into the next so make sure you encourage the child to say the sound and rapidly move on to the next sound.	Short, clipped sounds – very easy to add an untidy 'uh' sound at the end e.g. 'buh' rather than 'b'.
f l m n r s v z sh th ng	Wonderful sounds that can go on for a long time e.g. 'mmmmmmmmm'. Make the most of these sounds when playing the blending games with the child.	
h p	Practise saying these sounds in a breathy way rather than 'huh' and 'puh'.	Breathy sounds – very easy to add an untidy 'uh' sound at the end e.g. 'huh' rather than 'h'.
a e i o u a-e ee i-e o-e u-e er ow oy oo aw air ar	These are vowel sounds and are quite flexible and can be spoken for an extended time for emphasis.	If overextended, these can become distorted e.g. with the sound 'ee' there is a tendency to add a 'y' sound at the end.
y z	Practise saying them clearly. A good strategy is to start to say a word containing the sound e.g. yes. Start to say it but stop without saying the 'e' 's' part of the word. In this way you say the pure 'y' sound.	Treat very carefully. These are always followed by another sound in words e.g. yes, wet. When we say them on their own we tend to say 'yuh' and 'wuh'.

Developing sensory perception and processing skills

An aspect of learning to read and spell which is frequently overlooked is the role of the child's sensory perceptual and processing abilities.

We are surrounded by things in our environment that stimulate our senses. We notice and respond to things we see, hear, touch, taste and smell. How our body and brain receive this information is termed perception, and how the brain interprets, organises, stores and responds to these stimuli is termed processing.

One way we perceive the world is through the things we hear; this is termed auditory perception and processing. Auditory perception does not relate to 'how well our ears work' but how we perceive and respond to the things we hear. Individuals with auditory perceptual difficulties may appear to 'hear things differently' from others and this may affect their ability to process verbal information. Indeed, children with these difficulties are likely to struggle with attention and listening, following verbal instructions and keeping up with teacher explanations. Auditory perception and processing can be separated into different aspects, including: auditory discrimination, auditory fusion, auditory memory, auditory sequential memory and auditory tracking, all of which are explored in activities within this programme. More specifically there is an aspect of auditory processing that relates to the processing of speech sounds or phonemes within words. This is called phonological processing, and children with difficulties in this area are likely to struggle with acquiring age appropriate reading and spelling skills.

In this book there are activities and worksheets for each of the seven sets of sounds which work on and develop the child's auditory perception and processing of simple speech sounds or phonological processing.

These are **Activities 1–7 Sound target – Story sheet, Sound target – Tongue twister fun, Odd one out, What sound am I? Same or different? How many did you hear? What comes next?** Instructions for these activities are at the top of the individual sheets, and learning objectives are as follows:

Activity	Learning objectives
1 Sound target story	**Auditory attention and tracking**: Actively listen to and follow to the end auditory information in the form of a story. **Phonological discrimination**: Discriminate between different sounds and identify words that start with a target sound.
2 Tongue twister fun	**Auditory attention and tracking**: Actively listen to and follow to the end auditory information in the form of a tongue twister. **Auditory sequential memory**: Remember and recall verbally a sequence of words heard.
3 Odd one out	**Auditory attention and tracking**: Actively listen to and follow to the end auditory information in the form of a list of words. **Phonological discrimination**: Discriminate between different sounds, identify the starting sound of words and identify which word has a different target sound.
4 What sound am I?	**Auditory attention and tracking**: Actively listen to and follow to the end auditory information in the form of a list of words. **Phonological discrimination**: Discriminate between different sounds and identify the starting sound of words. **Auditory recall memory**: Remember and recall verbally a word heard.
5 Same or different?	**Auditory attention and tracking**: Actively listen to and follow to the end auditory information in the form of word pairs. **Phonological discrimination**: Discriminate between different sounds, identify the starting sound of words and identify whether they are the same or different.
6 How many did you hear?	**Phonological and auditory fusion**: Recognise gaps between sounds and words.

Activity	Learning objectives
7 What comes next?	**Auditory attention and tracking**: Actively listen to and follow to the end auditory information in the form of a sequence of sounds. **Phonological sequential memory**: Remember and recall a sequence of sounds heard. **Phonological and auditory processing**: Identify patterns within the sounds and identify the sound which would come next in the sequence.

Children can work on these auditory activities **before, as well as after**, they are introduced to the sound spellings that represent them, as these activities have no visual component.

Another way we perceive the world is visually, using our eyes to see; this is termed visual perception. Visual perception does not relate to 'how well our eyes work' but how we perceive and respond to the things we see. Individuals with visual perceptual difficulties may appear to 'see the world differently' from others and this may affect their ability to process visual figures, shapes and forms in their environment. Since letters are visual figures, children with underlying visual perceptual and processing difficulties are likely to struggle to get to grips with letters and words for reading and spelling. Visual perception can be separated into different aspects, including: visual discrimination, spatial relationships, visual memory, visual sequential memory, visual closure, form constancy and visual tracking, all of which are explored within the programme.

In this book there are activities and worksheets for each of the seven sets of sounds which work on and develop the child's visual perception and processing of simple sound spellings.

These are **Activities 11–20 Sound spelling tracker, Spot the sound spelling, Remembering sound spellings, Colour the picture, Which Is the same? Bits missing, Busy sound spellings, Where Am I? Remembering lots of sound spellings, Tracking sound spellings.** Instructions for these activities are at the top of the individual sheets, and learning objectives are as follows:

Activity	Learning objectives
11 Sound spelling tracker	**Tracking**: Visually track, left to right, through a list of sound spellings. **Visual discrimination**: Discriminate between visually similar sound spellings to identify a target sound spelling.
12 Spot the sound spelling	**Visual discrimination**: Discriminate between visually similar sound spellings to identify a target sound spelling.
13 Remembering sound spellings	**Visual memory**: Recall and identify a single sound spelling from memory.
14 Colour the picture	**Visual discrimination**: Discriminate between visually similar sound spellings to identify a target sound spelling.
15 Which is the same?	**Form constancy**: Generalise the form of sound spellings. Recognise sound spellings when not in a typical presentation.

16 Bits missing	**Visual closure**: Identify sound spellings from a visually incomplete picture.
17 Busy sound spellings	**Figure ground**: Identify sound spellings from a visually complex presentation.
18 Where am I?	**Spatial relations**: Perceive the position / spatial orientation of sound spellings on the page. Accurately reproduce sound spellings on the page to match a given position / spatial orientation.
19 Remembering lots of sound spellings	**Visual sequential memory**: Remember and recall a sequence of sound spellings. Complete a sequence of sound spellings.
20 Tracking sound spellings	**Tracking**: Visually track, left to right, through a list of sound spellings. **Visual discrimination**: Discriminate between visually similar forms to isolate and identify target sound spellings.

Children should work on these visual activities **after** the sounds and sound spellings have been introduced, as described later in this chapter.

A third way we perceive the world is through the movements our bodies make to interact with our environment. This is our kinaesthetic sense and in relation to reading and spelling refers to the fine movements our fingers, wrist, hand, arm and shoulder make to form the letters in written words.

Children with special educational needs benefit from experiencing a variety of sensory experiences when learning something new. When learning to write a sound spelling, providing different sensory experiences not only enables the child to learn the movement pattern associated with forming the sound spelling but also reinforces the relationship between the sound and the sound spelling.

Here are some different experiences you could provide for the child to write the sound spellings. During each activity, encourage the child to **say the corresponding sound at the same time as writing the sound spelling – Activity 10 Sensory writing.**

Consider using a variety of:

- substrates to write in e.g. write in sand, shaving foam, glitter, flour, gravel, syrup – use a finger then try using a stick or other writing tool for a different type of sensory feedback;
- writing surfaces e.g. magnetic or gel board, blackboard, textured paper, whiteboard, tablet (using drawing apps);
- writing tools e.g. thin pencil, thick pencil, biro, felt tip pen, ink, crayon, chalk, paint on brush, paint on finger, vibrating pen, light up pen, stylus on tablet;
- textured sound spellings – finger tracing 'letter' shape e.g. sandpaper letters, wooden letters, gel letters, raised texture letters, foam letters;
- sound spelling templates e.g. writing over feint letters, dotted letters, writing letters in guidelines, tracing letters;

- gross (large) motor movements e.g. forming big letters in the air, writing big letters on a large whiteboard or blackboard, using both sides of a big double-sided blackboard for mirrored bilateral movements to form letters, moving their body into the shape of the letter;
- sensory input e.g. adult writing the letter on the child's back or forearm without them seeing, investigating and identifying letters in a feely bag, writing with scented pens etc.

The child could also explore all of the above with 'eyes closed'. This removes the visual component of the activity and requires the child to focus entirely on their kinaesthetic sense. This helps to develop a 'movement' or 'muscle' memory for forming the letter and remembering its shape.

Activity 21 Writing the sound spellings works specifically on conventional 'pen and paper' sound spelling formation. Instructions are given at the top of the individual sheet.

The learning objectives for Activities 10 and 21 are as follows:

Activity	Learning objectives
10 Sensory writing	**Letter formation**: Accurately form the letter that makes up a sound spelling **Kinaesthetic awareness**: Develop the 'muscle memory' associated with formation of target sound spellings.
21 Writing the sound spellings	**Letter formation**: Form the letter that makes up a sound spelling with: accuracy, size consistency size and spatial awareness of the line. **Kinaesthetic awareness**: Develop the 'muscle memory' associated with formation of target sound spellings.

Multisensory writing strategy

Phonics for Pupils with Special Educational Needs has an overarching multisensory approach to teaching which integrates visual, auditory and kinaesthetic processing while enhancing and supporting learning and acquisition of skills.

From this point on, whenever the child forms or writes a sound spelling, require them to **ALWAYS *say the associated sound at the same time as writing it***. This applies to when writing single sound spellings or when writing a sequence of sound spellings to make a word.

In this way all the senses are engaged:

- the **visual** sense (seeing the sound spelling form),
- the **auditory** sense (hearing the sound) and
- the **kinaesthetic** sense (feeling the specific movement associated with forming the sound spelling shape).

The three sensory experiences are simultaneously processed, making connections in the brain between the different aspects of the information and maximising the child's chance of remembering it.

Introducing the sounds and their sound spellings

When introducing a new set of sounds and sound spellings you may wish to introduce a sound a day until all the sounds in the set have been covered or you may wish to introduce all the sounds on the same day. Which of these options you choose will depend on the learning needs of the children you are teaching, particularly their ability to recall visual and auditory information.

Introducing each sound is simply a matter of presenting a sound spelling visually and telling the children what sound it represents. A more child-friendly way of describing this is to say that the sound spelling is a 'picture of the sound'. In this way you are presenting the visual and auditory information associated with each sound spelling and it is this information that children need to remember and use in their reading and spelling.

So, for example, we might introduce a new sound in this way, using the sound spelling cards in the programme **Activity 8 Sound spelling cards**:

Visual "Look at this". **s**

Auditory "This is a picture of the sound 's'".

Introducing the kinaesthetic sense alongside the visual and auditory aspects helps to reinforce the association between visual figure (sound spelling) and auditory information (sound).

So, we could add a third component to our introduction:

Kinaesthetic "When we want to write a word with the 's' **sound** in it we have to draw this picture to **spell** the sound. It is a **sound spelling** for the sound 's'. Let's draw this sound spelling together".
Teacher and child either draw the shape in the air (teacher models and supports the child's movement) or trace a template provided.

In this way the child will be introduced to the sounds in a set and their sound spellings, but they will require lots and lots of experience of them to retain the necessary information to begin to use sound spellings and sounds to support their reading and spelling.

The sound spelling cards can be used to carry out simple matching exercises, remembering to work in both directions: sound > sound spelling and sound spelling > sound.

A well-established children's favourite, which reinforces the relationship between the sound and the sound spelling, is **Activity 9, Sound spelling bingo**, which has a variety of presentations, as described on the sheets.

Tackling the 'k' sound

In Book 1, basic sounds are introduced and for the majority of these a single sound spelling is learned. The focus of the book is the first concept, 'Letters represent sounds' and keeps things simple for the children to understand.

There is one sound, however, that needs to be considered carefully at this stage and that is the sound 'k'.

This sound can be represented in more than one way, that is with the sound spellings: **c** and **k**. Since these two sound spellings appear in many simple, commonly used CVC words, it is important for the child to be able to work with both of them and so it is necessary to briefly consider that third concept at this stage. This is the first (although not the last) time the child experiences concept 3, 'Some sounds are represented by more than one sound spelling'.

Activity 8a Investigating the sound 'k' requires the child to look at a selection of words all containing the sound 'k' and sort them into two lists based on their 'k' sound spellings; that is whether they have a **c** or **k** sound spelling. This activity is only required in set 3 of this book although the third concept is more fully explored in Book 3 onwards with more complex sounds. Instructions are given at the top of the sheet.

The learning objectives for the activities described are as follows:

Activity	Learning objectives
8 Sound spelling cards	Identify and match the appropriate sound spelling to its sound. identify and match the appropriate sound to its sound spelling.
8a Investigating a sound	Identify all the sound spellings that represent the target sound.
9 Sound spelling bingo	Identify and match the appropriate sound spelling to its sound.

A focus on b and d

By Set 5, the child has investigated the sounds 'b' and 'd' and discovered their sound spellings **b** and **d**. These two sound spellings are commonly confused by children with visual perceptual difficulties causing difficulties with reading and spelling words. For this reason, there are additional activities in Set 5 that focus solely on **b** and **d** so that the child has an opportunity to explore the properties of these visual figures side by side.

As well as developing the child's understanding of sounds and sound spellings, the programme also teaches and develops the key skills of blending, segmenting and phoneme manipulation.

Skill 1 – blending for reading

Blending is the ability to push sounds together to make a word and is a key skill in reading. It is important that blending is taught as an active or ***dynamic*** process – pushing the sounds together as the child moves through the word and listening for the word forming.

The dynamic blending technique

- When the child is reading a word, ask them to say the sounds as you simultaneously move your pen or finger underneath or above the word (without obscuring the letters) so that you are indicating which sound spellings to think about.
- Have the child say the sounds in a ***dynamic*** blended fashion (connecting the sounds and pushing them together).

  Rather than the child saying separate sounds quickly one after the other, e.g. 'm' 'a' 'n', have the child actively push the sounds into each other without a gap, e.g. 'mmaaann'. In this way the child simply has to listen and then say the word they heard forming. It may be helpful to point out to the child that it sounds like we are saying the word very slowly and ask them what the word would be if we speeded it up.

  Be aware of the need to say the sounds clearly and purely. Some sounds are more difficult to blend as they are clipped, e.g. 'b', 'p', 't', 'd' etc. When reading words with these sounds in you will have to make sure the child says the sound and very rapidly moves on to the next sound. This avoids the child distorting the clipped sound; if it takes too long they are forced to artificially stretch it out before blending it into the next.
- Model this dynamic blending technique for the child.
- When working on any task with the child be aware of the need to gently correct their blending technique and encourage them to actively push the sounds together, modelling the technique if necessary.

Blending activities

A place to read (Activity 22)

Even before starting on set 1 work, the 'A place to read' activity helps to introduce the dynamic blending technique, concentrating on phonological processing without involving letters. This activity can then be continued as the child works through the sets with the teacher word list provided.

In this activity you will model the dynamic blending technique for the child, who will then tell you what word they heard forming. As you blend the sounds you will point to visual prompts (green dots) that indicate where in the word you are. The child does not have to see sound spellings to do this activity. This activity not only models a good blending technique, it teaches the child to listen for the word forming.

- Set out the appropriate 'Place to read' card in front of the child; two green dots for VC words and three for CVC words. At the end of the dots there is a picture of a mouth which prompts the child to say the word that they heard forming. Cards are found at the end of this chapter.

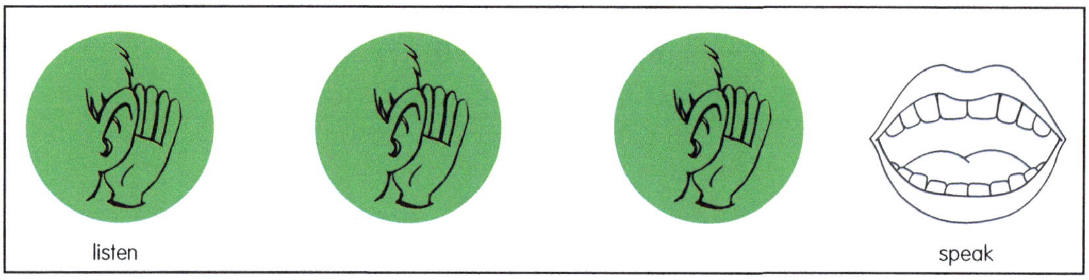

- Choose a word to present to the child from the word list in the appropriate chapter. Note that the number of meaningful words it is possible to generate is small in the early sets but gets larger as the child experiences more sounds by working through the programme. You can always include words from previous sets to refresh awareness of all the sounds.
- Say the sounds in the word one by one, pushing them together as you go. Make sure that you push the sounds into one another, 'picking up' sounds as you move through the word, e.g. if the word is **sat** then dynamic blending would sound like 'sssaaat' rather than three separate sounds 's' 'a' 't' spoken quickly.
- Point to the visual prompts on the card (green dots). Move across the page through the dots at the same time that you say the sounds. You should be pointing to the dot that corresponds to the sound in the word.

  For example:

- Ask the child to say what word they heard slowly forming. With practise you should be able to simply point to the visual prompt (the picture of the mouth) to remind them to say the word without having to say anything like, 'What is the word?' This is quite important as the very act of asking the question might interrupt their auditory processing and reduce their chances of successfully identifying the word.

Practising this activity **before** starting set 1 work will prepare the child for learning how to blend dynamically and effectively but is also useful for children who are struggling to master blending and who would continue to benefit from this activity as they progress through the sets.

Dynamic blending – Word cards (Activity 23)

There are word cards in each section of the book relating to the sounds being explored. Practise dynamic blending, as described above, to read the words on the cards. The colour of the letters gets increasingly darker as the child works through the word, acting as a visual signal that they are picking up sounds as they go and pushing them together, ready to listen for the word forming. Model this process for the child if necessary.

Blending bricks* (Activity 24)

Use some large plastic construction bricks for this activity. The teacher word list will help you choose words to use. You will need the correct number of bricks – you will need a brick for each sound in the word. Present the bricks separately with a sound spelling written on each using a non-permanent whiteboard pen (this can be wiped off), e.g.

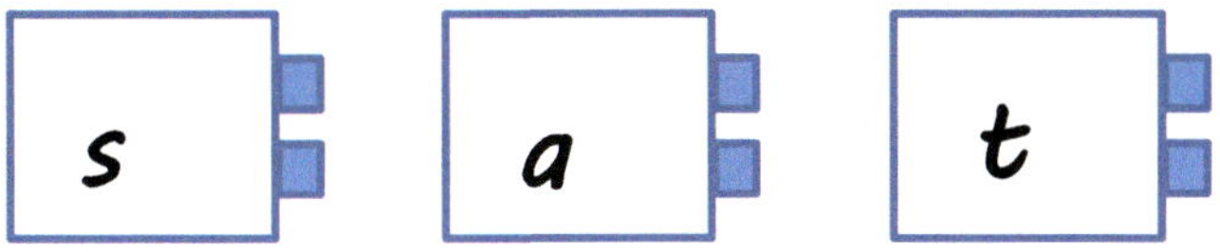

Ask the child to push the bricks together in order and say the sounds, dynamically blending as they go through the word.

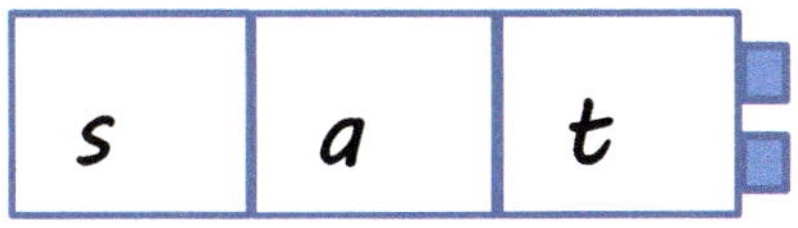

When finished, ask the child to say the word they heard forming. Model this process for the child if necessary. This activity is a concrete way of demonstrating the reading process, e.g. **three** sounds (**three** bricks) are pushed together to make **one** word (**one** solid 'wall' of bricks).

Speed blending* (Activity 25)

Using the target sound word cards, present a word to the child. You will require the child to say the sounds, dynamically blending, as you move your pen across the sound spellings and through the word. However, there are some rules the child must follow for this game. The child must say the sound for as long as the pen is under the sound spelling and is not allowed to move to the next

*Activities with an asterisk (*) do not require a worksheet.

sound until you move your pen. In this way you control the child's blending and progression through the word. As soon as the child says the last sound, they are to shout out the word, *but* as soon as they say the last sound *you* shout out the word too. Whoever is first wins.

Reveal and blend* (Activity 26)

This is an advanced blending activity and should only be carried out when the child has gained some confidence in using the dynamic blending technique.

Using the target sound word cards, present a word to the child, covering it with a blank top card. Slowly pull back the top card revealing the sound spellings one by one. Ask the child to say the sounds, dynamically blending, as each sound spelling is revealed. When finished, ask the child to say the word they heard forming. Model this process for the child if necessary.

Flippies (Activity 27)

Flippies are sets of cards that are clipped together so that when the child runs their finger along the sound spellings the individual cards flip up. This provides a kinaesthetic as well as auditory and visual experience for the child when reading the word. Follow the instructions on the sheet to make the flippies out of card.

Present the flippy to the child. Ask the child to move their finger across the cards, saying each sound (in a dynamic, blended fashion) as each sound spelling 'flips up'. When finished, ask the child to say the word they heard forming. Model this process for the child if necessary.

There is a blank template at the end of this section, so you can make your own bespoke flippies.

The learning objectives for these activities are as follows:

Activity	Learning objectives
22 A place to read	State a word formed when sounds are blended.
23 Dynamic blending target sound word cards	Use the dynamic blending strategy to read words. Read words containing the target sound represented by all possible sound spellings.
24 Blending bricks	Actively push sounds together using the dynamic blending strategy for reading words.
25 Speed blending	Use the dynamic blending strategy to read words. Rapidly say what word can be heard forming when blending.
26 Reveal and blend	Use the dynamic blending strategy to read words.
27 Flippies	Use the dynamic blending strategy to read words.

Skill 2 – sequential segmenting for spelling

Segmenting is the ability to split words up into their component sounds in sequence and is a key skill in spelling. The child needs to isolate each sound and match a sound spelling to that sound to successfully spell a word. It is important that the child is taught to segment sequentially through the word as this is how to access sounds in words to be able to spell them effectively.

The sequential segmenting technique

When supporting a child to spell a word it is helpful to provide visual prompts to indicate where to listen for a sound, e.g. draw lines or dots on a whiteboard or piece of paper.

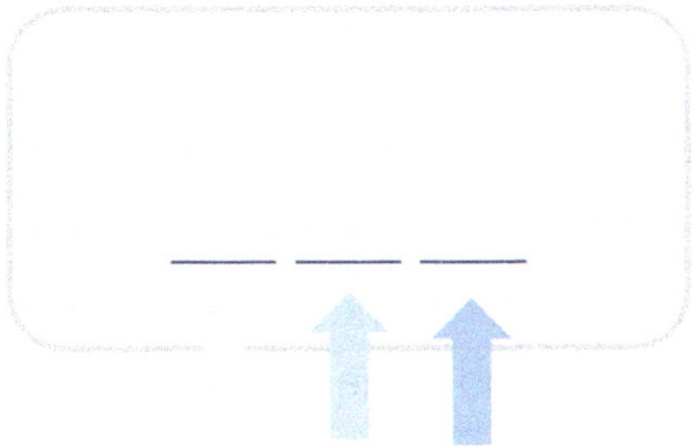

- Say the word in a dynamic blended style and at the same time move your finger across the board along all the lines. Your finger should be pointing to the line that corresponds to the sound in the word as you say it.
- Pointing to the first line, ask the child, "What sound can you hear ***here*** in the word.......?"
- Repeat the word (saying it in a dynamic blended style and moving your finger along the lines, as above) and then the question. You may need to repeat this several times, especially when this activity is new to the child, and you may need to emphasise the target sound to support the child to identify it.
- Once the child has identified the sound, ask them to write the matching sound spelling on the appropriate line.

  At this stage avoid using language such as 'first', 'initial' and 'beginning' which requires the child to think about the position in the word, as this requires additional cognitive processing. Using this technique, the visual prompts of the lines and your finger to indicate the 'place to listen', removes the burden of this extra cognitive task.
- Once the child has identified the 'initial' sound and written the sound spelling, move on to the 'middle' sound using the same technique and then the 'final' sound. Note that although it is useful for professionals to talk using positional language, take care to avoid labels such as 'medial', 'second', 'middle', 'next', 'final', 'last', 'third' or 'end'. Instead point to the place to listen and ask the child what sound they hear, 'here'.
- By working sequentially through the word, the child has identified the sounds and can then match sound spellings and so successfully spell the word. This simple technique can be used to spell any word.

- At some stage in the programme the child may be able to cope with use of positional language and indeed it is useful when supporting spelling, particularly in other curriculum areas. There is no specific point at which this happens for all children; timing is individual to each child. Teachers and teaching assistants will need to be aware of when this subtle shift occurs and choose appropriate strategies to support spelling.

Segmenting activities

A place to listen (Activity 28)

Even before starting on set 1 work, the 'A place to listen' activity helps to introduce the sequential segmenting technique, concentrating on phonological processing with a visual prompt without involving letters. This activity could be continued as the child works through the sets with the word lists provided.

This activity prepares the child for segmenting words as part of the process of learning to spell.

- Set out an appropriate 'place to listen' card in front of the child. There are two cards with dots on for VC words and three cards with dots on for CVC words. The position of the red dot on the card indicates the position of the target sound in the word. Cards are found at the end of this chapter.

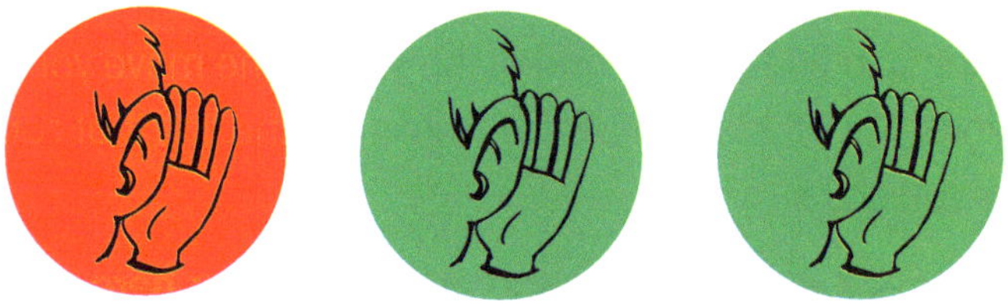

- Choose a word to present to the child from the word list in the appropriate chapter. Note that the number of meaningful words it is possible to generate is small in the early stages but gets larger as the child experiences more sounds by working through the programme.
- Follow the instructions above for the sequential segmenting strategy, asking the child what sound they can hear, *here* (pointing to the red dot).
- If the child finds it difficult to identify the sound, allow your finger to linger on the target sound dot and emphasise the sound so it is easier to isolate.
- The child is not required to write or match a sound spelling so this activity is purely aural.

At first the child will need lots of experience and practise to be able to consistently identify the initial sound in lots of different words. Once the child is confidently identifying the initial sound then move on to the middle sound using the same technique and the appropriate card. Similarly, once the child is confident in identifying the middle sound then move on to the final sound using the same technique and the appropriate card.

Practising this activity before starting set 1 work will prepare the child for learning how to segment sequentially and effectively but is also useful for children who are struggling to master segmenting and who would continue to benefit from this activity as they progress through the sets.

Segmenting bricks* (Activity 29)

Use some large plastic construction bricks for this activity. The teacher word list will help you choose words to use. Present the bricks already pushed together, a brick for each sound with a sound spelling written on each using a non-permanent whiteboard pen (this can be wiped off). Ask the child to pull the bricks apart in order and say the sounds one by one, as they go through the word, removing a brick at a time. Model this process for the child if necessary.

Alternatively present the child with unmarked bricks already pushed together such that there is a brick for each sound. Say a word to the child and ask them to pull apart the bricks, one by one in order and say the sounds that make up the word. Then ask the child to write the corresponding sound spelling on each brick.

Sound boxes (Activity 30) and How many sounds? (Activity 31)

These activities are worksheet based and instructions are written at the top of the sheet.

Phoneme frame* (Activity 32)

There is a phoneme frame with three boxes available at the end of this section. Copy this onto card and place it in an individual transparent file pocket-wallets (you can now write on this using non-permanent whiteboard pens and it will wipe off). Use the frame to work on 2 and 3 sound words. The teacher word list will help you choose words to use. Work through the activity in this way:

- Place the frame in front of the child and place a counter underneath each box.
- Present the chosen word orally.
- Say the word in a dynamic blended style and at the same time move your finger across the frame across all the boxes. Your finger should be pointing to the box that corresponds to the sound in the word as you say it.
- Ask the child to tell you all the sounds in the word, one by one. As the child says each sound they push a counter into the box.
- If the child needs support, use the sequential segmenting technique described earlier.

An extension activity could be to ask the child to match a sound spelling to each sound and write it under the box.

The learning objectives for these activities are as follows:

Activity	Learning objectives
28 A place to listen	Identify sounds in target positions within the word.
29 Segmenting bricks	Actively pull words apart using the sequential segmenting strategy to identify all the sounds in a word.

Activity	Learning objectives
30 Sound boxes	Identify all the sounds in a word. Use the sequential segmenting strategy to spell words.
31 How many sounds?	Identify all the sounds in a word. Use the sequential segmenting strategy to spell words.
28 Phoneme frame	Identify all the sounds in a word. Use the sequential segmenting strategy to spell words.

Skill 3 – phoneme manipulation

Phoneme manipulation is the ability to slide sounds in and out of words and is important when reading and spelling.

The *Phonics for Pupils with Special Educational Needs* programme includes activities and worksheets to work on this skill.

Activities 33–36 Sound swap, Read – Delete – Spell, Read – Add – Spell, Sound exchange, work on phoneme manipulation and instructions are written at the top of the worksheet.

When working on phoneme manipulation with a child, remember to use the sequential segmenting and dynamic blending techniques as appropriate.

The learning objectives for these activities are as follows:

Activity	Learning objectives
33 Sound swap	Swap, add or delete sounds in words to make meaningful words.
34 Read – Delete – Spell	Delete a sound from words to make meaningful words.
35 Read – Add – Spell	Add a sound to words to make meaningful words.
36 Sound exchange	Swap, add or delete sounds in words to make meaningful words.

Reading and spelling activities

From 37 onwards the activities are designed to give the child the opportunity to overlearn the relationships between sounds and sound spellings and gain experience in applying their skills, knowledge and understanding of sounds and sound spellings to read and spell single words and words in the context of sentences. The programme also incorporates reading at text level by sharing an appropriate book, usually at the end of a teaching session.

Activities 37–46 focus on reading single words.

Reading words with target sounds (Activity 37)

In each chapter of the book there is a set of cards made up of words containing the target sounds being explored. Practise dynamic blending, as described earlier, using the cards. Model this process for the child if necessary.

Reading high frequency words (Activity 38)

In each chapter of the book there is a set of cards with high frequency words relating to the sounds being explored. Practise dynamic blending, as described earlier, using the cards. Model this process for the child if necessary. High frequency words are discussed in greater detail later in this section of the book.

Activities 39–46 Reading race, Spot the word, Remembering words, Which Is the word?, Word splits, Busy words, Remembering lots of words and **Hidden words** have instructions written at the top of the worksheet with learning objectives as follows:

Activity	Learning objectives
37 Reading words with target sounds	Use the dynamic blending strategy to read words. Read words containing the target sounds. Develop automaticity of reading words.
38 Reading high frequency words	Use the dynamic blending strategy to read high frequency words. Read words containing the target sounds. Develop automaticity of reading high frequency words.
39 Reading race	Use the dynamic blending strategy to read words. Read words containing the target sounds. Develop reading speed and fluency.
40 Spot the word	Track, left to right, through a list of words. Use the dynamic blending strategy to read words. Identify words that are the same as a target word.
41 Remembering words	Use the dynamic blending strategy to read words. Recall and identify a single word from memory.
42 Which is the word?	Use the dynamic blending strategy to read words. Read words containing the target sound represented by all possible sound spellings. Recognise and identify real and nonsense words.
43 Word splits	Identify a word from a visually incomplete picture.
44 Busy words	Identify words from a visually complex presentation.
45 Remembering lots of words	Use the dynamic blending strategy to read words. Remember and recall a sequence of words. Complete a sequence of words.
46 Hidden words	Track, left to right, through a list of symbols. Discriminate between symbols and sound spelling letters. Isolate sound spellings and read the word.

Activities 47–52 focus on spelling single words.

Word build (Activity 47)

Copy the word build activity sheet onto card and cut out the cards, clipping the cards for each word together. You will need a whiteboard and pen. Work through the activity in this way:

- Present the picture to the child and talk about what word it might represent.
- Place the sound spelling cards on the whiteboard in front of the child but make sure they are mixed up randomly.
- Draw a line for each sound in the word on the whiteboard, e.g. two lines for a VC word, three lines for a CVC word.
- Using the sequential segmenting technique ask the child what sounds they can hear in the word. When the child has identified a sound correctly they can then choose its matching sound spelling from the cards available and place it on the appropriate line. In this way they build up the word.

Activities 48, 49 and 50 Finish the word 1, Finish the word 2 and Finish the word 3 – have instructions written at the top of the worksheet.

Spelling with sound spelling cards (Activity 51)

Present a range of sound spelling cards to the child and allow them to select and use them to build a given word. Drawing the appropriate number of lines on a whiteboard may be useful to support the child. Use the teacher word list to help select appropriate words. Support the child to self-correct when errors are made.

Spelling challenge (Activity 52)

The spelling challenge sheets provide the child with a structured method for practising and learning to spell the high frequency words. Work with the child through the sheets in this way:

bad	b a d	b a d
___ ___ ___		____________

- Encourage the child to read the word on the left then look at the same word in the middle.
- Encourage the child to notice the sound spellings that represent each of the sounds, e.g. 'bad' 'b' 'a' 'd' is represented by the sound spellings **b a d** – the sound spellings are spread out to make this clear.

- Ask the child to write over the grey sound spellings one by one, saying the corresponding sound at the same time as writing each sound spelling.
- Next, notice that there are two sets of lines, one made up of a number of small lines and the other a solid line. The number of small lines corresponds to the number of sounds in the word.
- Ask the child to write the sound spellings one by one on the small lines in the first set of lines, saying the corresponding sound at the same time as writing each sound spelling, e.g. **b a d**.
- Now ask the child to write the word, sound spelling by sound spelling, on the solid line, once again saying the corresponding sound at the same time as writing each sound spelling, e.g. **b a d**.

The child has now written the word three times and has made important connections between the sounds in the word and the sound spellings we write. Next time the child wants to write that word they can use the sounds (which they can access from the spoken word using the sequential segmenting technique) as a prompt to write the sound spellings in the right order and so spell the word.

To make the activity more challenging you could cover the words so that the child does not have a visual cue when writing the word on the lines. The child could then check their own work.

The learning objectives for all these activities are as follows:

Activity	Learning objectives
47 Word build	Use the sequential segmenting strategy to spell words. Spell words containing the target sound.
48 Finish the word 1	Use the sequential segmenting strategy to identify the initial sound in a word. Complete a word by adding a missing sound spelling.
49 Finish the word 2	Use the sequential segmenting strategy to identify the middle sound in a word. Complete a word by adding a missing sound spelling.
50 Finish the word 3	Use the sequential segmenting strategy to identify the final sound in a word. Complete a word by adding a missing sound spelling.
51 Spelling with sound spelling cards	Use the sequential segmenting strategy to spell words with the aid of visual prompts. Proofread spelling and self-correct as required.
52 Spelling challenge	Use the sequential segmenting strategy to spell words with the aid of visual prompts. Develop automaticity of spelling high frequency words.

Activities 53–56 Read the sentence, Oops! Correct the spelling, Spot the spelling, Writing challenge focus on reading and spelling words in sentences and have instructions written at the top of each sheet, with learning objectives as follows:

Activity	Learning objectives
53 Read the sentence	Use the dynamic blending strategy to read words. Read sentences closely matched to phonic knowledge with fluency and accuracy.
54 Oops! Correct the spelling	Proofread spelling and identify words that are misspelled. Use the sequential segmenting strategy to spell words.
55 Spot the spelling	Use the dynamic blending strategy to read words. Read sentences closely matched to phonic knowledge with fluency and accuracy. Complete sentences with single words to demonstrate understanding of meaning. Use the sequential segmenting strategy to spell words.
56 Writing challenge	Read sentences closely matched to phonic knowledge with fluency and accuracy. Remember and verbally recall a sequence of words read. Recall and write a sequence of words. Use the sequential segmenting strategy to spell words. Spell words containing the target sound.

An overview of all the activities in Book 1 are shown in the following table.

Table 3 Overview of *Phonics for Pupils with Special Educational Needs* – activities and resources Book 1

Aspect	Activities	Covered in this chapter	1	2	3	4	5	6	7
Auditory processing	1. Sound target story		✓	✓	✓	✓	✓	✓	✓
	2. Tongue twister fun		✓	✓	✓	✓	✓	✓	✓
	3. Odd one out		✓	✓	✓	✓	✓	×	✓
	4. What sound am I…?		✓	✓	✓	×	✓	×	✓
	5. Same or different?		✓	✓	✓	×	✓	×	✓
	6. How many did you hear?		✓	✓	✓	×	✓	×	✓
	7. What comes next?		✓	✓	✓	✓	✓	✓	✓
Introducing the sound and sound spelling	8. Sound spelling cards	✓	✓	✓	✓	✓	✓	✓	✓
	8a. Investigating the sound 'k'	✓	×	×	✓	×	×	×	×
	9. Sound spelling bingo		✓	✓	✓	✓	✓	✓	✓
	10. Sensory writing*	✓							

Aspect	Activities	Covered in this chapter	1	2	3	4	5	6	7
Visual processing	11. Sound spelling tracker		×	✓	✓	✓	✓	✓	✓
	12. Spot the sound spelling		✓	✓	✓	✓	✓	✓	✓
	13. Remembering sound spellings		✓	✓	✓	✓	✓	✓	✓
	14. Colour the picture		✓	✓	✓	✓	✓	×	×
	15. Which is the same?		✓	✓	✓	✓	✓	✓	✓
	16. Bits missing		✓	✓	✓	✓	✓	✓	✓
	17. Busy sound spellings		✓	✓	✓	✓	✓	✓	✓
	18. Where am I?		✓	✓	✓	✓	✓	✓	✓
	19. Remembering lots of sound spellings		✓	✓	✓	✓	✓	✓	✓
	20. Tracking sound spellings		✓	✓	✓	✓	✓	✓	✓
	21. Writing the sound spellings		✓	✓	✓	✓	✓	✓	✓
Skill – dynamic blending	22. A place to read	✓	✓	✓	✓	✓	✓	✓	✓
	23. Dynamic blending	✓	✓	✓	✓	✓	✓	✓	✓
	24. Blending bricks*	✓							
	25. Speed blending*	✓							
	26. Reveal and blend*	✓							
	27. Flippies	✓	✓	✓	✓	✓	✓	✓	✓
Skill – segmenting	28. A place to listen	✓	✓	✓	✓	✓	✓	✓	✓
	29. Segmenting bricks*	✓							
	30. Sound boxes		✓	✓	✓	✓	✓	✓	✓
	31. How many sounds?		✓	✓	✓	✓	✓	✓	✓
	32. Phoneme frame*	✓							
Skill – phoneme manipulation	33. Sound swap		✓	✓	✓	✓	✓	✓	✓
	34. Read – Delete – Spell		✓	✓	✓	✓	✓	×	✓
	35. Read – Add – Spell		×	✓	✓	✓	✓	×	✓
	36. Sound exchange		×	✓	✓	✓	✓	✓	×
Reading words	37. Reading words with the target sounds		✓	✓	✓	✓	✓	✓	✓
	38. Reading high frequency words		✓	✓	✓	✓	✓	✓	✓
	39. Reading race		✓	✓	✓	✓	✓	✓	✓
	40. Spot the word		✓	✓	✓	✓	✓	✓	✓
	41. Remembering words		✓	✓	✓	✓	✓	✓	✓
	42. Which is the word?		✓	✓	✓	✓	✓	✓	✓
	43. Word splits		✓	✓	✓	✓	✓	✓	✓

Aspect	Activities	Covered in this chapter	1	2	3	4	5	6	7
	44. Busy words		✓	✓	✓	✓	✓	✓	✓
	45. Remembering lots of words		✓	✓	✓	✓	✓	✓	✓
	46. Hidden words		✓	✓	✓	✓	✓	✓	✓
Spelling words	47. Word build	✓	✓	✓	✓	✓	✓	✓	✓
	48. Finish the word 1 – initial sound		✓	✓	✓	✓	✓	✓	✓
	49. Finish the word 2 – middle sound		✓	✓	✓	✓	✓	✓	✓
	50. Finish the word 3 – Final sound		✓	✓	✓	✓	✓	✓	✓
	51. Spelling with sound spelling cards	✓							
	52. Spelling challenge	✓	✓	✓	✓	✓	✓	✓	✓
Working in sentences	53. Read the sentence		×	×	✓	✓	✓	✓	✓
	54. Oops! Correct the spelling		×	×	✓	✓	✓	✓	✓
	55. Spot the spelling		×	×	✓	✓	✓	✓	✓
	56. Writing challenge		×	×	✓	✓	✓	✓	✓
Text reading	57. Reading book*	✓							

Note that some of the activities, indicated by an asterisk*, do not require a corresponding worksheet and these are described and explained in this introductory section. Not all activities are applicable to all sections of the programme and for these worksheets and resources are not available, as indicated by a cross.

High frequency words

The high frequency words are the most common words used in written English and many programmes focus heavily on learning these as 'sight words'. This programme does not take this approach. A child with special educational needs is less likely to find success with a 'visual only' strategy than when using a multisensory approach to reading and spelling, and many such children struggle to learn and remember a bank of sight words in this way.

Even if we explore the auditory or phonic aspect of high frequency words early on in the programme, explicitly working on them as a group in their own right would mean we have to carry out focus work on a multitude of key sounds all at the same time, which would be very confusing for the child. Yet, the very point about these words is that they are 'high frequency' and so are likely to appear in even simple text and pupils may encounter them very early in the programme. This presents us with a dilemma.

The solution is that the programme takes a gentler approach to high frequency words with a longer-term view of the situation and does not explicitly teach them as a separate group of words requiring their own focus and teaching materials.

The high frequency words are studied when the child works on the appropriate focus sound as they work through the programme. At the end of this section of the book is a list of the high frequency words organised according to the key sounds in the word and the point at which they fit into the programme.

Most importantly, high frequency words are also dealt with as they naturally arise in the context of the child's reading or writing. The same dynamic blending strategy is used for reading and the same sequential segmenting strategy is used for spelling, but the teacher or teaching assistant steps in to support the child with just that little bit of knowledge that they lack.

The strategies for dealing with reading and spelling high frequency words are as follows:

Scaffolding reading high frequency words

A scaffolding approach is taken to support a child to read high frequency words when they naturally crop up when reading. The teacher or teaching assistant uses their knowledge of what the child has learned and understood so far to enable them to support in just the right way and provide only the information that the child lacks.

For example, a child working at the set 3 level encounters the word **seen** in a story book.

As the teacher or teaching assistant you know that they have worked on the sounds 's' and 'n' and so you can assume that they know them and can work with them. You also know that the child has not yet worked on the 'ee' sound and it is the sound spelling **ee** which will potentially cause them difficulties.

- Encourage the child to start decoding the word and for them to begin by identifying and saying the sound 's'.
- As they move on to the next sound spelling, gently interrupt them and point to the **ee** sound spelling (drawing a ring around or underlining the two letters can help the child to notice the sound spelling).
- Pointing to the **ee** sound spelling say, "This is a picture of the sound 'ee'. You haven't done this sound yet, but you will. This is 'ee'.
- Support the child to start over and dynamically blend the 's' and 'ee' sounds together.
- The child can then continue on through the word independently, identify the 'n' sound, dynamically blending to get the word 'seen'.

In this way the child has actually decoded 66% of the word, blended 100% of it and concluded what the word is (or 'read' it) themselves.

When supporting reading in this way, there is never a need to simply supply a whole word for the child.

Scaffolding spelling high frequency words

Similarly, a scaffolding approach is taken to support a child to spell high frequency words when they naturally crop up when writing. The teacher or teaching assistant uses their knowledge of what the child has learned and understood so far to enable them to support in just the right way and provide only the information that the child lacks.

For example, a child working at the set 3 level is doing a writing task and wishes to spell the word 'said'.

As the teacher or teaching assistant you know that they have worked on the sounds 's' and 'd' and so you can assume that they know them and can work with them. You also know that the child has not yet worked on the 'e' sound and it is the sound spelling **ai** which will potentially cause them difficulties.

- Draw three lines on a whiteboard, one line for each sound in the word.
- Using the sequential segmenting technique encourage the child to identify the first sound they can hear in the word 'said'.
- Invite the child to match a sound spelling for the sound 's'.
- Using the sequential segmenting technique encourage the child to identify the next (middle) sound they can hear in the word 'said'.
- The child will be able to identify the 'e' sound but will not be able to match the appropriate sound spelling. Gently interrupt them, saying, "Yes, there is an 'e' sound here. You haven't investigated this sound fully yet but you will. We use this way of writing 'e' in this word". Write in the ai sound spelling on the line for the child.
- The child can then continue on through the word, identify the 'd' sound, and match a sound spelling to the sound.
- If the child then copies the word from the whiteboard into their book require them to say each sound at the same time as writing the appropriate sound spelling.

These gentle approaches to the high frequency words primes the child for the time when they can work on them more fully.

Listening to a child read

Teaching a child to efficiently decode words is only one part of reading. Alongside this, children need to understand what they have read, included in which is the ability to 'read between the lines and beyond the text', and develop an interest and enthusiasm for stories, poetry and writing. All teachers strive to generate in their pupils a 'love of books'.

Although this programme does not address the specifics of reading comprehension it does set a place for it and the development of an interest and enthusiasm for reading at all levels, by encouraging pupil and teacher to share a book and talk about what they have read.

Activity 57 Reading book

The last **quarter** of any teaching session should be devoted to reading a book with the child, supporting them to apply their increasing knowledge, skills and understanding to read the text.

This gives you an opportunity to gently correct errors as they read by highlighting sound spellings, referencing sounds, providing information about sounds they have not yet covered, correcting them when they use the wrong sound, pointing out where they have missed out or added sounds and by supporting and modelling a good dynamic blending technique.

During this activity also take time to enjoy sharing a book with the child. Stimulate their interest in the story, poem or text by talking about it and asking questions to support their understanding of what they have read. The content of this discussion and the depth to which texts can be explored will depend on the child's age and cognitive abilities but some suggestions about areas of questioning and discussion are given below:

- Identify the general 'topic' of the text
- Identify where a story takes place
- Identify the main character(s)
- Identify what is happening and be aware of the sequence of events
- Identify characters, places and objects in illustrations and pictures
- Be aware of the importance of key events in the text
- Make connections between the text and personal experiences
- Draw conclusions about events in the text
- Make predictions about what might happen next
- Identify cause, effect and consequences within the text
- Make connections between the text and the child's prior knowledge or experience
- Describe the main character
- Express opinions about a character's actions or speech
- Express opinions about their enjoyment of the story or otherwise
- Identify different genres of writing and express preferences

Choosing the right book

There are several book series that take a phonics approach to writing and produce books that focus on a key sound or groups of sounds. These books are really useful if they match the sound(s) that the child is working on from this programme, as the child is likely to experience a higher level of success when reading these, which is a great confidence boost. Be aware that the language in these books can be a little unnatural or stilted as the writers are restricted by which words are available for them to use to write the story.

Other books that do not take this phonics approach are just as accessible, but the child is likely to require much more adult support. The child is more likely to encounter high frequency words (refer to the section on high frequency words) that they have not yet focused on within the programme. Since a higher level of adult support may be required, the child may feel less successful when reading these books.

No type of book is better than another. A mixture of books is preferable to balance the child's diet of reading material to make it as rich and interesting as possible whilst allowing the child to experience success and independence.

Pace

When sharing a book with learner readers the flow and pace of reading may be stalled if the child has to be supported to decode several words in a sentence. This may mean that the child will lose track of the meaning of what they have been reading. If this is the case, at the end of each sentence stop and re-read it for the child so that they can focus on language and meaning. This is a good opportunity to talk about the story, characters and events.

A few more considerations

By now you should have a good overview of the programme, how it works and how to begin to deliver it, but there are a few other aspects that it are worth taking time to consider and reflect on which will help you when working with a child or a group of children.

Regional variations

Earlier in this chapter there was reference to the number of sounds in spoken English and the fact that this varies according to regional differences associated with accent and pronunciation.

For example, in most of the UK the words **book**, **cook** and **look** are pronounced with an 'u' sound in the middle but in some areas an 'oo' sound is used. There is a subtle difference in the pronunciation of the 'u' sound in words like **bus** and **run** in different parts of the UK and of course there is the classic 'castle' and 'bath' debate where the **a** sound spelling represents the sound 'ar' for some people but 'a' for others.

When creating the content of the programme every effort was made to reduce the impact of these differences by careful selection of example words. However, it is important for you as a practitioner to be selective about the words presented to your child or group of children and **always** follow your local pronunciations. In the rare event of you finding in the programme a word is out of place then just avoid it and remember to deal with it in a section appropriate to you and the child.

Terminology

Many phonics programmes use terminology that children with special educational needs find difficult to understand, remember and use. In *Phonics for Pupils with Special Educational Needs* this terminology is kept to a minimum and is made as child friendly as possible. Labels such as phoneme, grapheme, short vowel, long vowel, digraphs, trigraphs, dipthong and spilt-vowel digraph are not used in this programme.

Knowing these terms does not have a direct impact on a child's functional reading and spelling accuracy and performance. Instead accessible terms such as sound, sound spelling and split sound spelling are used.

Tricky words

Phonics for Pupils with Special Educational Needs' view of written language means that nearly all words can be decoded and there are very few 'common exception' or 'tricky' words. Please refer to the list of high frequency words which also shows how these common words are coded.

There are some words that do appear to be truly 'tricky' and difficult to decode. Investigation of their origins and history can be quite revealing. Encountering these words in the course of their reading presents an opportunity to talk about this with the child at a level that is appropriate to their cognitive abilities.

the	When pronounced as 'thee', e.g. before words starting with a vowel or used for emphasis, it is easy to decode as 'th' 'ee'. Otherwise this is often pronounced as 'thuh'. The 'uh' sound is a Schwa (which is covered extensively in Book 7). The easiest way to describe this is an 'untidy' or 'sloppy' sound.
one	Originally pronounced using an 'u' sound, like in the phrase 'a good 'un'. The 'wun' pronunciation appeared in the south-west of England in the 14th century and spread rapidly.
once	Its history mirrors that of the word 'one'.
two	From the old English **twa** which contained pronounced consonants and an 'a-e' sound 'tway'. The reason for the shift to the 'too' pronunciation is no longer known.

friend	Decodable but unique – the sound spelling **ie** represents the sound 'e' in this word. This word is investigated when working on the 'e' sound in Book 4.
people	Decodable but unique – the sound spelling **eo** represents the sound 'ee' in this word. This word is investigated when working on the 'ee' sound in Book 4.
minute	Middle English from the Latin **minutus** (meaning small) pronounced with an 'oo' sound. This is another example of a Schwa.
hour	From the Latin **hora**. Although the 'h' hasn't been pronounced since Roman times, the **h** has persisted to distinguish it visually from the word **our**.
busy	From the Old English **bisig** originally referring to 'having a care or anxious'. Later it referred to being occupied doing something. Spelling shifted from **i** to **u** in the 15th century for a reason no longer known.
business	Source is the same as above **bisgnes**. The original meaning, referring to **busyness** as 'the state of being busy', has become obsolete and replaced by today's meaning and spelling.
iron	From the Celtic word **isarnon**, which means holy metal (metal made into swords for the Crusades), the Old English word was **iren**.
Mr	A contraction of the word **M**iste**r** – taking just the first and last letter as a short form of the word.
Mrs	A contraction of the word **M**ist**r**e**s**s – taking the first and last letter and the middle letter r as a short from of the word 'missus' (which is in itself a short form of mistress which is an out-dated formal title for a woman).

Planning

At the end of this section there is a lesson planner which can be used to plan teaching sessions and track pupil progression through the programme.

All possible activities are listed on the planner which could be viewed as a menu of activities.

To use the lesson planner, simply date the column and strike through the small box corresponding to each activity you plan to do in the session. ⧅ You can cross check through once completed. ☒

This provides a simple visual map of the pupil(s)' progress through the programme.

There is space to write brief notes and a larger space at the bottom of the planner where dynamic teacher assessment notes can be written on individual pupil responses / errors, teacher reflections and next steps for the pupil or group.

Structuring a session

Teaching sessions can be of any length but should always include as wide a range of activities as possible. The activities are grouped according to the focus of the activity and this is made clear on the planning sheet:

- Auditory (phonological) processing without visuals
- Introducing the sounds and sound spellings
- Visual processing and sound spellings
- Dynamic blending
- Sequential segmenting
- Phoneme manipulation
- Reading words
- Spelling words
- Working in sentences
- Reading text

Sessions should be planned to ensure that over time there is even coverage of all these aspects and all activities available. As a general rule, all sessions should finish with reading text, a book, either listening to the child read or a shared reading activity in a group.

Note that for each chapter in the book there is a corresponding answer sheet for your information.

The tasks

Children with special educational needs are often easily distracted and find it difficult to concentrate for long periods on the same task. For this reason, it is recommended that the individual activities are time limited rather than task limited.

For example, if a child starts a worksheet with support but after five minutes or so has only completed two items then stop there, record that the sheet is incomplete and move on to the next activity. The child can always continue work on the incomplete sheet in a subsequent session. It is better to keep the lesson interesting and varied to maintain a high level of engagement rather than finish a worksheet for the sake of it. Depending on the child, activities should only last around five to six minutes.

Progress through the programme

Do not feel that a child or group of children must go through every single activity and worksheet in the programme. If you have introduced a set of sounds and sound spellings and the child is able to reliably and consistently recall the sound(s) when shown a sound spelling and identify the sound spellings when told the sound, then move them on to the next set. Remember that the child takes all previous sounds and their sound spellings with them into the next section, so nothing is ever left behind.

And finally...

You now have an overview of the programme, its approach to written language, how to teach the key skills and the important techniques required to support a child or group of children.

You have all the tools necessary to expand the child's knowledge of sounds and sound spellings, teaching them to become readers and spellers.

Lesson planner Book 1

Name(s):			Date		Date		Date		Date		Date	
Book 1 Focus set:				**Notes**		**Notes**		**Notes**		**Notes**		**Notes**
Auditory processing without Visuals	1	Sound target story										
	2	Tongue twister fun										
	3	Odd one out										
	4	What sound am I?										
	5	Same or different?										
	6	How many did you hear?										
	7	What comes next?										
Introducing the sound and sound spellings	8	Using spelling cards										
	8a	Investigating the sound 'k' set 3 only										
	9	Sound spelling bingo										
	10	Sensory writing*										
Visual processing sound spellings	11	Sound spelling tracker										
	12	Spot the sound spelling										
	13	Remembering sound spellings										
	14	Colour the picture										
	15	Which is the same?										
	16	Bits missing										

Name(s):		Date		Date		Date		Date		Date	
Book 1 Focus set:			**Notes**		**Notes**		**Notes**		**Notes**		**Notes**
	17 Busy sound spellings										
	18 Where am I?										
	19 Remembering lots of sound spellings										
	20 Tracking sound spellings										
	21 Writing the sound spellings										
Dynamic blending	22 A place to read										
	23 Dynamic blending										
	24 Blending bricks*										
	25 Speed blending*										
	26 Reveal and blend*										
	27 Flippies										
Sequential segmenting	28 A place to listen										
	29 Segmenting bricks*										
	30 Sound boxes										
	31 How many sounds?										
	32 Phoneme frame*										
Phoneme manipulation	33 Sound swap										
	34 Read – Delete – Spell										
	35 Read – Add – Spell										
	36 Sound exchange										
Reading words	37 Reading words with the target sounds										
	38 Reading high frequency words										

Name(s):		Date		Date		Date		Date		Date	
Book 1 Focus set:			**Notes**		**Notes**		**Notes**		**Notes**		**Notes**
	39 Reading race										
	40 Spot the word										
	41 Remembering words										
	42 Which is the word?										
	43 Word splits										
	44 Busy words										
	45 Remembering lots of words										
	46 Hidden words										
Spelling words	47 Word build										
	48 Finish the word 1 – Initial sound										
	49 Finish the word 2 – Middle sound										
	50 Finish the word 3 – Final sound										
	51 Spelling with sound spelling cards										
	52 Spelling challenge										
Working in sentences	53 Read the sentence										
	54 Oops! correct the spelling										
	55 Spot the spelling										
	56 Writing challenge										
Reading text	57 Reading book*										
Observation / assessment notes											

Word list

Set	V, VC & CVC words				
1 s a t p	**a**	**at**	**pat** **sat** **tap**		
2 i n m d	am an **in** it	dad **did** dim **din** dip mad	man map mat nap nip nit	pad pan pin pip pit sad	sip sit tad tan tin
3 g o c k	on	can cap cat cod **cog** cop	cot dig dog dot gap got	keg kid kit mop nod not	pop pot tig tog top
4 e u r	up	cup cut den get men met mug mum	net nut peg pen pet put rag ram	ran rap rat red rid rig rim rip	rug run set sun ten
5 h b f l	if	bad bag ban bat bed beg bet bib big bin bit	bob bud bug bun bus cab fan fat fed fib fog	fun had hat hen hid him hip hit hop hot hug	lad lap led leg let lid lip lit log lot peg
6 j v w x	box fix fox	jam jet jog	jug van vet	wag wax web	wet wig win
7 y z	yam yap	yes yet	zag zap	zig zip	

High frequency word list

The following list is the high frequency words organised according to the sounds in the word and in relation to the programme. Each word is explored at an appropriate point in the programme, as indicated. Of course, children are likely to encounter these words at earlier stages in their reading as they share books and will be guided to decode them, with a 'heads up' to sounds not yet studied.

Book	Structure / sound(s)	Top 100 High frequency words	Top 101–200 High frequency words
1	**Set 1 VC** **CVC**	a at sat	
1	**Set 2 VC** **CVC**	in it did	am an dad man
1	**Set 3 VC** **CVC**		on can cat dog got not top
1	**Set 4 VC** **CVC**		up get mum put* ran red run sun
1	**Set 5 VC** **CVC**		if bad bed big but fun had hat him hot let
1	**Set 6** **CVC**		fox
1	**Set 7** **CVC**		yes
2	**All sets** **VCC**	and ask* it's	end
2	**All sets** **CVCC**	help just went	best fast* last* lost lots must next wind
2	**All sets** **CCVC**	from	gran stop
2	**All sets** ***CCVCC+***		didn't grandad plant*
3	**sh**		fish wish

Book	Structure / sound(s)	Top 100 High frequency words	Top 101–200 High frequency words
3	th	that this them then with	bath* path*
3	ng		along king long thing
3	ch		much children
3	k	back	duck
3	f	off	
3	l	will	fell still tell
3	s		across miss
4	o-e	don't go no old so	cold going most told boat grow snow window
4	z	as his is	clothes has us
4	ee	be he me she we see very	began he's been feet green keep need queen sleep three tree each eat sea tea even here these only really
4	a-e	day came made make they	away may play say way gave take great again* baby
4	er	her were	after ever every never over under different first girl word work we're

Book	Structure / sound(s)	Top 100 High frequency words	Top 101–200 High frequency words
4	e	again* said head	any many friend
4	ow		down how now town about found our out round shout
5	oy		boy
5	oo	do into to you look* too	today food room took* through
5	u	put* look looks come love some could	book good looking took something couldn't would coming another mother other
5	i-e	by my I I'm like time	fly find I'll inside liked night right
5	aw	for all call saw your	morning or small water thought before more door
5	air	there their	there's bear air chair

Book	Structure / sound(s)	Top 100 High frequency words	Top 101–200 High frequency words
5	ar	are	after* can't fast* father last* car dark garden hard park
6	s		horse house mouse place
6	l		animals people
6	b		rabbit
6	d	looked called	jumped pulled cried suddenly
6	o	was	want wanted gone
6	i		live lived
6	u-e		use
Advanced Consonants			
6	f		laugh
6	g		eggs ghost
6	h		who whose
6	j		giant magic
6	k		school
6	m		climb
6	n		know
6	p		floppy stopped
6	r		narrator
6	t		better little
6	v		I've
6	w		what when where which white why
6	z		because please

* These words may be explored at different points in the programme depending on variations in regional pronunciation.

A place to read cards

A place to read VC

A place to read CVC

A place to listen cards

A place to listen — VC initial sound

A place to listen — VC final sound

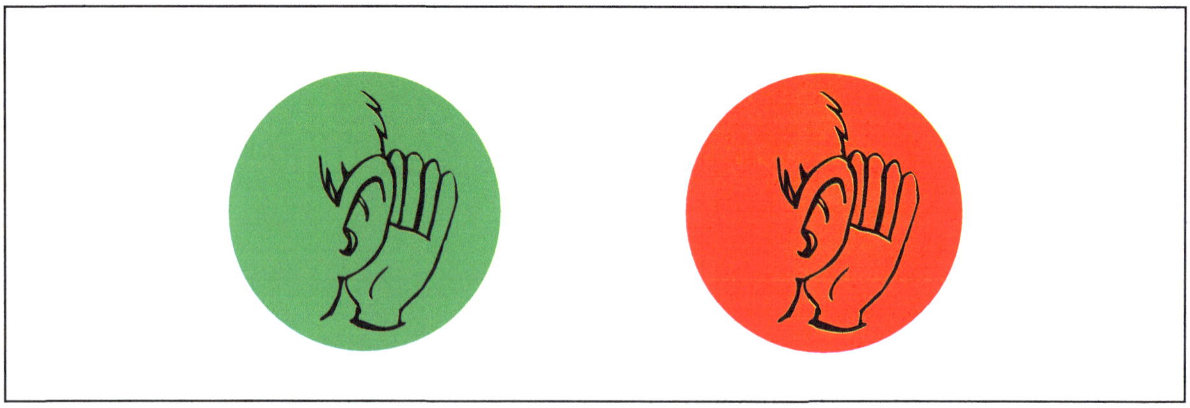

A place to listen cards

A place to listen **CVC initial sound**

A place to listen **CVC middle sound**

A place to listen **CVC middle sound**

Phoneme frame

Phoneme frame 1: up to three sounds

Blank flippies template

Flippies blank – for words with up to four sound spellings

Print out on card and cut out.
Stack them with the biggest (the complete word) on the bottom and in decreasing size so that the smallest is on the top.
Make sure the left-hand edge of the cards are flush. Staple the cards together on the left-hand side.
When the child runs a finger over the cards the sound spellings flip up. Ask the child to say the sounds and match to the flips.

Sounds and their sound spellings 1 poster

a	cat

o	go
o-e	home
oa	boat
ow	grow
oe	toe
ough	though

ea	dream
ee	seen
y	happy
e	be
ie	field
e-e	eve
i	ski

a-e	made
a	angel
ai	train
ay	play
ea	steak
ey	they
eigh	eight

er	her
ur	burn
ir	bird
ear	learn
or	word
our	colour
ar	collar
re	centre
ere	were

e	red
ea	head
a	many
ai	said
ie	friend

ou	loud
ow	down
ough	plough

oi	soil
oy	boy

oo	moon
u	truth
u-e	rule
ew	grew
o	do
ui	suit
ou	soup
ue	blue

u	put
o	month
oo	book
ou	touch
o-e	come
oul	could

i-e	kite
i	mind
y	by
igh	night
ie	pie

or	for
au	haunt
aw	saw
ore	more
ar	war
al	walk
our	your
a	also
oar	roar
ough	bought
augh	taught

air	hair
ere	there
are	care
ear	bear

ar	star
a	father
al	calm
ear	heart

o	got
a	want
au	fault

i	sit
y	myth

u	music
u-e	cube
ew	few
ue	cue

Sounds and their sound spellings 2 poster

s	sat
c	city
sc	scent
ss	less
st	listen
ce	dance
se	house

t	top
tt	better
bt	doubt

p	pet
pp	happy

m	man
mm	summer
mn	hymn
mb	lamb

n	not
kn	knot
nn	sunny
gn	gnat

d	dog
dd	ladder
ed	wagged

g	get
gg	wiggle
gu	guard
gue	plague
gh	ghost

c	can
k	kid
ck	duck
ch	chemist
que	plaque

r	rat
wr	wrong
rr	hurry
rh	rhythm

b	bat
bb	robber
bu	build

f	fun
ph	phone
ff	stuff
gh	cough

h	hat
wh	whose

l	lamp
ll	bell
le	little
el	travel
il	pupil
al	metal
ol	symbol

j	jam
g	giant
ge	large
dge	bridge

v	van
ve	have

w	wig
wh	which

x	fox
xc	except
cc	accept

y	yes

z	zip
s	his
zz	buzz
ze	freeze
se	noise

sh	ship
s	sugar
ch	machine

th	think

ng	ring

ch	chip
tch	match

qu	quit

SECTION 1

SET 1 SOUNDS AND SOUND SPELLINGS

s a t p

Auditory discrimination is the ability to hear differences between sounds. Good auditory discrimination helps us to recognise and identify the sounds in words and so interpret them correctly. Children with poor auditory discrimination may confuse sounds and misinterpret things they have heard. Their spelling and writing may reflect their confusion over what sounds they heard in a word. **Auditory attention and tracking** is the ability to actively listen and follow auditory information from beginning to end. Good auditory attention and tracking helps us to follow a conversation, a story read out loud or a set of instructions, being able to focus on key information. Children with poor auditory attention and tracking may find it difficult to follow and respond appropriately to what is being said to them.

This story contains lots of words that start with the sounds 's', 'a', 't' and 'p', in but you will focus on just one 'target' sound. Read the story out loud. Encourage the child to listen carefully and spot any word that starts with the 'target' sound. When a target word has been read, the child indicates that they have heard and spotted it by tapping the table, putting up a hand or any other agreed signal, but without shouting out. Stop reading and discuss the word, making any error correction necessary. If a word is missed, re-read the sentence. Do not show the story to the children. The target words are highlighted below for you: 's', 'a', 't' and 'p'. Repeat on another occasion focusing on a different target sound.

Activity 1 Sound target – Story sheet Set 1

Sam loves tasty sausages. Sam can eat six sausages a day and on Tuesdays tries seven!
Sam would have them for breakfast, dinner and tea.
If you ask Sam what his favourite food is, he shouts, "Sausages!"
Sam's birthday is in September. When it was his birthday his mum said, "Let's have a super party!"
It was a great party with lots of games to play and plenty of singing and dancing. After tea they played pass the parcel.
Sam's cake was covered in sweet treats shaped like sausages!
Best of all was the present… Sam got a real live sausage dog puppy!
Sam called her Tammy.

Please Note: The focus of activity is the *sound* in the word, NOT what *letter* is in the word.

Auditory discrimination is the ability to hear differences between sounds. Good auditory discrimination helps us to recognise and identify the sounds in words and so interpret them correctly. Children with poor auditory discrimination may confuse sounds and misinterpret things they have heard. Their spelling and writing may reflect their confusion over what sounds they heard in a word. **Auditory sequential memory** is the ability to remember and recall a series of things that they have heard. Children with poor auditory sequential memory may find it difficult to remember information given earlier in a conversation or set of instructions and may struggle to recall the sequence of sounds in a word.

The sentences contain lots of words beginning with one of the target sounds 's', 'a', 't' or 'p'.
Read the sentence to the child several times; invite them to join in as you say it and gradually recall it on their own.
Ask them to say it as quickly as they can and have some fun with it. After some practise, ask the child if they can identify which sound they hear a lot in the tongue twister. Perhaps they can make up their own?
Note that the vocabulary included in these tongue twisters may be unfamiliar to the child, especially the adjectives. If appropriate, talk about unfamiliar words and discuss their meaning.
Break this task into a number of shorter tasks over a number of lessons if necessary.

Activity 2 Sound target – Tongue twister fun Set 1

Super Sue sings silly songs.

Scary snakes slide slowly on sand.

Angry Ali's ankles ache.

Amazing ants avoid aliens.

Tricky Tom tickles terrible tigers.

Trusty trains travel on true tracks.

Put pink pickles on pale pizza.

Pretty parrots paint purple pictures.

Auditory discrimination is the ability to hear differences between sounds. Good auditory discrimination helps us to recognise and identify the sounds in words and so interpret them correctly. Children with poor auditory discrimination may confuse sounds and misinterpret things they have heard. Their spelling and writing may reflect their confusion over what sounds they heard in a word. **Auditory attention and tracking** is the ability to actively listen and follow auditory information from beginning to end. Good auditory attention and tracking helps us to follow a conversation, a story read out loud or a set of instructions, being able to focus on key information. Children with poor auditory attention and tracking may find it difficult to follow and respond appropriately to what is being said to them.

This activity focuses the child on listening to short lists of words starting with the sounds 's', 'p', 't' and 'a'. The words get increasingly complex, as does the number of words the child has to listen to.

Read out the words and ask the child to identify the odd one out, the word that *does not* start with the same sound as the others. Do not show the words to the child. The odd one out is highlighted for you.
Break this task into a number of shorter tasks over a number of lessons if necessary.

Activity 3 Odd one out — Set 1

1.	sad	sat	**pen**	2.	pin	**ten**	pip
3.	tap	tan	**put**	4.	**top**	sit	sad
5.	pan	**sum**	pop	6.	**sun**	tip	tum
7.	pond	**test**	past	8.	sent	sand	**tops**
9.	**pest**	sink	sing	10.	tent	**soft**	tank
11.	stop	stab	**plan**	12.	**trap**	pram	plug
13.	trip	**snap**	twin	14.	skin	slip	**plop**
15.	**trust**	stamp	stand	16.	stink	**plank**	stump
17.	pin	pop	**sad**	put			
18.	tin	**sip**	top	ten			
19.	**peg**	sit	sun	set			

Auditory discrimination is the ability to hear differences between sounds. Good auditory discrimination helps us to recognise and identify the sounds in words and so interpret them correctly. Children with poor auditory discrimination may confuse sounds and misinterpret things they have heard. Their spelling and writing may reflect their confusion over what sounds they heard in a word. **Auditory recall memory** is the ability to remember and recall something that they have just heard. Children with poor auditory recall memory may find it difficult to remember sounds and words and respond appropriately.

Read the list of words below clearly, asking the child to listen carefully. All words start with an 's', 'a', 't' or 'p' and get increasingly complex. At random points, tap the table and stop reading, asking the child to remember and say the last word you said. Then ask them to tell you what the first sound in the word is.

Break this task into a number of shorter tasks over a number of lessons if necessary.

Activity 4 What sound am I? Set 1

1.	at	sad	pip	ten	am	pot	ted
2.	sit	tap	sun	pan	an	put	sat
3.	top	pat	sip	peg	tin	set	pup
4.	ant	past	sand	tank	and	sent	pink
5.	test	sink	ask	soft	pest	spit	twig
6.	skin	trap	skip	twin	plan	trip	spin
7.	stamp	trust	stand	stink	plank	tramp	
8.	prank	stump	trend	slump	strap	splint	
9.	pain	stain	train	paint	saint	tame	
10.	steam	peel	seem	team	scream	tree	

Auditory discrimination is the ability to hear differences between sounds. Good auditory discrimination helps us to recognise and identify the sounds in words and so interpret them correctly. Children with poor auditory discrimination may confuse sounds and misinterpret things they have heard. Their spelling and writing may reflect their confusion over what sounds they heard in a word.

Read out the pairs of words. Ask the child to tell you whether or not they start with the same sound. The words get increasingly complex. Word pairs that start with the same sound are highlighted.

Break this task into a number of shorter tasks over a number of lessons if necessary.

Activity 5 Same or different? Set 1

1. at - am
2. sit - sad
3. pin - ten
4. sip - pop
5. top - an
6. pet - pad
7. tan - tip
8. sat - pen
9. sun - put
10. pot - pip
11. and - ant
12. send - soft
13. test - tank
14. pink - sent
15. past - sand
16. sink - tent
17. snap - skin
18. trap - plan
19. stop - spin
20. twig - trip
21. plop - spot
22. stamp - stand
23. plank - trust
24. strip - strap
25. tramp - stink
26. splint - sprint

Auditory fusion is the ability to hear the subtle gaps between sounds and words. Children with poor auditory fusion may get lost in conversations and when following a list of instructions given verbally.

Say the sounds or read the words in the list one after another at a brisk pace so that there are no obvious gaps between the sounds or the words. Ask the child to listen carefully and then tell you how many sounds or words you have said. All the words start with the sound 's', 'a', 't' or 'p' and get increasingly complex.

Break this task into a number of shorter tasks over a number of lessons if necessary.

Activity 6 How many did you hear? Set 1

1. s – p – t – s
2. a – s – t
3. p – p – s – a – t
4. s – s – s
5. t – p – s – a
6. t – s – a – p – t
7. s – a – a
8. p – p
9. sun – sit – ten – put
10. tap – pin – at
11. sit – pop – pan – top
12. tan – pet
13. sad – pip – pen
14. top – pad - sum
15. ant – am – ask – and
16. sip – an – a - tap
17. soft – test – past
18. sand - send
19. tank – sent – pond – pest – sand
20. snap – skip – twig
21. trip – plop
22. slim – slap - trap
23. twist - stink
24. stamp – trust – stand
25. plank – stump – trend
26. strip – strap
27. splint – am – stamp – trust
28. ask – test – plan
29. slip – trap - snap
30. print – and – ant - sprint

Auditory attention and tracking is the ability to actively listen and follow auditory information from beginning to end. Good auditory attention and tracking helps us to follow a conversation, a story read out loud or a set of instructions, being able to focus on key information. Children with poor auditory attention and tracking may find it difficult to follow and respond appropriately to what is being said to them. **Auditory sequential memory** is the ability to remember and recall a series of things that they have heard. Children with poor auditory sequential memory may find it difficult to remember information given earlier in a conversation or a set of instructions and may struggle to recall the sequence of sounds in a word.

In this activity the child has to process the auditory information but also respond by working out the pattern and stating the next sound in the sequence. Read out the list of sounds with a clear space between each. Ask the child to listen and work out what sound would come next. Answers are in red.

Break this task into a number of shorter tasks over a number of lessons if necessary.

Activity 7 What comes next? Set 1

1. s p s p s p ...... s
2. t p t p t p ...... t
3. a t a t a t ...... a
4. p a p a p a ...... p
5. t t a t t a t t a ...... t
6. s s t s s t s s t ...... s
7. p a a p a a p a a ...... p
8. s p p s p p s p p ...... s
9. s s t t s s t t ...... s
10. p p s s p p s s ..... p
11. t t a a t t a a ...... t
12. a a p p a a p p ...... a
13. s s a s s a s s a ...... s
14. t t p t t p t t p ...... t
15. p s p p s p p s p ...... p
16. t s s t s s t s ...... s
17. p t a p t a p t a ...... p
18. s p t s p t s p t ...... s
19. s a p s a p s a p ...... s
20. t p s t p s t p s ...... t
21. s t t p s t t p s t t p ...... s
22. a p p t a p p t a p p t ...... a
23. t a a s t a a s t a a s ...... t
24. p s s a p s s a p s s a ...... p

Print out the cards below to use when introducing the sounds and sound spellings.

Activity 8 Sound spelling cards Set 1

a	s
t	p

There are six different bingo cards and a set of individual sound spelling cards which can be copied and cut out.
Each child is given their own bingo card. Shuffle the sound spelling cards, select and 'call' the sound spellings, one by one, from the top of the pile. There are a number of ways to do this, depending on the focus for the pupils:

- show the selected sound spelling and say the sound – child matches visual figures with auditory reinforcement
- show the selected sound spelling only – child matches visual figures without auditory reinforcement
- say the sound for the selected sound spelling but do not show it to the children – child processes the auditory information and matches to a visual figure.

When a child has a sound spelling on their card they can cover it with a counter or write over the sound spelling on the bingo card, writing in between the lines as a guide, saying the sound as they write. If they have more than one of a sound spelling on the card then they must only cover one and wait for that sound spelling to be called again. The first person to cover all their sound spellings is the winner.

Activity 9 Sound spelling bingo Set 1

a	a
t	p

t	t
p	a

p	s
p	a

s	t
a	p

s	p
t	s

s	t
a	s

a	a	a	a	a
a	p	p	p	p
p	p	t	t	t
t	t	t	s	s
s	s	s	s	

Visual discrimination is the ability to see differences between objects that are similar. Good visual discrimination helps keep us from getting confused when looking at shapes and forms in the environment. Children with poor visual discrimination may find it difficult to recognise letters, may confuse letters such as b and d and may find it difficult to identify mathematical symbols.

Focus on one sound spelling e.g. **s** (say the sound 's' and point to the matching sound spelling rather than using the letter name when talking to the child).
Ask the child to look at all the sound spellings and indicate or put a ring round all the letters matching the target.

Break this task into a number of shorter tasks over a number of lessons if necessary.

Activity 12 Spot the sound spelling Set 1

p t s t a

a p

s a s t

s p

a t

p s

t a

Visual memory is the ability to remember and identify a shape or picture that we have previously seen. Children with poor visual memory may struggle to remember pictures, figures, shapes, letters and numbers and may have difficulties with reading, writing and number work.

Ask the child to look at the sound spelling in the yellow box for at least five seconds, covering the white box underneath. Then cover the yellow box so that the sound spelling cannot be seen and reveal the choice of sound spellings in the white box below. Ask the child to select the matching sound spelling from the white box.

Break this task into a number of shorter tasks over a number of lessons if necessary.

Activity 13 Remembering sound spellings Set 1

s
s a

t
p t

a
s a

p
t p

t
s t p

s
a p s

Visual discrimination is the ability to see differences between objects that are similar. Good visual discrimination helps keep us from getting confused when looking at shapes and forms in the environment. Children with poor visual discrimination may find it difficult to recognise letters, may confuse letters such as b and d and may find it difficult to identify mathematical symbols.

Ask the child to colour in the shapes according to the sound spelling colour key at the bottom.

Activity 14 Colour the picture Set 1

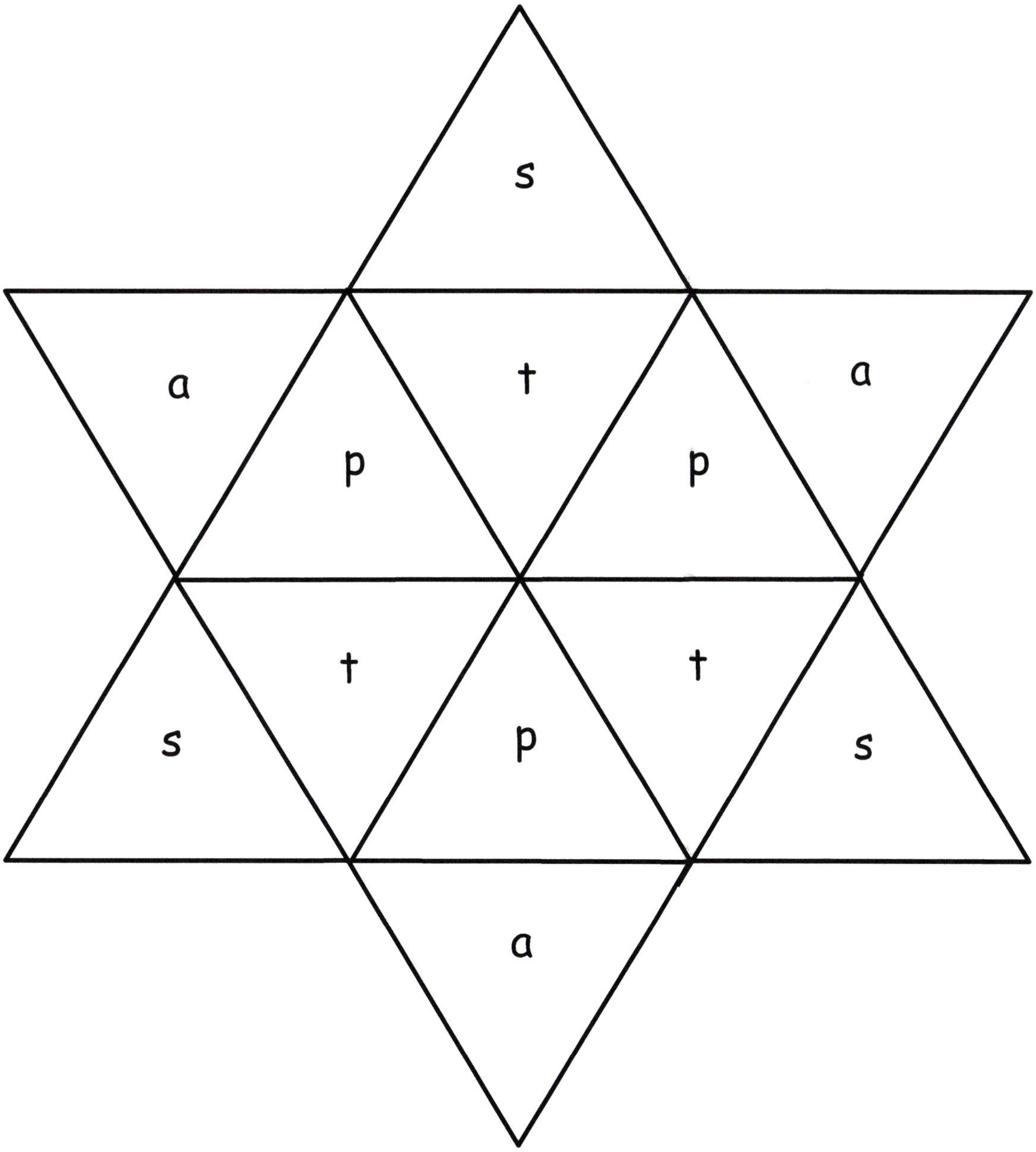

Colour p red s yellow t orange a brown

Form constancy is the ability to generalise forms and figures and identify them even if they are slightly different from that usually seen. This skill helps us distinguish differences in size, shape, and orientation or position. Children with poor form constancy may frequently reverse letters and numbers.

Ask the child to look at the letter on the left and match to a letter on the right (written differently), drawing a line to connect each.

Activity 15 Which is the same? Set 1

p	a
a	s
t	p
s	t
s	t
t	a
p	p
a	s

Visual closure is the ability to identify an object, shape or symbol from a visually incomplete or disorganised presentation and to see where the different parts of a whole fit together, i.e. to recognise something when seeing only part of it. This skill helps us understand things quickly because our visual system doesn't have to process every detail to recognise what we're seeing.

Ask the child to look at the sound spelling in the white box then track left to right along the row.
Ask the child to indicate or put a ring around the sound spelling that is the same as the sound spelling in the white box.

Break this task into a number of shorter tasks over a number of lessons if necessary.

Activity 16 Bits missing Set 1

p	p	t	s
s	a	s	p
a	s	a	p
t	t	p	a
p	p	s	a
s	s	a	p

Figure ground is the ability to find patterns or shapes when hidden within a busy background without getting confused by surrounding images. This skill keeps children from getting lost in the details, for example when looking at pictures in books or reading. Children with poor figure ground become easily confused with too much print on the page, affecting their concentration and attention.

Ask the child to look at the sound spellings which are overlapping. Ask the child to first find and count all the 's' sound spellings (refer to the sound not the letter name), then the **t** etc. Ask the child to write down how many of each sound spelling they found.

Break this task into a number of shorter tasks over a number of lessons if necessary.

Activity 17 Busy sound spellings Set 1

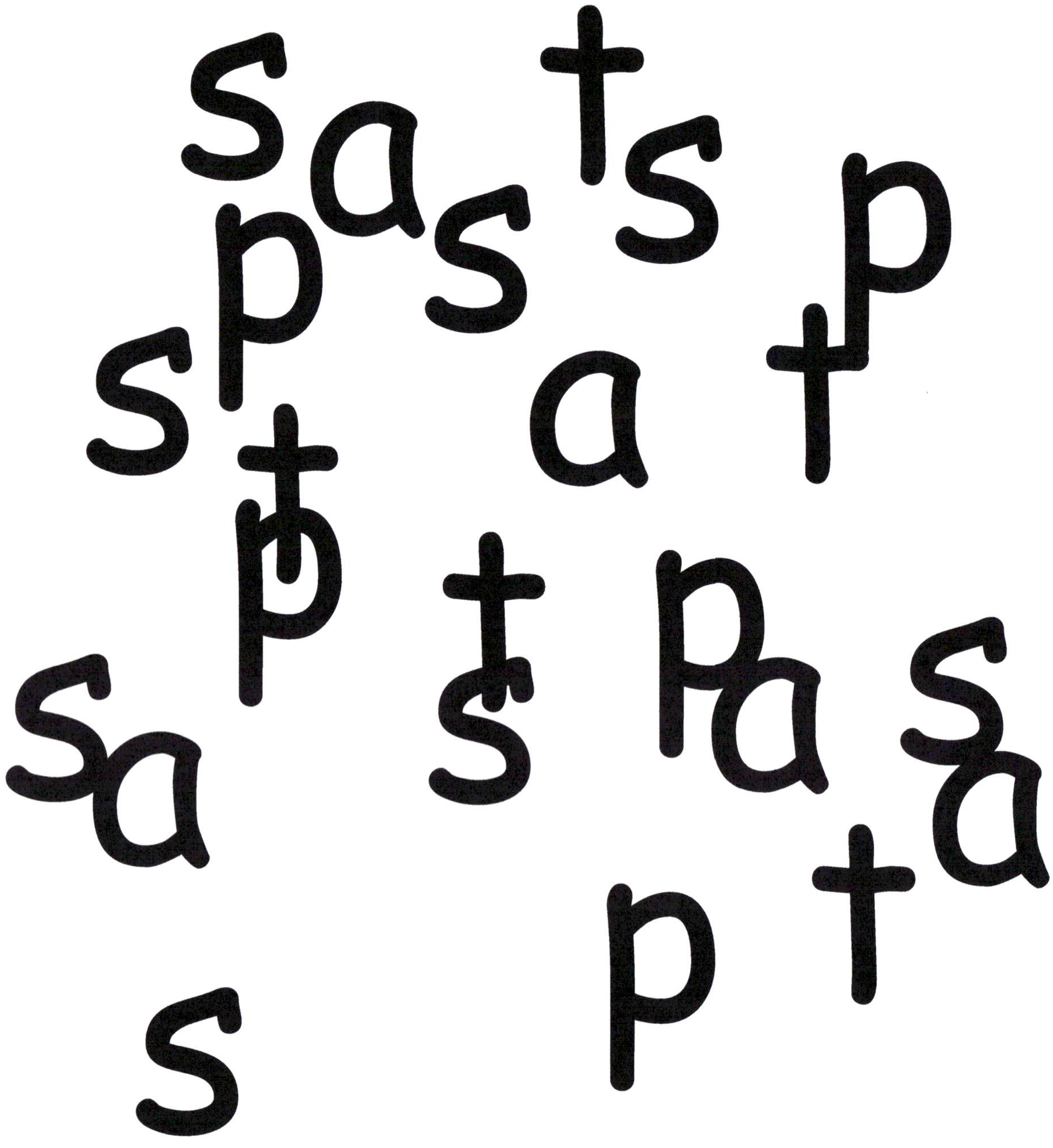

Spatial relations is the ability to perceive the position of objects in relation to ourselves and to each other. This skill helps children to understand relationships between symbols and letters. Children with poor spatial relations may find it difficult to write letters in the correct orientation, write consistently starting at the margin and write letters of the same size.

In the first part, ask the child to copy the sound spellings on the line underneath in exactly the same places as they appear above.
In the second part, ask the child to copy the words on the line underneath in exactly the same places, saying the matching sound as they write each sound spellings.
Break this task into a number of shorter tasks over a number of lessons if necessary.

Activity 18 Where am I? Set 1

a p s

p t a p

pat a tap

at sat sap

Visual sequential memory is the ability to remember sequences of figures, symbols and shapes. Children with poor visual sequencing struggle to remember a sequence of letters and follow visual patterns. They may have difficulties writing a sequence of letters to form a word and a sequence of words to form a sentence.

Ask the child to look at the sound spellings in the yellow box for at least five seconds, covering the white box underneath. Then cover the yellow box so that the sound spellings cannot be seen and reveal the sequence of sound spellings in the white box below. Ask the child to remember the missing sound spelling and write it in the space.

Break this task into a number of shorter tasks over a number of lessons if necessary.

Activity 19 Remembering lots of sound spellings Set 1

s	a
_	a

t	a
t	_

a p
_ p

p t
t _

t p s
t p _

s p t
s _ t

Tracking is the ability to follow a sequence of symbols. The eyes need to focus on the symbols in order and not look randomly at the symbols on the page. This is an important skill for reading and writing where letters and words are written from left to right and the reader is required to work down a page from the top to the bottom.

Choose a target sound spelling for the child to find. Ask the child to look at the sound spellings, tracking from left to right and down the page.
When they find the target sound spelling the child indicates or puts a ring around it. Repeat with a different sound spelling.

Break this task into a number of shorter tasks over a number of lessons if necessary.

Activity 20 Tracking sound spellings Set 1

s a s p t s a a p t
p s t s p a t a p s

p t s p a t s p t a t s s
a t s p p a t s p t a p a
s t a p p t s a s t p a t

p p t s a p s t s t a p t s p a a p t
s p a a p t t a p t s s p a t p a p t
s t a s t t p a t s s t p p a s t p a

t s a p t s a p t t s p t p a s t a s
p t s t a p s p t a p t a s p t s a t
s a p t s t t p a s s p a t p a t p s

Having introduced the sounds and their corresponding sound spellings it is important that the child is given the opportunity to practise forming the sound spellings. As discussed in the introductory chapter, the child should be provided with lots of sensory and kinaesthetic experiences of forming the sound spellings in a variety of media as well as writing on conventional paper.

In this activity the child can practise forming the sound spellings by copying over the grey sound spellings which act as a guide. Encourage the child to say the sound at the same time as writing the sound spelling. The child can then practise writing the sound spellings within the boxes underneath which focuses the child on the spatial relationship between the sound spelling as it forms and the surrounding visual environment.

Activity 21 Writing sound spellings Set 1

a a a a a

a a a a a a a

a						

s s s s s

s s s s s s s

t t t t t

t t t t t t t

p p p p p

p p p p p p p

Blending is the ability to push sounds together to make a word and is a key skill in reading. Blending is a dynamic activity where the child actively pushes the sounds together and listens to the word forming.

Activity 22 'A place to read' prepares the child for blending sounds themselves as part of the process of learning to read. You will model the dynamic blending technique for the child who will then tell you what word they can hear forming. Refer to the full explanation of the 'A place to read' activity in the 'Working through the programme' section.

Segmenting, the ability to split words up into their component sounds in sequence, is a key skill in spelling. The child needs to isolate each sound and match a sound spelling to successfully spell a word.

Activity 28 'A place to listen' activity prepares the child for segmenting words as part of the process of learning to spell. Refer to the full explanation of the 'A place to listen' activity in the 'Working through the programme' section.

Below is a list of words to use for both activities. At this early stage in the programme there are very few meaningful words which can be generated from the sounds studied in set 1.

Activity 22 A place to read — Set 1
Activity 28 A place to listen

at

pat

sat

tap

This set of cards is made up of words containing the target sounds for set 1. Copy onto card and cut out. Practise dynamic blending for reading, as described in the 'Working through the programme' section, using these cards. Notice that the letters get gradually darker as the child works through the word, a visual signal that they are pushing together the sounds and preparing them to listen to the word forming. Model this process for the child if necessary.

Activity 23 Dynamic blending Set 1

at	sat
pat	tap

Print out onto card and cut out.
Stack them with the biggest (the complete word) on the bottom and in decreasing size so that the smallest is on the top.
Make sure the left-hand edge of the cards are flush. Staple the cards together on the left-hand side.
When the child runs a finger over the cards the sound spellings flip up. Ask the child to say the sounds and match to the flips.

Flippies

Set 1

s	s a	s a t
p	p a	p a t
t	t a	t a p

Read the clue on the left for the child.
Use the clue to work out what the answer word is.
Encourage the child to think about the sounds in the word and write a sound spelling for each sound in the boxes on the right, one by one.
The first one is done as an example for you.
Explain that they may not need to use all the boxes and so some are shaded in.
Break this task into a number of shorter tasks over a number of lessons if necessary.

Activity 30 Sound boxes Set 1

Clue	Sound boxes		
	t	a	p

Look ________ the TV.			
The boy ________ on the chair.			
I want __ biscuit.			

Support the child to read the words on the left one by one.
For each word support the child to work out what sounds are in the word and count them.
Then support the child to cross out any boxes that are not needed.
In each of the boxes in the middle, have the child write the sound spelling to match each sound.
In the last column the child writes how many sounds there are in the word.
Break this task into a number of shorter tasks over a number of lessons if necessary.

Activity 31 How many sounds? Set 1

Word	Sound spellings					How many sounds?
at	a	t				2
sat	s	a	t			3
tap						
a						
Pat						

During this activity the child will get the chance to slide sounds in and out of words, i.e. practise phoneme manipulation. Sounds will be swapped, added or taken away. Print the sound spellings on card and cut out.

Build a starting word from the prompt list, demonstrating dynamic blending as you move the sound spelling cards into place.

Repeat the word, running your finger along the cards so that it corresponds with the sounds within the word.

Ask the child to change the word to the next word on the prompt list. As you say the new word run your finger under the cards so that it corresponds with the sounds within the word and gives the child the chance to hear and see what is different.

The child can then swap the appropriate sound spelling cards.

Activity 33 Sound swap Set 1

Sound swap s a t p

List 1	List 2
at	pat
sat	sat
pat	at
tat	a
tap	at
sap	tat

s	a	t
t	p	

Support the child to read the word in the first column. Then, referring to the second column, ask the child what sound they are going to take away.
Then ask the child to think about what word would be made if the sound in the second column was taken out of the word, in this case from the beginning of it.
Remind the child to think about the sounds, blend dynamically and listen to the word forming.
Have the child write out the new word on the line at the end, sounding out the word as they write each sound spelling.

There are very few meaningful words which can be generated from the sounds in this set so this is just an example of similar work as the child progresses through the programme.

Activity 34 Read – Delete – Spell Set 1

Read	Read without this sound	Spell the new word
sat	's'	____________
at	't'	____________
pat	'p'	____________

This set of cards is made up of words containing the target sounds for set 1. Copy onto card and cut out. Practise dynamic blending for reading, as described in the 'Working through the programme' section, using these cards. Model this process for the child if necessary.

Activity 37 Reading words with target sounds Set 1

at	sat
pat	tap

This set of cards is made up of the high frequency words containing the target sounds for set 1. Copy onto card and cut out.

Practise dynamic blending for reading, as described in the 'Working through the programme' section, using these cards. Model this process for the child if necessary.

Activity 38 Reading high frequency words Set 1

a	at
sat	

Starting at 'a' have the child read each of the words as quickly as possible tracking along the line one by one until they get to 'pat'.
Support the child to read the words by giving information about sounds and supporting dynamic blending but do not supply the whole word.
Time how long it takes to read all the words and record the time at the bottom of the page.
Repeat at a later point, e.g. at the end of the lesson or the following day, and see if the child can beat their *own* previous time.

Activity 39 Reading race — Set 1

a at tap sat pat

1 _____ minutes ____ seconds
2 _____ minutes ____ seconds
3 _____ minutes ____ seconds

Visual discrimination is the ability to see differences between objects that are similar. Good visual discrimination helps keep us from getting confused when looking at shapes and forms in the environment. Children with poor visual discrimination may find it difficult to recognise letters, may confuse letters such as b and d and may find it difficult to identify mathematical symbols.

Ask the child to look at the word in the pink box then track along the row looking at the other words. The child indicates or puts a ring around the word that is the same as the one in the pink box.

Break this task into a number of shorter tasks over a number of lessons if necessary.

Activity 40 Spot the word Set 1

a	p	s	a
at	at	ap	pa
sat	sat	pat	tap
tap	pat	sat	tap
pat	tap	pat	sat

Visual memory is the ability to remember and identify a shape or picture that we have previously seen. Children with poor visual memory may struggle to remember pictures, figures, shapes, letters and numbers and may have difficulties with reading, writing and number work.

Ask the child to look at the word in the yellow box for at least five seconds, covering the white box underneath. Then cover the yellow box so that the letter cannot be seen and reveal the choice of words in the white box below. Ask the child to select the matching word from the white box.

Break this task into a number of shorter tasks over a number of lessons if necessary.

Activity 41 Remembering words Set 1

sat
sat at

tap
pat tap

at
sat at

pat
tap pat

tap
tap sat pat

sat
at sat pat

Form constancy is the ability to generalise forms and figures and identify them even if they are slightly different from that usually seen. This skill helps us distinguish differences in size, shape, and orientation or position. Children with poor form constancy may frequently reverse letters and numbers.

Ask the child to look at the word in the orange box then track along the row looking at the other words. The child indicates or puts a ring around the word that is the same as the one in the orange box.

Break this task into a number of shorter tasks over a number of lessons if necessary.

Activity 42 Which is the word? Set 1

a	o	a	c
at	if	it	at
sat	set	sat	sit
tap	tap	top	tip
pat	pet	pit	pat

Visual closure is the ability to identify an object, shape or symbol from a visually incomplete or disorganised presentation and to see where different parts of a whole fit together, i.e. to recognise something when seeing only part of it. This skill helps us understand things quickly because our visual system doesn't have to process every detail to recognise what we're seeing.

Ask the child to look at the large word and then at the choice of smaller words underneath. The child indicates or puts a ring around the word that is the same as the big word.

Break this task into a number of shorter tasks over a number of lessons if necessary.

Activity 43 Word splits Set 1

at

at it

sat

sat pat

pat

tap pat

Figure ground is the ability to find patterns or shapes when hidden within a busy background without getting confused by surrounding images. This skill keeps children from getting lost in the details, for example when looking at pictures in books or reading. Children with poor figure ground become easily confused with too much print on the page, affecting their concentration and attention.

Ask the child to look at the words which are overlapping. Ask the child to first find all the words. Some words are written more than once. How many of each word are there?

Break this task into a number of shorter tasks over a number of lessons if necessary.

Activity 44 Busy words Set 1

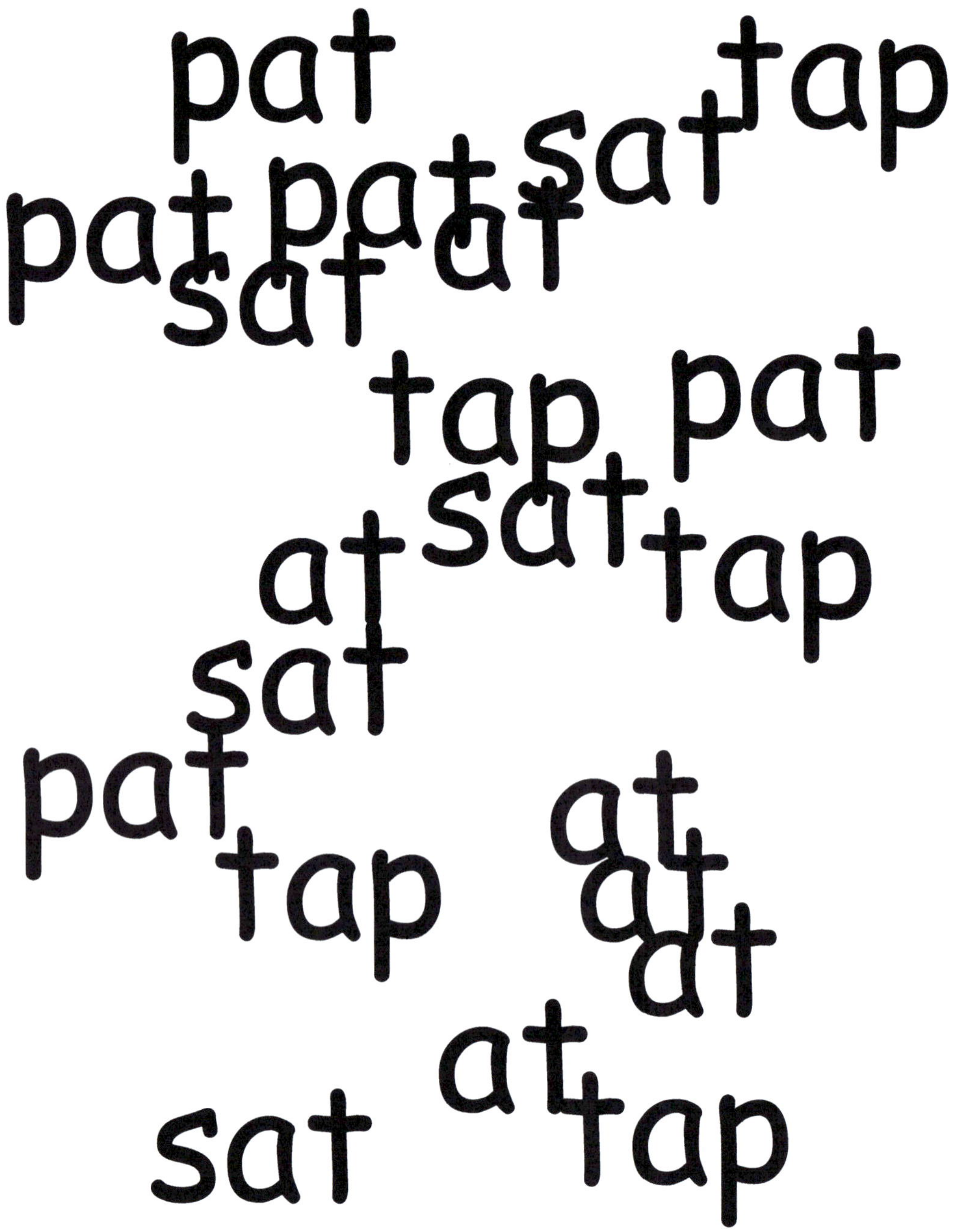

Visual sequential memory is the ability to remember sequences of figures, symbols and shapes. Children with poor visual sequencing struggle to remember a sequence of letters and follow visual patterns. They may have difficulties writing a sequence of letters to form a word and a sequence of words to form a sentence.

Ask the child to look at the words in the yellow box for at least five seconds, covering the white box underneath. Then cover the yellow box so that the words cannot be seen and reveal the sequence of words in the white box below. Ask the child to remember the missing word and write it in the space.

Break this task into a number of shorter tasks over a number of lessons if necessary.

Activity 45 Remembering lots of words Set 1

sat at
_____ at

tap pat
tap _____

at pat
____ pat

tap sat
tap ____

at	sat	pat
____	sat	pat

tap	at	sat
tap	____	sat

Tracking is the ability to follow a sequence of letters, figures or symbols. The eyes need to focus on the symbols in order and not look randomly at the symbols on the page. This is an important skill for reading and writing where letters and words are written from left to right and the reader is required to work down a page from the top to the bottom.

Ask the child to look at the symbols and sound spellings and track from left to right. When the child finds a group of sound spellings then they indicate or put a circle around them all. The child then reads the word.

Break this task into a number of shorter tasks over a number of lessons if necessary.

Activity 46 Hidden words Set 1

◣◁↘▲at→↔▷▲←▲▽sat⇦▲▽⇨▲⇦⇨
⇦tap⇦▲▷▽↘▽pat⇦▷↓▽⇦↘⇨ at⇨▲⇦

▲at▲▷△▷⇨pat←▲▷↔sat▲↗⇨↘▽↘⇕↦
tap⇦▷▼⇕↔▽⇕↔sat▷←⇕↔↗ at⇨⇦▷⇕←

at→↔▷▲▲▷△▷⇨pat←▲sat▲↘⇦↗↦⇨
↗⇨ sat↘↘▽↘⇕↦tap⇦▷▼⇕↔▽⇕at▲△↔

ψιρτtapδωθνσatπωψρωαpatφπλ
ωωνsatμρδφυδτsatωφνδεatεδωφ

Prior to working with the child, read through the instructions in the 'Working through the programme' section.

Activity 47 Word build Set 1

a	t		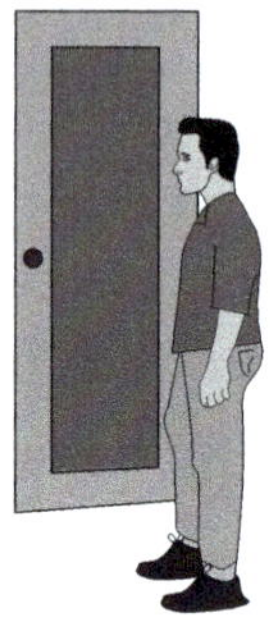
p	a	t	
s	a	t	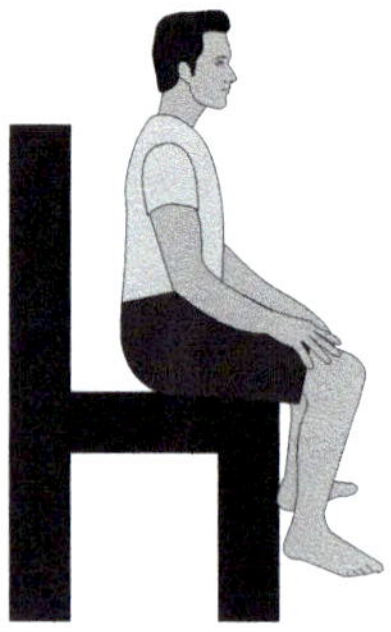
t	a	p	

Support the child to look at the picture and work out what the word is.
Then support the child to work out the initial sound in the word and match a sound spelling in the gap provided.
The 'Place to listen' technique should be used to support this.
Read through the 'Place to listen' instructions in the 'Working through the programme' section of this book prior to working with the child.
Ask the child to read the completed word using the dynamic blending technique.

Activity 48 Finish the word 1 Set 1

	_ a t
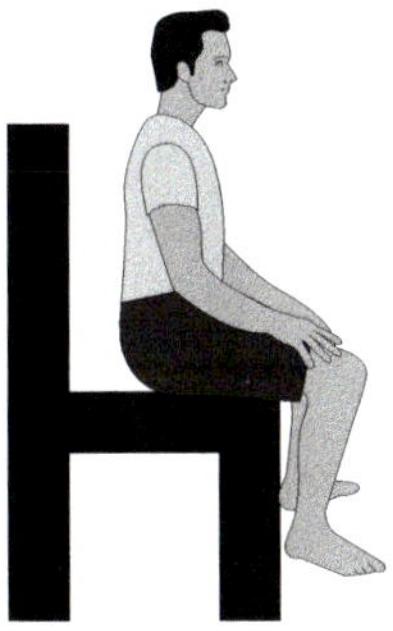	_ a t
	_ a p

Support the child to look at the picture and work out what the word is.
Then support the child to work out the middle sound in the word and match a sound spelling in the gap provided.
The 'Place to listen' technique should be used to support this.
Read through the 'Place to listen' instructions in the 'Working through the programme' section of this book prior to working with the child.
Ask the child to read the completed word using the dynamic blending technique.

Activity 49 Finish the word 2 Set 1

	t _ p
	p _ t
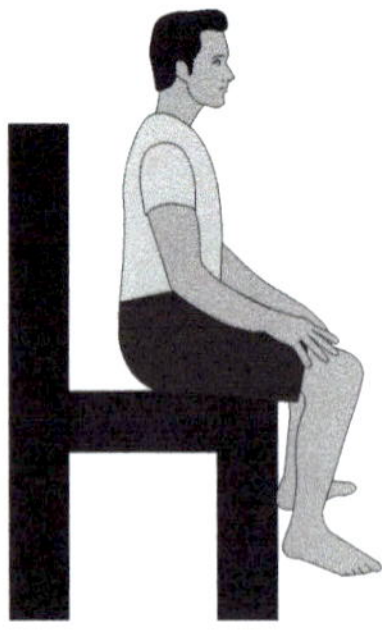	s _ t

Support the child to look at the picture and work out what the word is.
Then support the child to work out the final sound in the word and match a sound spelling in the gap provided.
The 'Place to listen' technique should be used to support this.
Read through the 'Place to listen' instructions in the 'Working through the programme' section of this book prior to working with the child.
Ask the child to read the completed word using the dynamic blending technique.

Activity 50 Finish the word 3 — Set 1

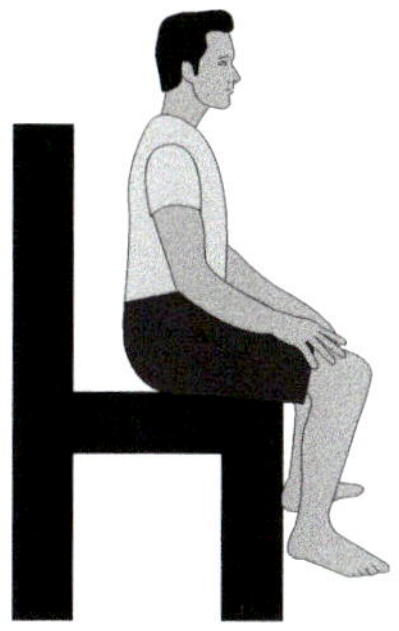

s a _

t a _

p a _

Read the instructions in the introduction of this book to guide you on how to work through this spelling practise sheet with the child.

Activity 52 Spelling challenge — Set 1

at	a	t		at	___ ___	___________
sat	s	a	t	sat	___ ___ ___	___________
tap	t	a	p	tap	___ ___ ___	___________

Answers Set 1: s a t p

Page 14
Activity 12 Spot the sound spelling

s 5
a 5
t 5
p 4

Page 20
Activity 17 Busy sound spellings

s 8
a 5
t 5
p 5

Page 30
Activity 30 Sound boxes

pat
at
sat
a

Page 31
Activity 31 How many sounds?

tap	3
a	1
pat	3

Page 33
Activity 34 Read – Delete – Spell

at
a
at

Page 42
Activity 44 Busy words

pat	5
at	6
tap	5
sat	5

Page 47
Activity 48 Finish the word 1

pat
sat
tap

Page 48
Activity 49 Finish the word 2

tap
pat
sat

Page 49
Activity 50 Finish the word 3

sat
tap
pat

SECTION 2

SET 2 SOUNDS AND SOUND SPELLINGS

i n m d

Auditory discrimination is the ability to hear differences between sounds. Good auditory discrimination helps us to recognise and identify the sounds in words and so interpret them correctly. Children with poor auditory discrimination may confuse sounds and misinterpret things they have heard. Their spelling and writing may reflect their confusion over what sounds they heard in a word. **Auditory attention and tracking** is the ability to actively listen and follow auditory information from beginning to end. Good auditory attention and tracking helps us to follow a conversation, a story read out loud or a set of instructions, being able to focus on key information. Children with poor auditory attention and tracking may find it difficult to follow and respond appropriately to what is being said to them.

This story contains lots of words that start with the sounds 'i', 'm', 'n' and 'd', but you will focus on just one 'target' sound.
Read the story out loud. Encourage the child to listen carefully and spot any word that starts with the 'target' sound. When a target word has been read, the child indicates that they have heard and spotted it by tapping the table, putting up a hand or any other agreed signal, but without shouting out. Stop reading and discuss the word, making any error correction necessary. If a word is missed, re-read the sentence. Do not show the story to the children. The target words are highlighted below for you: 'i', 'm', 'n' and 'd'. Repeat on another occasion focusing on a different target sound.

Activity 1 Sound target – Story sheet Set 2

Mum was mad. She sat down in the middle of the garden and sighed.
Mum loved her garden and she was incredibly proud of it.
She had so many new flowers: marigolds, daffodils and mimosa.
But her favourite were her daisies. They were massive and majestic.
Her neighbours all admired them immensely.
The problem with them was Misty. No, not mist - like fog! Misty, her daughter's pet rabbit. Misty had escaped and munched her way through all of mum's daisies! It was a disaster! Mum was miserable.
She would never get those flowers back.
Suddenly mum felt a tickle on her hand. A small cold nose was nuzzling her. Mum laughed. She could not stay mad with such a naughty but delightful rabbit like Misty.

Please Note: The focus of activity is the *sound* in the word, NOT what *letter* is in the word.

Auditory discrimination is the ability to hear differences between sounds. Good auditory discrimination helps us to recognise and identify the sounds in words and so interpret them correctly. Children with poor auditory discrimination may confuse sounds and misinterpret things they have heard. Their spelling and writing may reflect their confusion over what sounds they heard in a word. **Auditory sequential memory** is the ability to remember and recall a series of things that they have heard. Children with poor auditory sequential memory may find it difficult to remember information given earlier in a conversation or set of instructions and may struggle to recall the sequence of sounds in a word.

The sentences contain lots of words beginning with one of the target sounds 'i', 'm', 'n' or 'd'.
Read the sentence to the child several times; invite them to join in as you say it and gradually recall it on their own.
Ask them to say it as quickly as they can and have some fun with it. After some practise, ask the child if they can identify which sound they hear a lot in the tongue twister. Perhaps they can make up their own?
Note that the vocabulary included in these tongue twisters may be unfamiliar to the child, especially the adjectives. If appropriate, talk about unfamiliar words and discuss their meaning.
Break this task into a number of shorter tasks over a number of lessons if necessary.

Activity 2 Sound target – Tongue twister fun Set 2

Interesting Izzy invents inky ice-cream.
Itchy insects ignore igloos.

Naughty Nancy noshes nuts.
Nina's new needles knit noodles.

Magic Mandy mixes minty milk.
Mush a mango, make a mess!

Do dogs dance with dusty donkeys?
Dozy ducks dream of dancing daisies.

Auditory discrimination is the ability to hear differences between sounds. Good auditory discrimination helps us to recognise and identify the sounds in words and so interpret them correctly. Children with poor auditory discrimination may confuse sounds and misinterpret things they have heard. Their spelling and writing may reflect their confusion over what sounds they heard in a word. **Auditory attention and tracking** is the ability to actively listen and follow auditory information from beginning to end. Good auditory attention and tracking helps us to follow a conversation, a story read out loud or a set of instructions, being able to focus on key information. Children with poor auditory attention and tracking may find it difficult to follow and respond appropriately to what is being said to them.

This activity focuses the child on listening to short lists of words starting with the sounds 'i', 'm', 'n' and 'd'. The words get increasingly complex, as does the number of words the child has to listen to. Later items include words starting with sounds from previous sets.

Read out the words and ask the child to identify the odd one out, the word that *does not* start with the same sound as the other two. Do not show the words to the child. The odd one out is highlighted for you.
Break this task into a number of shorter tasks over a number of lessons if necessary.

Activity 3 Odd one out — Set 2

1.	in	ink	**map**	2.	mop	man	**nap**
3.	dad	**nip**	did	4.	**dog**	men	mum
5.	**it**	nit	nod	6.	den	**mat**	dig
7.	melt	mend	**nest**	8.	damp	**ink**	desk
9.	**dent**	mask	mint	10.	mast	maps	**dump**
11.	drop	drip	**spot**	12.	trip	**drag**	twig
13.	**drink**	stamp	stand	14.	strip	**drank**	splint
15.	did	dad	dip	**nap**			
16.	man	mop	**ink**	men			
17.	**desk**	melt	mask	mend			

Auditory discrimination is the ability to hear differences between sounds. Good auditory discrimination helps us to recognise and identify the sounds in words and so interpret them correctly. Children with poor auditory discrimination may confuse sounds and misinterpret things they have heard. Their spelling and writing may reflect their confusion over what sounds they heard in a word. **Auditory recall memory** is the ability to remember and recall something that they have just heard. Children with poor auditory recall memory may find it difficult to remember sounds and words and respond appropriately.

Read the list of words below clearly, asking the child to listen carefully. All words start with an 'i', 'm', 'n' or 'd' and get increasingly complex. At random points, tap the table and stop reading, asking the child to remember and say the last word you said. Then ask them to tell you what the first sound in the word is.

Break this task into a number of shorter tasks over a number of lessons if necessary.

Activity 4 What sound am I? Set 2

1.	in	did	man	nap	not	dad	it
2.	mat	nit	dig	it	mad	nod	dog
3.	dip	in	men	nut	mug	nip	den
4.	ink	its	mask	nest	damp	mist	dent
5.	mend	dump	melt	desk	nest	mint	next
6.	drop	drag	drip	drift	drink	draft	
7.	mean	need	deep	meat	neat	deed	
8.	made	name	date	nail	daze	mate	
9.	nine	mile	dine	mine	night	died	
10.	moon	noon	drew	mood	do	droop	

Auditory discrimination is the ability to hear differences between sounds. Good auditory discrimination helps us to recognise and identify the sounds in words and so interpret them correctly. Children with poor auditory discrimination may confuse sounds and misinterpret things they have heard. Their spelling and writing may reflect their confusion over what sounds they heard in a word.

Read out the pairs of words. Ask the child to tell you whether or not they start with the same sound. The words get increasingly complex. Word pairs that start with the same sound are highlighted.

Break this task into a number of shorter tasks over a number of lessons if necessary.

Activity 5 Same or different? Set 2

1. in - it
2. did -dad
3. map - not
4. net - nod
5. dog - men
6. nip - den
7. mop - met
8. mad - dip
9. nut - it
10. mat - man
11. ink - its
12. melt - damp
13. desk - dump
14. mist - dent
15. mint - nest
16. drop - drag
17. drift - drink
18. mean - deep
19. need - neat
20. note - mole
21. moan - nope
22. name - date
23. mail - nail
24. main - made

Auditory fusion is the ability to hear the subtle gaps between sounds and words. Children with poor auditory fusion may get lost in conversations and when following a list of instructions given verbally.

Say the sounds or read the words in the list one after another at a brisk pace so that there are no obvious gaps between the sounds or words. Ask the child to listen carefully and then tell you how many sounds or words you have said. All the words start with the sound 'i', 'm', 'n' or 'd' and get increasingly complex.

Break this task into a number of shorter tasks over a number of lessons if necessary.

Activity 6 How many did you hear? Set 2

1. i - n - i - d
2. m - d - n
3. d - d - m - i - n
4. m - m - n - m
5. d - m - n
6. d - i - m - n - d
7. i - d - m
8. m - i - d - n
9. men - did - net
10. in - met - not
11. dad - map - ink - nap
12. mat - nip
13. net - man - mum - dot - dog
14. den - mop - nod
15. its - mist - damp
16. nest - desk
17. mend - next - melt
18. dump - mint - dent - mast
19. drag - drop
20. drift - drip - draft - drink
21. neat - mean - deep
22. deal - meet
23. nail - main - date - made
24. mail - name - make
25. note - moan
26. mole - nope - dole

Auditory attention and tracking is the ability to actively listen and follow auditory information from beginning to end. Good auditory attention and tracking helps us to follow a conversation, a story read out loud or a set of instructions, being able to focus on key information. Children with poor auditory attention and tracking may find it difficult to follow and respond appropriately to what is being said to them. **Auditory sequential memory** is the ability to remember and recall a series of things that they have heard. Children with poor auditory sequential memory may find it difficult to remember information given earlier in a conversation or a set of instructions and may struggle to recall the sequence of sounds in a word.

In this activity the child has to process the auditory information but also respond by working out the pattern and stating the next sound in the sequence. Read out the list of sounds with a clear space between each. Ask the child to listen and work out what sound would come next. Answers are in red.

Break this task into a number of shorter tasks over a number of lessons if necessary.

Activity 7 What comes next? Set 2

1. m d m d m d ...... m
2. i m i m i m i
3. m n m n m n ...... m
4. n i n i n i ...... n
5. m m i m m i m m i ...... m
6. d d n d d n d d n ...... d
7. m n n m n n m n n ...... m
8. d i i d i i d i i ...... d
9. d d m m d d m m ...... m
10. i i n n i i n n i i n n i
11. m m i i m m i i m m i i ...... m
12. m m n n m m n n m m n n ...... m
13. m m d m m d m m ...... d
14. n n d n n d n n d ...... n
15. i m m i m m i m m i
16. m n n m n n m n n ...... m
17. i m d i m d i m d i
18. n d m n d m n d m ...... n
19. n d i n d i n d i ...... n
20. m n i m n i m n i ...... m
21. d i i m d i i m d i i m ...... d
22. i n n d i n n d i n n d i
23. n m m i n m m i n m m i ...... n
24. n d d m n d d m n d d m ...... n

Print out the cards below to use when introducing the sounds and the sound spellings.

Activity 8 Sound spelling cards Set 2

i	m
n	d

There are six different bingo cards and a set of individual sound spelling cards which can be copied and cut out.
Each child is given their own bingo card. Shuffle the sound spelling cards, select and 'call' the sound spellings, one by one, from the top of the pile. There are a number of ways to do this, depending on the focus for the pupils:

- show the selected sound spelling and say the sound – child matches visual figures with auditory reinforcement
- show the selected sound spelling only – child matches visual figures without auditory reinforcement
- say the sound for the selected sound spelling but do not show it to the children – child processes the auditory information and matches to a visual figure.

When a child has a sound spelling on their card they can cover it with a counter or write over the sound spelling on the bingo card, writing in between the lines as a guide, saying the sound as they write. If they have more than one of a sound spelling on the card then they must only cover one and wait for that sound spelling to be called again. The first person to cover all their sound spellings is the winner.

Activity 9 Sound spelling bingo Set 2

m	m
i	n

i	i
n	m

n	d
n	m

d	i
m	n

d	n
i	d

d	i
m	d

i	i	i	i	i
i	m	m	m	m
m	m	n	n	n
n	n	n	d	d
d	d	d	d	

Visual discrimination is the ability to see differences between objects that are similar. Good visual discrimination helps keep us from getting confused when looking at shapes and forms in the environment. Children with poor visual discrimination may find it difficult to recognise letters, may confuse letters such as b and d and may find it difficult to identify mathematical symbols.

Ask the child to look at the sound spelling in the yellow box then track along the row looking at the other sound spellings. The child indicates or puts a ring around the sound spelling that is the same as the one in the yellow box.

Break this task into a number of shorter tasks over a number of lessons if necessary.

Activity 11 Sound spelling tracker Set 2

i	n	i	a	m
m	n	m	p	a
n	m	p	d	n
i	a	m	i	n
d	p	t	d	a
n	a	m	n	d
d	p	t	d	a

Visual discrimination is the ability to see differences between objects that are similar. Good visual discrimination helps keep us from getting confused when looking at shapes and forms in the environment. Children with poor visual discrimination may find it difficult to recognise letters, may confuse letters such as b and d and may find it difficult to identify mathematical symbols.

Focus on one sound spelling e.g. **i** (say the sound 'i' and point to the matching sound spelling rather than using the letter name when talking to the child).
Ask the child to look at all the sound spellings and indicate or put a ring round all the letters matching the target.

Break this task into a number of shorter tasks over a number of lessons if necessary.

Activity 12 Spot the sound spelling Set 2

i n i d i m

d

m i n m n

n n d

d n d

i m i

d n m d

Visual memory is the ability to remember and identify a shape or picture that we have previously seen. Children with poor visual memory may struggle to remember pictures, figures, shapes, letters and numbers and may have difficulties with reading, writing and number work.

Ask the child to look at the sound spelling in the yellow box for at least five seconds, covering the white box underneath. Then cover the yellow box so that the sound spelling cannot be seen and reveal the choice of sound spellings in the white box below. Ask the child to select the matching sound spelling from the white box.

Break this task into a number of shorter tasks over a number of lessons if necessary.

Activity 13 Remembering sound spellings Set 2

m
n m

d
p d

i
i t

n
m n

d
p d a

m
n m a

Visual discrimination is the ability to see differences between objects that are similar. Good visual discrimination helps keep us from getting confused when looking at shapes and forms in the environment. Children with poor visual discrimination may find it difficult to recognise letters, may confuse letters such as b and d and may find it difficult to identify mathematical symbols.

Ask the child to colour in the shapes according to the sound spelling colour key at the bottom.

Activity 14 Colour the picture Set 2

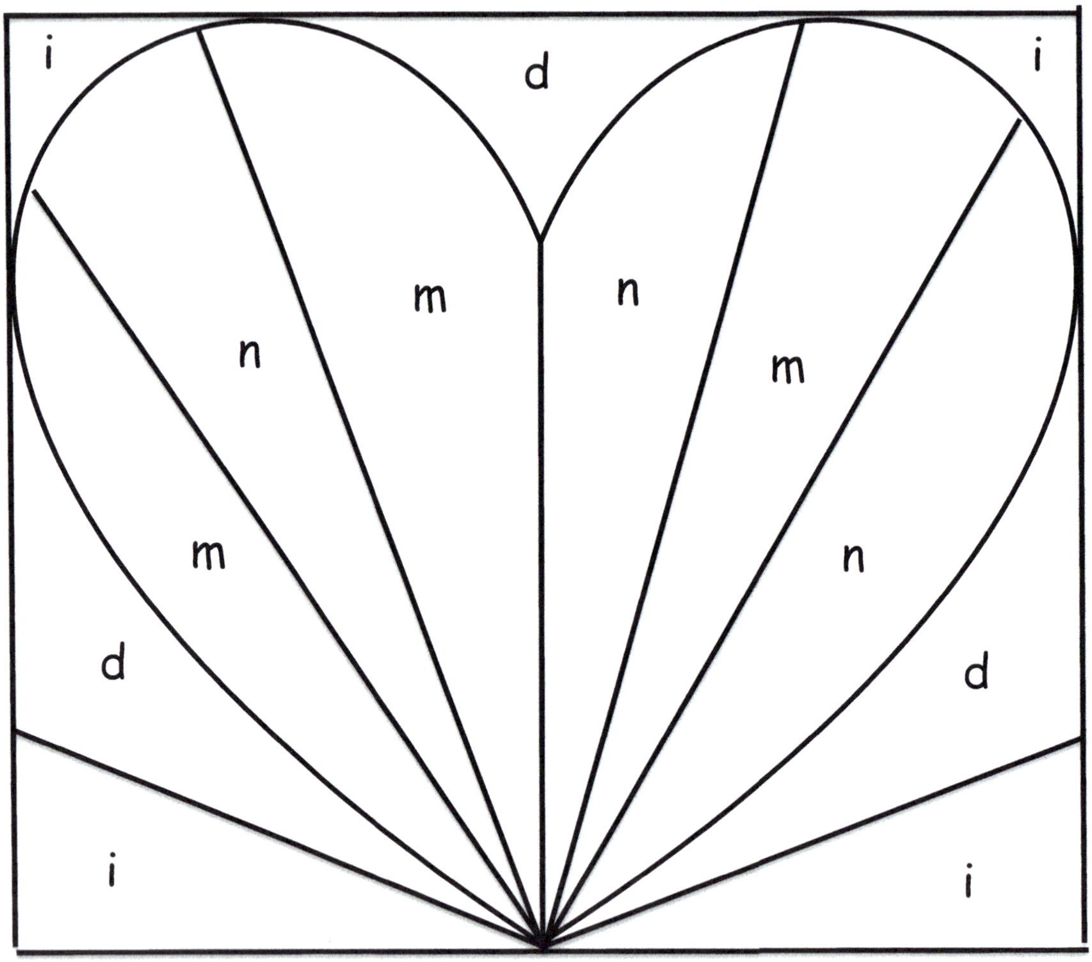

Colour m red n pink d yellow i orange

Form constancy is the ability to generalise forms and figures and identify them even if they are slightly different from that usually seen. This skill helps us distinguish differences in size, shape, and orientation or position. Children with poor form constancy may frequently reverse letters and numbers.

Ask the child to look at the letter on the left and match to a letter on the right (written differently), drawing a line to connect each.

Activity 15 Which is the same? Set 2

i	d
m	n
n	i
d	m
m	i
i	d
n	m
d	n

Visual closure is the ability to identify an object, shape or symbol from a visually incomplete or disorganised presentation and to see where the different parts of a whole fit together, i.e. to recognise something when seeing only part of it. This skill helps us understand things quickly because our visual system doesn't have to process every detail to recognise what we're seeing.

Ask the child to look at the sound spelling in the white box then track left to right along the row.
Ask the child to indicate or put a ring around the sound spelling that is the same as the sound spelling in the white box.

Break this task into a number of shorter tasks over a number of lessons if necessary.

Activity 16 Bits missing Set 2

m	n	m	p
	m	a	n
	d	p	n
	a	n	m
	i	t	d
	p	d	a

Figure ground is the ability to find patterns or shapes when hidden within a busy background without getting confused by surrounding images. This skill keeps children from getting lost in the details, for example when looking at pictures in books or reading. Children with poor figure ground become easily confused with too much print on the page, affecting their concentration and attention.

Ask the child to look at the sound spellings, which are overlapping. Ask the child to first find and count all the 'd' sound spellings (refer to the sound not the letter name), then the 'i' etc. Ask the child to write down how many of each sound spelling they found.

Break this task into a number of shorter tasks over a number of lessons if necessary.

Activity 17 Busy sound spellings Set 2

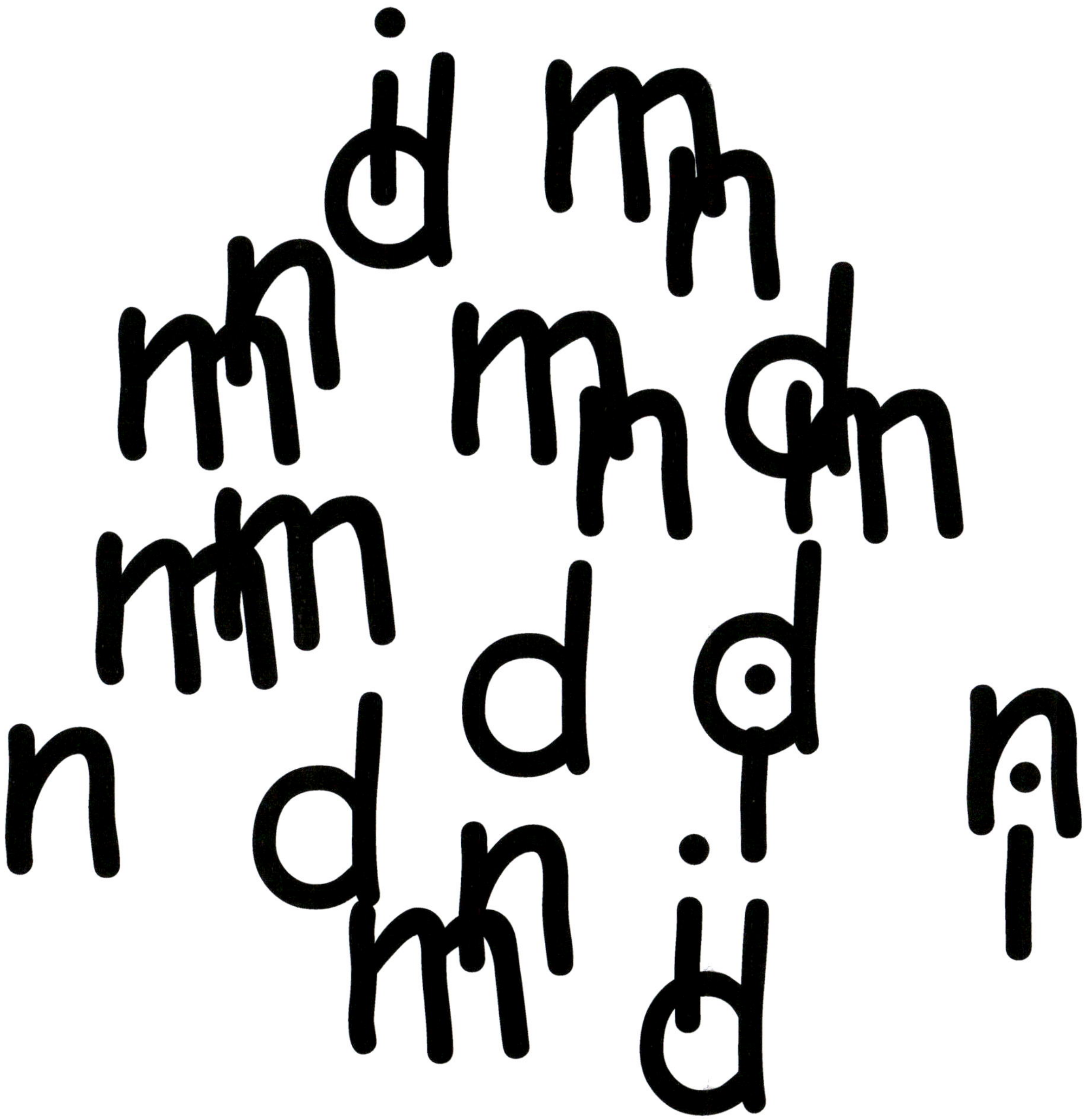

Spatial relations is the ability to perceive the position of objects in relation to ourselves and to each other. This skill helps children to understand relationships between symbols and letters. Children with poor spatial relations may find it difficult to write letters in the correct orientation, write consistently starting at the margin and write letters of the same size.

In the first part, ask the child to copy the sound spellings on the line underneath in exactly the same places as they appear above.
In the second part, ask the child to copy the words on the line underneath in exactly the same places, saying the matching sound as they write each sound spellings.
Break this task into a number of shorter tasks over a number of lessons if necessary.

Activity 18 Where am I? Set 2

m n d i

d m i n m

man in dim

sit nap

Visual sequential memory is the ability to remember sequences of figures, symbols and shapes. Children with poor visual sequencing struggle to remember a sequence of letters and follow visual patterns. They may have difficulties writing a sequence of letters to form a word and a sequence of words to form a sentence.

Ask the child to look at the sound spellings in the yellow box for at least five seconds, covering the white box underneath. Then cover the yellow box so that the sound spellings cannot be seen and reveal the sequence of sound spellings in the white box below. Ask the child to remember the missing sound spelling and write it in the space.

Break this task into a number of shorter tasks over a number of lessons if necessary.

Activity 19 Remembering lots of sound spellings Set 2

m n
_ n

t i
t _

d p
_ p

i t
_ t

n a m
n a _

a n m
a _ m

Tracking is the ability to follow a sequence of symbols. The eyes need to focus on the symbols in order and not look randomly at the symbols on the page. This is an important skill for reading and writing where letters and words are written from left to right and the reader is required to work down a page from the top to the bottom.

Choose a target sound spelling for the child to find. Ask the child to look at the sound spellings, tracking from left to right and down the page.
When they find the target sound spelling the child indicates or puts a ring around it. Repeat with a different sound spelling.

Break this task into a number of shorter tasks over a number of lessons if necessary.

Activity 20 Tracking sound spellings Set 2

m n d i n m m i d i
d m n d i i d n m i

m n m i d n d i m n i d i
m n d i m n i d i n m n i
d m i n i d m n m i d m n

i m n d p n i i d p m n m d p m i p n
d p i m i d p m n p p d i n m p m i d
p n d m p i n p m d m n d i m i d p i

t i m d i n t m p t m n i p d p t m n
m n d i m t p d t i d p t m n p m d i
n t i d p m m n d p t i p d i t m n m

Having introduced the sounds and their corresponding sound spellings it is important that the child is given the opportunity to practise forming the sound spellings. As discussed in the introductory chapter, the child should be provided with lots of sensory and kinaesthetic experiences of forming the sound spellings in a variety of media as well as writing on conventional paper.

In this activity the child can practise forming the sound spellings by copying over the grey sound spellings which act as a guide. Encourage the child to say the sound at the same time as writing the sound spelling. The child can then practise writing the sound spellings within the boxes underneath which focuses the child on the spatial relationship between the sound spelling as it forms and the surrounding visual environment.

Activity 21 Writing sound spellings Set 2

i i i i i

i i i i i i i

i						

n n n n n

n n n n n n n

m m m m m

m m m m m m m

d d d d d

d d d d d d d

Blending is the ability to push sounds together to make a word and is a key skill in reading. Blending is a dynamic activity where the child actively pushes the sounds together and listens to the word forming.

Activity 22 'A place to read' prepares the child for blending sounds themselves as part of the process of learning to read. You will model the dynamic blending technique for the child who will then tell you what word they can hear forming. Refer to the full explanation of the 'A place to read' activity in the 'Working through the programme' section.

Segmenting, the ability to split words up into their component sounds in sequence, is a key skill in spelling. The child needs to isolate each sound and match a sound spelling to successfully spell a word.

Activity 28 'A place to listen' activity prepares the child for segmenting words as part of the process of learning to spell. Refer to the full explanation of the 'A place to listen' activity in the 'Working through the programme' section.

Below is a list of words to use for both activities. Use words from the previous set if required.

Activity 22 A place to read Set 2
Activity 28 A place to listen

am an

in it

dad did dip

mad man map mat

nap nit nip

pad pan pin pip pit

sad sip sit

tan tin

This set of cards is made up of words containing the target sounds for set 2. Copy onto card and cut out. Practise dynamic blending for reading, as described in the 'Working through the programme' section, using these cards. Notice that the letters get gradually darker as the child works through the word, a visual signal that they are pushing together the sounds and preparing them to listen to the word forming. Model this process for the child if necessary.

Activity 23 Dynamic blending Set 2

am	in
it	man
nap	sad
sit	pan

Print out onto card and cut out.
Stack them with the biggest (the complete word) on the bottom and in decreasing size so that the smallest is on the top.
Make sure the left-hand edge of the cards are flush. Staple the cards together on the left-hand side.
When the child runs a finger over the cards the sound spellings flip up. Ask the child to say the sounds and match to the flips.

Flippies

Set 2 - a

d	d	i	d	i	d
m	m	a	m	a	n
s	s	i	s	i	t

Print out onto card and cut out.
Stack them with the biggest (the complete word) on the bottom and in decreasing size so that the smallest is on the top.
Make sure the left-hand edge of the cards are flush. Staple the cards together on the left-hand side.
When the child runs a finger over the cards the sound spellings flip up. Ask the child to say the sounds and match to the flips.

Flippies Set 2 - b

s	s a	s a d
m	m a	m a t
p	p i	p i n

Read the clue on the left for the child.
Use the clue to work out what the answer word is.
Encourage the child to think about the sounds in the word and write a sound spelling for each sound in the boxes on the right, one by one.
The first one is done as an example for you.
Explain that they may not need to use all the boxes and so some are shaded in.
Break this task into a number of shorter tasks over a number of lessons if necessary.

Activity 30 Sound boxes Set 2

Clue	Sound boxes		
Find this inside an apple.	p	i	p
Cook food in it.			
I __________ happy.			
Mum and __________.			
Sit on the floor on this.			

Support the child to read the words on the left one by one.
For each word support the child to work out what sounds are in the word and count them.
Then support the child to cross out any boxes that are not needed.
In each of the boxes in the middle, have the child write the sound spelling to match each sound.
In the last column the child writes how many sounds there are in the word.
Break this task into a number of shorter tasks over a number of lessons if necessary.

Activity 31 How many sounds? Set 2

Word	Sound spellings					How many sounds?
did	d	i	d			3
man						
am						
pin						
mat						
sit						
pan						
sad						
it						

During this activity the child will get the chance to slide sounds in and out of words, i.e. practise phoneme manipulation. Sounds will be swapped, added or taken away. Print the sound spellings on card and cut out.

Build a starting word from the prompt list, demonstrating dynamic blending as you move the sound spelling cards into place.

Repeat the word, running your finger along the cards so that it corresponds with the sounds within the word.

Ask the child to change the word to the next word on the prompt list. As you say the new word run your finger under the cards so that it corresponds with the sounds within the word and gives the child the chance to hear and see what is different.

The child can then swap the appropriate sound spelling cards.

Activity 33 Sound swap — Set 1 & 2

Sound swap i n m d

List 1	List 2
pip	sad
tip	sat
tap	sit
map	sip
mad	nip
mat	nap

s	a	t
p	p	i
n	m	d

Support the child to read the word in the first column. Then, referring to the second column, ask the child what sound they are going to take away.
Then ask the child to think about what word would be made if the sound in the second column was taken out of the word, in this case from the beginning of it.
Remind the child to think about the sounds, blend dynamically and listen to the word forming.
Have the child write out the new word on the line at the end, sounding out the word as they write each sound spelling.

Break this task into a number of shorter tasks over a number of lessons if necessary.

Activity 34 Read – Delete – Spell Set 2

Read	Read without this sound	Spell the new word
am	'm'	______________
pan	'p'	______________
pit	'p'	______________
tin	't'	______________
man	'm'	______________

Support the child to read the word in the first column. Then, referring to the second column, ask the child to think about what word would be made if the sound in the second column was added in front of the word. Remind the child to think about the sounds, blend dynamically and listen to the word forming.
Have the child write out the new word on the line at the end, sounding out the word as they write each sound spelling.

Break this task into a number of shorter tasks over a number of lessons if necessary.

Activity 35 Read – Add – Spell Set 2

Read	Read with this sound at the beginning	Spell the new word
at	's'	sat
in	'p'	______
at	'm'	______
it	's'	______
an	'm'	______

Support the child to read the words on the left, one by one.
For each word read the clue to the child and work out what the answer word is.
Explain to the child that they will need to either: add a sound, take away a sound or change a sound to make the answer word
e.g. sip > slip > lip > lap.
Have the child write out the new word on the line on the right, saying each sound as they write each sound spelling.
An example is done for you.
Break this task into a number of shorter tasks over a number of lessons if necessary.

Activity 36 Sound exchange — Set 2

Starting word	Clue	New word
at	Left sitting down	sat
tin	Not out	______
pad	Unhappy	______
pip	Just a little drink	______
an	Cook food in it	______
sit	Which one? Point to ____	______
map	Push to get water	______
at	____ a dog on the head!	______
nip	Find in apples and oranges	______

This set of cards is made up of words containing the target sounds for set 2. Copy onto card and cut out. Practise dynamic blending for reading, as described in the 'Working through the programme' section, using these cards. Model this process for the child if necessary.

Activity 37 Reading words with target sounds Set 2

dip	mad
mat	nap
pan	pip
sad	sip
sit	tin

This set of cards is made up of the high frequency words containing the target sounds for set 2. Copy onto card and cut out.
Practise dynamic blending for reading, as described in the 'Working through the programme' section, using these cards. Model this process for the child if necessary.

Activity 38 Reading high frequency words Set 2

in	it
did	am
an	dad
man	

Starting at 'in' have the child read each of the words as quickly as possible tracking along the line one by one until they get to 'sad'.
Support the child to read the words by giving information about sounds and supporting dynamic blending but do not supply the whole word.
Time how long it takes to read all the words and record the time at the bottom of the page.
Repeat at a later point, e.g. at the end of the lesson or the following day, and see if the child can beat their *own* previous time.

Activity 39 Reading race — Set 2

in man sit nap sad

1 _____ minutes ____ seconds
2 _____ minutes ____ seconds
3 _____ minutes ____ seconds

Visual discrimination is the ability to see differences between objects that are similar. Good visual discrimination helps keep us from getting confused when looking at shapes and forms in the environment. Children with poor visual discrimination may find it difficult to recognise letters, may confuse letters such as b and d and may find it difficult to identify mathematical symbols.

Ask the child to look at the word in the pink box then track along the row looking at the other words. The child indicates or puts a ring around the word that is the same as the one in the pink box.

Break this task into a number of shorter tasks over a number of lessons if necessary.

Activity 40 Spot the word Set 2

in	it	in	an
am	an	in	am
did	did	dad	pad
sit	sat	sip	sit
man	pan	mad	man

Visual memory is the ability to remember and identify a shape or picture that we have previously seen. Children with poor visual memory may struggle to remember pictures, figures, shapes, letters and numbers and may have difficulties with reading, writing and number work.

Ask the child to look at the word in the yellow box for at least five seconds, covering the white box underneath. Then cover the yellow box so that the letter cannot be seen and reveal the choice of words in the white box below. Ask the child to select the matching word from the white box.

Break this task into a number of shorter tasks over a number of lessons if necessary.

Activity 41 Remembering words Set 2

map
map man

dad
did dad

in
in it

man
map man

pip
pit pip pad

map
nap man map

Form constancy is the ability to generalise forms and figures and identify them even if they are slightly different from that usually seen. This skill helps us distinguish differences in size, shape, and orientation or position. Children with poor form constancy may frequently reverse letters and numbers.

Ask the child to look at the word in the orange box then track along the row looking at the other words. The child indicates or puts a ring around the word that is the same as the one in the orange box.

Break this task into a number of shorter tasks over a number of lessons if necessary.

Activity 42 Which is the word? Set 2

it	it	in	at
an	it	an	in
dad	sad	mad	dad
pip	pip	sip	nap
map	man	map	mat

Visual closure is the ability to identify an object, shape or symbol from a visually incomplete or disorganised presentation and to see where different parts of a whole fit together, i.e. to recognise something when seeing only part of it. This skill helps us understand things quickly because our visual system doesn't have to process every detail to recognise what we're seeing.

Ask the child to look at the large word and then at the choice of smaller words underneath. The child indicates or puts a ring around the word that is the same as the big word.

Break this task into a number of shorter tasks over a number of lessons if necessary.

Activity 43 Word splits Set 2

it
at   it
sit
sit   pat
dad
dad   pad
map
mat   map

Figure ground is the ability to find patterns or shapes when hidden within a busy background without getting confused by surrounding images. This skill keeps children from getting lost in the details, for example when looking at pictures in books or reading. Children with poor figure ground become easily confused with too much print on the page, affecting their concentration and attention.

Ask the child to look at the words, which are overlapping. Ask the child to first find all the words. Some words are written more than once. How many of each word are there?

Break this task into a number of shorter tasks over a number of lessons if necessary.

Activity 44 Busy words Set 2

it am it
am sad
did man
man
did it did it
it pip
sad pip pip pip
sad sad did
it pip am
man

Visual sequential memory is the ability to remember sequences of figures, symbols and shapes. Children with poor visual sequencing struggle to remember a sequence of letters and follow visual patterns. They may have difficulties writing a sequence of letters to form a word and a sequence of words to form a sentence.

Ask the child to look at the words in the yellow box for at least five seconds, covering the white box underneath. Then cover the yellow box so that the words cannot be seen and reveal the sequence of words in the white box below. Ask the child to remember the missing word and write it in the space.

Break this task into a number of shorter tasks over a number of lessons if necessary.

Activity 45 Remembering lots of words Set 2

sad	mat
____	mat

pin	tip
pin	____

man	did	
____	did	

dad	pit	
dad	____	

am	it	an
____	it	an

map	tin	sip
map	____	sip

Tracking is the ability to follow a sequence of letters, figures or symbols. The eyes need to focus on the symbols in order and not look randomly at the symbols on the page. This is an important skill for reading and writing where letters and words are written from left to right and the reader is required to work down a page from the top to the bottom.

Ask the child to look at the symbols and sound spellings and track from left to right. When the child finds a group of sound spellings then they indicate or put a circle around them all. The child then reads the word.

Break this task into a number of shorter tasks over a number of lessons if necessary.

Activity 46 Hidden words Set 2

↘▲↘dad→↔▷▲sit⇦▲▽⇨am⇨⇦tip⇦▲
▷▽↘▽man⇦▷↓▽⇦↘⇨did⇨▲⇦pan▲⇨

▲mat▲▷⇦⇨in←▲▷↔an▲↗▽⇦↘↕↱▽⇨
mad⇦▷▼↕↔⇦▽↕↔nap▷▲←↕↗tin⇨⇦↕⇦

→↔▷it▲▷△▷⇨pin←▶↙▲map▲↘⇦↗↱⇨
↗⇨sad↘↘▽↘↕↱tan⇦▷▼↕↔▽↕pip▲△↔

ρ γ η ι φ m a p δ ω θ ν σ a m π ω ρ ω α s a d φ π
λ ω ρ ν t i n μ δ φ υ η τ s i t ω φ ν ε η d i d ε δ ω φ

Prior to working with the child, read through the instructions in the 'Working through the programme' section.

Activity 47 Word build Set 2

i	n		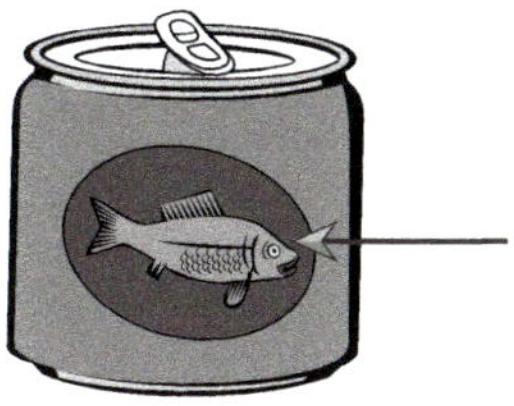
d	a	d	
p	i	n	
s	a	d	

m	a	p	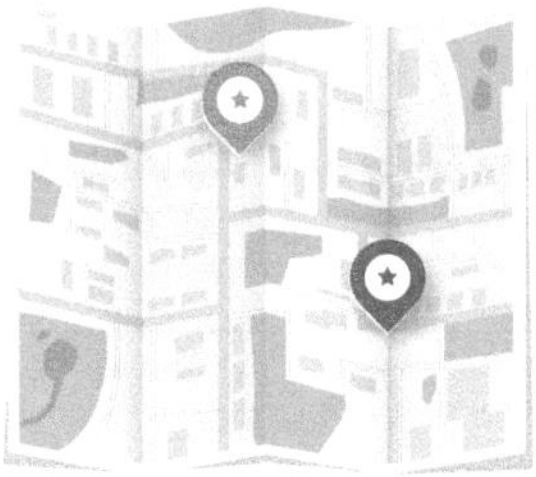
t	i	n	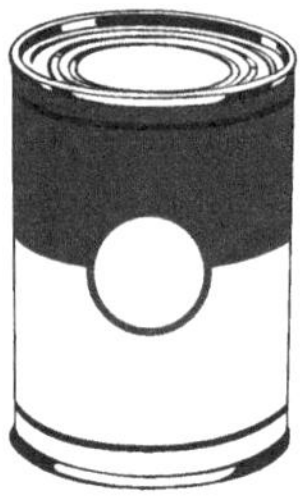
m	a	n	

Support the child to look at the picture and work out what the word is.
Then support the child to work out the initial sound in the word and match a sound spelling in the gap provided.
The 'Place to listen' technique should be used to support this.
Read through the 'Place to listen' instructions in the 'Working through the programme' section of this book prior to working with the child.
Ask the child to read the completed word using the dynamic blending technique.

Activity 48 Finish the word 1 Set 2

_ a d

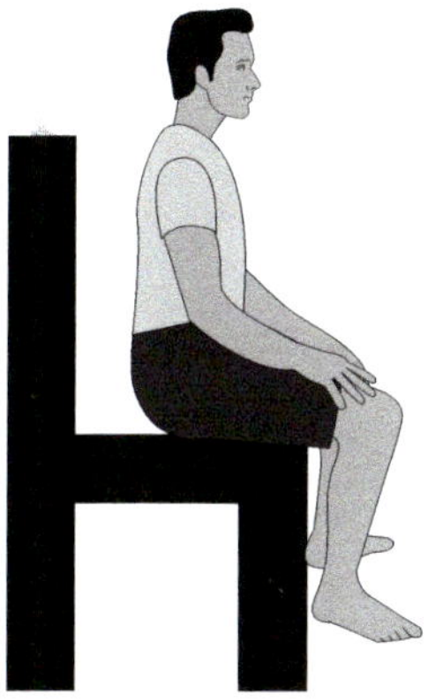

_ i t

_ a n

_ i p

Support the child to look at the picture and work out what the word is.
Then support the child to work out the middle sound in the word and match a sound spelling in the gap provided.
The 'Place to listen' technique should be used to support this.
Read through the 'Place to listen' instructions in the 'Working through the programme' section of this book prior to working with the child.
Ask the child to read the completed word using the dynamic blending technique.

Activity 49 Finish the word 2 Set 2

n _ p

m _ n

t _ n

s _ d

Support the child to look at the picture and work out what the word is.
Support the child to look at the picture and work out what the word is.
Then support the child to work out the final sound in the word and match a sound spelling in the gap provided.
The 'Place to listen' technique should be used to support this.
Read through the 'Place to listen' instructions in the 'Working through the programme' section of this book prior to working with the child.
Ask the child to read the completed word using the dynamic blending technique.

Activity 50 Finish the word 3 — Set 2

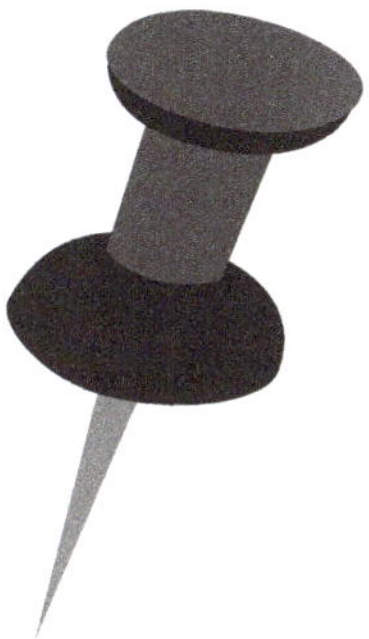

p i _

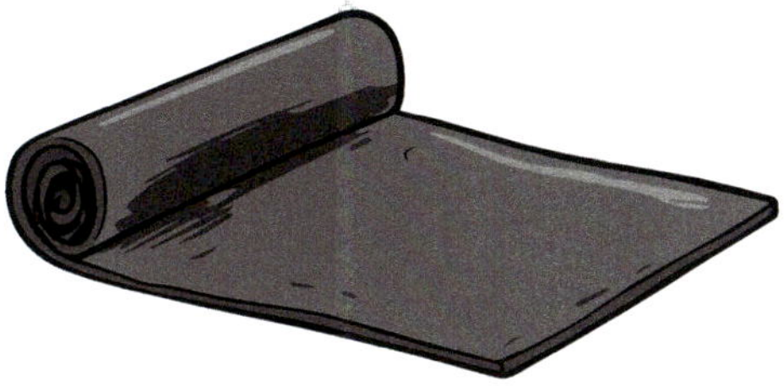

m a _

s i _

d a _

Read the instructions in the introduction of this book to guide you on how to work through this spelling practise sheet with the child.

Activity 52 Spelling challenge — Set 2

am	a m	a m	__ __	______
an	a n	a n	__ __	______
in	i n	i n	__ __	______
it	i t	i t	__ __	______
dad	d a d	d a d	__ __ __	______

did	d i d	did	__ __ __	__________
man	m a n	man	__ __ __	__________
sad	s a d	sad	__ __ __	__________
sit	s i t	sit	__ __ __	__________

Answers — Set 2: i n m d

Page 67
Activity 12 Spot the sound spelling

i 6
n 7
m 5
d 7

Page 73
Activity 17 Busy sound spellings

i 4
n 6
m 7
d 6

Page 84
Activity 30 Sound boxes

pan
am
dad
mat

Page 85
Activity 31 How many sounds?

man	3	am	2
pin	3	mat	3
sit	3	pan	3
sad	3	it	2

Page 88
Activity 34 Read – Delete – Spell

at
a
at

Page 89
Activity 35 Read – Add – Spell

pin
mat
sit
man

Page 90
Activity 36 Sound exchange

in	sad
sip	pan
it	tap
pat	pip

Page 99
Activity 44 Busy words

it	6
am	3
did	4
sad	4
man	3
pip	5

Page 105
Activity 48 Finish the word 1

dad	sit
pan	pip

Page 106
Activity 49 Finish the word 2

nap	man
tin	sad

Page 107
Activity 50 Finish the word 3

pin	mat
sip	dad

SECTION 3

SET 3 SOUNDS AND SOUND SPELLINGS

gock

Auditory discrimination is the ability to hear differences between sounds. Good auditory discrimination helps us to recognise and identify the sounds in words and so interpret them correctly. Children with poor auditory discrimination may confuse sounds and misinterpret things they have heard. Their spelling and writing may reflect their confusion over what sounds they heard in a word. **Auditory attention and tracking** is the ability to actively listen and follow auditory information from beginning to end. Good auditory attention and tracking helps us to follow a conversation, a story read out loud or a set of instructions, being able to focus on key information. Children with poor auditory attention and tracking may find it difficult to follow and respond appropriately to what is being said to them.

This poem contains lots of words that start with the sounds 'g', 'o', and 'k', but you will focus on just one 'target' sound.
Read the poem out loud. Encourage the child to listen carefully and spot any word that starts with the 'target' sound. The sound 'k' can be represented by the sound spellings **c** and **k** in words.
When a target word has been read, the child indicates that they have heard and spotted it by tapping the table, putting up a hand or any other agreed signal, but without shouting out. Stop reading and discuss the word, making any error correction necessary. If a word is missed, re-read the sentence. Do not show the story to the children. The target words are highlighted below for you: 'g', 'o' and 'k'. Repeat on another occasion focusing on a different target sound.

Activity 1 Sound target – Story sheet — Set 3

Can a cat go on a kite?	No
Can an otter go on a cake?	Never
Can a ghost get in a cot?	Not at all
Can a car get in a lake?	I hope not
Can a kid grow a moustache?	Not yet
Can a garden grow orange fish?	Get out of here!
Can an octopus give me a gift?	I wish!
Can my gran give me a kiss?	Of course

Please Note: The focus of activity is the *sound* in the word, NOT what letter is in the word.

Auditory discrimination is the ability to hear differences between sounds. Good auditory discrimination helps us to recognise and identify the sounds in words and so interpret them correctly. Children with poor auditory discrimination may confuse sounds and misinterpret things they have heard. Their spelling and writing may reflect their confusion over what sounds they heard in a word. **Auditory sequential memory** is the ability to remember and recall a series of things that they have heard. Children with poor auditory sequential memory may find it difficult to remember information given earlier in a conversation or set of instructions and may struggle to recall the sequence of sounds in a word.

The sentences contain lots of words beginning with one of the target sounds 'g', 'o', or 'k'. The sound 'k' can be represented by the sound spellings **c** and **k** in words.
Read the sentence to the child several times, invite them to join in as you say it and gradually recall it on their own.
Ask them to say it as quickly as they can and have some fun with it. After some practise, ask the child if they can identify which sound they hear a lot in the tongue twister. Perhaps they can make up their own?
Note that the vocabulary included in these tongue twisters may be unfamiliar to the child, especially the adjectives. If appropriate, talk about unfamiliar words and discuss their meaning.
Break this task into a number of shorter tasks over a number of lessons if necessary.

Activity 2 Sound target – Tongue twister fun Set 3

Grinning geese guard glittering gates.

Green goblins growl at greedy grannies.

Odd Oscar is an orange octopus.

Kicking kangaroos cook crispy carrots.

Cute kittens curl in café corners.

Auditory discrimination is the ability to hear differences between sounds. Good auditory discrimination helps us to recognise and identify the sounds in words and so interpret them correctly. Children with poor auditory discrimination may confuse sounds and misinterpret things they have heard. Their spelling and writing may reflect their confusion over what sounds they heard in a word. **Auditory attention and tracking** is the ability to actively listen and follow auditory information from beginning to end. Good auditory attention and tracking helps us to follow a conversation, a story read out loud or a set of instructions, being able to focus on key information. Children with poor auditory attention and tracking may find it difficult to follow and respond appropriately to what is being said to them.

This activity focuses the child on listening to short lists of words starting with the sounds 'g', 'o', and 'k'. The sound 'k' can be represented by the sound spellings **c** and **k** in words. The words get increasingly complex as does the number of words the child has to listen to. Later items include words starting with sounds from previous sets.

Read out the words and ask the child to identify the odd one out, the word that *does not* start with the same sound as the others. Do not show the words to the child. The odd one out is highlighted for you.
Break this task into a number of shorter tasks over a number of lessons if necessary.

Activity 3 Odd one out — Set 3

1.	**on**	cap	cat	2.	kid	kit	**get**
3.	cop	**gap**	cot	4.	can	**off**	cab
5.	cod	can	**top**	6.	dog	got	get
7.	camp	sink	cask	8.	mask	cost	cast
9.	**dent**	mask	mint	10.	mast	maps	**dump**
11.	drop	drip	**spot**	12.	trip	**drag**	twig
13.	**drink**	stamp	stand	14.	strip	**drank**	splint
15.	did	dad	dip	**nap**			
16.	man	mop	**ink**	men			
17.	**desk**	melt	mask	mend			

Auditory discrimination is the ability to hear differences between sounds. Good auditory discrimination helps us to recognise and identify the sounds in words and so interpret them correctly. Children with poor auditory discrimination may confuse sounds and misinterpret things they have heard. Their spelling and writing may reflect their confusion over what sounds they heard in a word. **Auditory recall memory** is the ability to remember and recall something that they have just heard. Children with poor auditory recall memory may find it difficult to remember sounds and words and respond appropriately.

Read the list of words below clearly, asking the child to listen carefully. All the words start with a 'g', 'o', or 'k' and get increasingly complex. The sound 'k' can be represented by the sound spellings **c** and **k** in words. At random points, tap the table and stop reading, asking the child to remember and say the last word you said. Then ask them to tell you what the first sound in the word is.

Break this task into a number of shorter tasks over a number of lessons if necessary.

Activity 4 What sound am I? Set 3

1.	got	on	can	kid	get	kit	cat
2.	cap	get	kip	cup	on	cot	got
3.	camp	grab	cost	glad	grip	crab	gran
4.	game	cake	came	gate	cape	cave	gain
5.	code	goat	goal	cone	coal	coat	
6.	green	cream	greet	creep	crease	creak	
7.	grew	clue	glue	crew	group	cruel	
8.	clown	gown	cloud	crowd	ground	growl	

Auditory discrimination is the ability to hear differences between sounds. Good auditory discrimination helps us to recognise and identify the sounds in words and so interpret them correctly. Children with poor auditory discrimination may confuse sounds and misinterpret things they have heard. Their spelling and writing may reflect their confusion over what sounds they heard in a word.

Read out the pairs of words. Ask the child to tell you whether or not they start with the same sound. The words get increasingly complex. Word pairs that start with the same sound are highlighted. The sound 'k' can be represented by the sound spellings **c** and **k** in words.

Break this task into a number of shorter tasks over a number of lessons if necessary.

Activity 5 Same or different? Set 3

1. on - in
2. can - cat
3. get - gap
4. kid - kit
5. cot - got
6. kip - on
7. cost - camp
8. grab - clap
9. grip - glad
10. crab - clip
11. grasp - clamp
12. gold - goal
13. coat - code
14. cream - clean
15. green - creep
16. growl - ground
17. cloud - clown
18. game - cake
19. grape - came
20. claim - cave
21. care - glare
22. grew - cruel

Auditory fusion is the ability to hear the subtle gaps between sounds and words. Children with poor auditory fusion may get lost in conversations and when following a list of instructions given verbally.

Say the sounds or read the words in the list one after another at a brisk pace so that there are no obvious gaps between the sounds or words. Ask the child to listen carefully and then tell you how many sounds or words you have said. All the words start with the sound 'g', 'o', or 'k' and get increasingly complex. The sound 'k' can be represented by the sound spellings **c** and **k** in words.

Break this task into a number of shorter tasks over a number of lessons if necessary.

Activity 6 How many did you hear? Set 3

1. g - k - g
2. k - c - g - o
3. g - g - k - o - o
4. g - k - o - o - g
5. k - c - g
6. o - g - k - k - o
7. g - c - g - g
8. g - c - g - o - k - g
9. can - cat - got
10. kit - cop - kid - on - gap
11. get - cop
12. kip - cup - got
13. camp - cast - cost
14. grip - crab - grab - clip
15. gran - clap
16. goat - coat - goal
17. grow - glow - crow - cloak
18. great - grey - crane - claim
19. grape - glade
20. clue - grew - cool
21. ground - count - growl - cow
22. green - greet - keen - keep

Auditory attention and tracking is the ability to actively listen and follow auditory information from beginning to end. Good auditory attention and tracking helps us to follow a conversation, a story read out loud or a set of instructions, being able to focus on key information. Children with poor auditory attention and tracking may find it difficult to follow and respond appropriately to what is being said to them. **Auditory sequential memory** is the ability to remember and recall a series of things that they have heard. Children with poor auditory sequential memory may find it difficult to remember information given earlier in a conversation or a set of instructions and may struggle to recall the sequence of sounds in a word.

In this activity the child has to process the auditory information but also respond by working out the pattern and stating the next sound in the sequence. Read out the list of sounds with a clear space between each. Ask the child to listen and work out what sound would come next. Answers are in red.

Break this task into a number of shorter tasks over a number of lessons if necessary.

Activity 7 What comes next? Set 3

1. g o g o g o ...... g
2. g k g k g k ...... g
3. o k o k o k ...... o
4. g g k g g k ...... g
5. o k k o k k ...... o
6. k k g k k g ...... k
7. o o g o o g ...... g
8. k k g g k k g g ...... k
9. o o g g o o g g ...... o
10. o o k k o o k k ...... o
11. g k o g k o g k o ...... g
12. k g o k g o k g o ...... k
13. k g o o k g o o ...... k
14. o k g g o k g g ...... o
15. o g k k o g k k ...... o
16. k k g g o o k k g g o o ...... k
17. k k o o g g k k o o g g ...... k
18. k g g g o k g g g o ...... k
19. g k k k o g k k k o ...... g
20. g o o o k g o o o k ...... g
21. g k g o g k g o ...... g
22. o g o k o g o k ...... o
23. g g k k o g g k k o ...... g
24. o o k k g o o k k g ...... o

Print out the cards below to use when introducing the sounds and sound spellings.

Activity 8 Sound spelling cards Set 3

g	o
c	k

This activity results in the child discovering that two sound spellings, c and k, represent the sound 'k' in written words.

Support the child to read the word **can**, work out the sound spelling corresponding to the sound 'k' and highlight it. The child has discovered the sound spelling **c** represents the sound 'k'. Ask the child to write the **c** sound spelling as a heading on the small line in the box on the can, then write the word **can** on the line underneath. Encourage the child to say each sound at the same time as writing each sound spelling. For example, the child writes **c** and says 'k', writes **a** and says 'a' and writes **n** and says 'n'.

Move on to the next word, **keg**, and support the child to read it, work out the sound spelling corresponding to the sound 'k' and highlight it. Ask the child to write the **k** sound spelling as a heading on the small line in the box on the keg, then write the word **keg** on the line underneath. Encourage the child to say each sound at the same time as writing each sound spelling. For example, the child writes **k** and says 'k', writes **e** and says 'e' and writes **g** and says 'g'.

Then work through the rest of the words one by one, sorting the words into **c** and **k** word lists as above. Point out to the child that this shows that there are two ways to write the sound 'k' when we hear it in a word. Good readers and spellers remember which of these sound spellings go in which word.

Break this task into a number of shorter tasks over a number of lessons if necessary.

Activity 8a Investigating the sound 'k' *Set 3 only*

can	kit	cap
keg	cat	kid
Kim	cod	cot

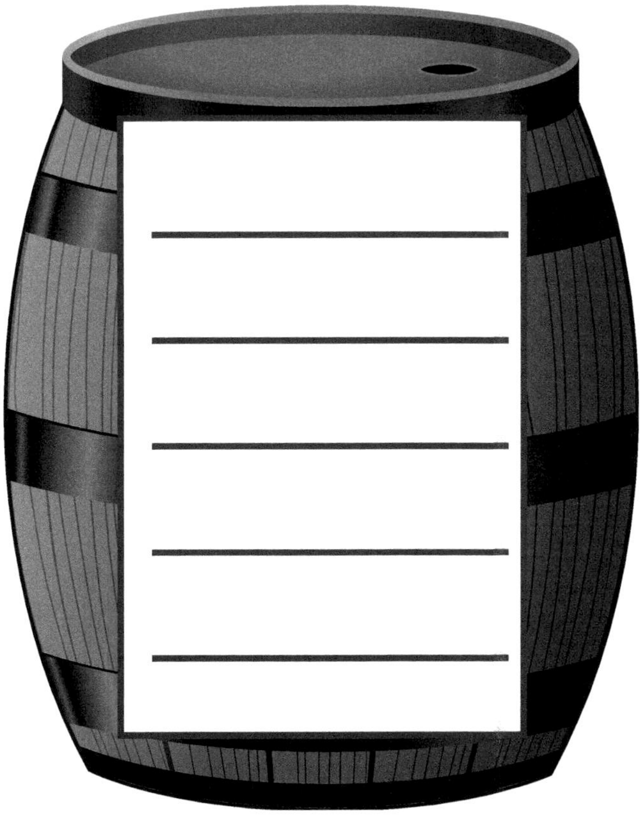

There are six different bingo cards and a set of individual sound spelling cards which can be copied and cut out.

Each child is given their own bingo card. Shuffle the sound spelling cards, select and 'call' the sound spellings, one by one, from the top of the pile. There are a number of ways to do this, depending on the focus for the pupils:

- show the selected sound spelling and say the sound – child matches visual figures with auditory reinforcement
- show the selected sound spelling only – child matches visual figures without auditory reinforcement
- say the sound for the selected sound spelling but do not show it to the children – child processes the auditory information and matches to a visual figure.

When a child has a sound spelling on their card they can cover it with a counter or write over the sound spelling on the bingo card, writing in between the lines as a guide, saying the sound as they write. If they have more than one of a sound spelling on the card then they must only cover one and wait for that sound spelling to be called again. The first person to cover all their sound spellings is the winner.

Activity 9 Sound spelling bingo Set 3

g	c
o	k

c	g
c	o

c	k
k	g

o	k
c	c

g	o
o	c

o	g
g	k

g	g	g	g	g
g	o	o	o	o
o	o	c	c	c
c	c	c	k	k
k	k	k	k	

Visual discrimination is the ability to see differences between objects that are similar. Good visual discrimination helps keep us from getting confused when looking at shapes and forms in the environment. Children with poor visual discrimination may find it difficult to recognise letters, may confuse letters such as b and d and may find it difficult to identify mathematical symbols.

Ask the child to look at the sound spelling in the yellow box then track along the row looking at the other sound spellings. The child indicates or puts a ring around the sound spelling that is the same as the one in the yellow box.

Break this task into a number of shorter tasks over a number of lessons if necessary.

Activity 11 Sound spelling tracker — Set 3

g	p	g	a	d
k	t	k	d	g
c	c	a	s	o
g	p	d	a	g
o	c	a	o	d
k	t	d	k	p
c	a	c	s	o
o	o	s	c	a

Visual discrimination is the ability to see differences between objects that are similar. Good visual discrimination helps keep us from getting confused when looking at shapes and forms in the environment. Children with poor visual discrimination may find it difficult to recognise letters, may confuse letters such as b and d and may find it difficult to identify mathematical symbols.

Focus on one sound spelling e.g. **g** (say the sound 'g' and point to the matching sound spelling rather than using the letter name when talking to the child). Note when asking the child to find the sound spelling for the sound 'k' point to which of the two sound spellings you mean (**c** or **k**) and say, "This way of writing 'k'", rather than use letter names or describe them as 'curly c' and 'kicking k'.

Ask the child to look at all the sound spellings and indicate or put a ring round all the letters matching the target.

Break this task into a number of shorter tasks over a number of lessons if necessary.

Activity 12 Spot the sound spelling Set 3

g o k c o k g

o

c o k

o c k

k g g g

g k

k o

c o g

Visual memory is the ability to remember and identify a shape or picture that we have previously seen. Children with poor visual memory may struggle to remember pictures, figures, shapes, letters and numbers and may have difficulties with reading, writing and number work.

Ask the child to look at the sound spelling in the yellow box for at least five seconds, covering the white box underneath. Then cover the yellow box so that the sound spelling cannot be seen and reveal the choice of sound spellings in the white box below. Ask the child to select the matching sound spelling from the white box.

Break this task into a number of shorter tasks over a number of lessons if necessary.

Activity 13 Remembering sound spellings Set 3

k
k g

c
c g

o
g o

g
g k

k
c g k

g
c g k

Visual discrimination is the ability to see differences between objects that are similar. Good visual discrimination helps keep us from getting confused when looking at shapes and forms in the environment. Children with poor visual discrimination may find it difficult to recognise letters, may confuse letters such as b and d and may find it difficult to identify mathematical symbols.

Ask the child to colour in the shapes according to the sound spelling colour key at the bottom.

Activity 14 Colour the picture — Set 3

Colour c light green k dark green g yellow o blue

Form constancy is the ability to generalise forms and figures and identify them even if they are slightly different from that usually seen. This skill helps us distinguish differences in size, shape, and orientation or position. Children with poor form constancy may frequently reverse letters and numbers.

Ask the child to look at the letter on the left and match to a letter on the right (written differently), drawing a line to connect each.

Activity 15 Which is the same? Set 3

o	c
c	g
g	o
o	k
k	o
c	c
g	k
k	g

Visual closure is the ability to identify an object, shape or symbol from a visually incomplete or disorganised presentation and to see where the different parts of a whole fit together, i.e. to recognise something when seeing only part of it. This skill helps us understand things quickly because our visual system doesn't have to process every detail to recognise what we're seeing.

Ask the child to look at the sound spelling in the white box then track left to right along the row.
Ask the child to indicate or put a ring around the sound spelling that is the same as the sound spelling in the white box.

Break this task into a number of shorter tasks over a number of lessons if necessary.

Activity 16 Bits missing Set 3

	t	k	d
	p	d	g
	a	o	c
	c	s	a
	t	d	k
	p	g	d
	o	m	s
	k	d	c

Figure ground is the ability to find patterns or shapes when hidden within a busy background without getting confused by surrounding images. This skill keeps children from getting lost in the details, for example when looking at pictures in books or reading. Children with poor figure ground become easily confused with too much print on the page, affecting their concentration and attention.

Ask the child to look at the sound spellings, which are overlapping. Ask the child to first find and count all the **g** sound spellings (refer to the sound not the letter name), then the **o** etc. Ask the child to write down how many of each sound spelling they found.

Break this task into a number of shorter tasks over a number of lessons if necessary.

Activity 17 Busy sound spellings — Set 3

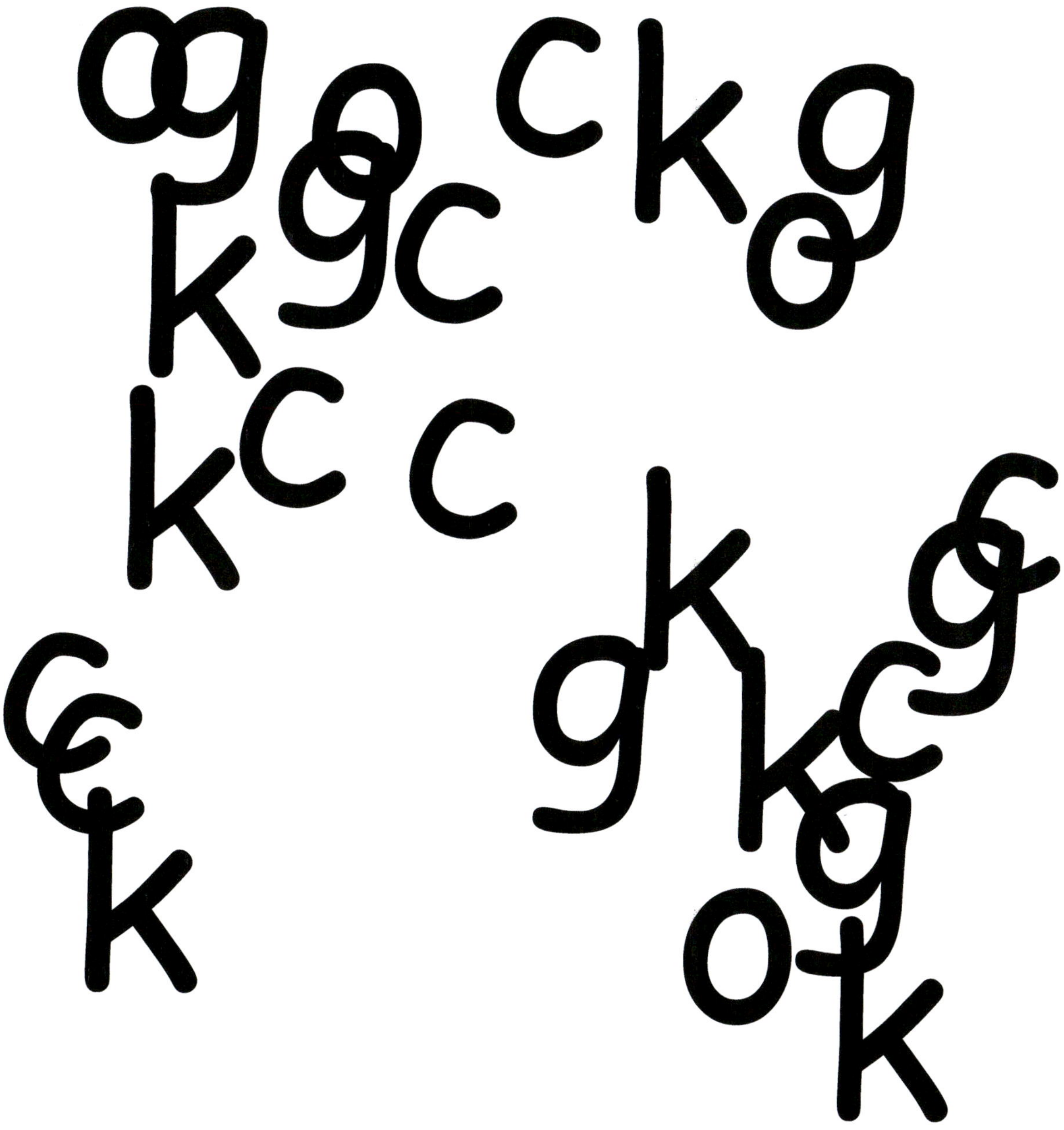

Spatial relations is the ability to perceive the position of objects in relation to ourselves and to each other. This skill helps children to understand relationships between symbols and letters. Children with poor spatial relations may find it difficult to write letters in the correct orientation, write consistently starting at the margin and write letters of the same size.

In the first part, ask the child to copy the sound spellings on the line underneath in exactly the same places as they appear above.
In the second part, ask the child to copy the words on the line underneath in exactly the same places, saying the matching sound as they write each sound spellings.
Break this task into a number of shorter tasks over a number of lessons if necessary.

Activity 18 Where am I? Set 3

o k c g

g c k o

cop kid on

dig pot

Visual sequential memory is the ability to remember sequences of figures, symbols and shapes. Children with poor visual sequencing struggle to remember a sequence of letters and follow visual patterns. They may have difficulties writing a sequence of letters to form a word and a sequence of words to form a sentence.

Ask the child to look at the sound spellings in the yellow box for at least five seconds, covering the white box underneath. Then cover the yellow box so that the sound spellings cannot be seen and reveal the sequence of sound spellings in the white box below. Ask the child to remember the missing sound spelling and write it in the space.

Break this task into a number of shorter tasks over a number of lessons if necessary.

Activity 19 Remembering lots of sound spellings Set 3

o k
_ k

c g
c _

k c
_ c

o g
_ g

g k o
g k _

k c g
k _ g

Tracking is the ability to follow a sequence of symbols. The eyes need to focus on the symbols in order and not look randomly at the symbols on the page. This is an important skill for reading and writing where letters and words are written from left to right and the reader is required to work down a page from the top to the bottom.

Choose a target sound spelling for the child to find. Ask the child to look at the sound spellings, tracking from left to right and down the page.
When they find the target sound spelling the child indicates or puts a ring around it. Repeat with a different sound spelling.

Break this task into a number of shorter tasks over a number of lessons if necessary.

Activity 20 Tracking sound spellings Set 3

c o c g k g k o g
k c g k o g g k o

g c o c k g c c k g o g c
k g c k g k c k o g g o k
g c o g k o c g k k o c g

k g c k g k c k o g g o k g c o g k g
c c k g o g c c k g c c g c o g k g c
c k g o g c c k g c c g c o g k o c g

g c c k g c c g c o g k g c c k g o g
c c k g c c k o g g o k g c o c k g c
c k g o g c c g c g c c k g c k o o g

Having introduced the sounds and their corresponding sound spellings it is important that the child is given the opportunity to practise forming the sound spellings. As discussed in the introductory chapter, the child should be provided with lots of sensory and kinaesthetic experiences of forming the sound spellings in a variety of media as well as writing on conventional paper.

In this activity the child can practise forming the sound spellings by copying over the grey sound spellings which act as a guide. Encourage the child to say the sound at the same time as writing the sound spelling. The child can then practise writing the sound spellings within the boxes underneath which focuses the child on the spatial relationship between the sound spelling as it forms and the surrounding visual environment.

Activity 21 Writing sound spellings Set 3

g g g g g

g g g g g g g

g						

o o o o o

o o o o o o o

c c c c c

c c c c c c c

k k k k k

k k k k k k k

Blending is the ability to push sounds together to make a word and is a key skill in reading. Blending is a dynamic activity where the child actively pushes the sounds together and listens to the word forming.

Activity 22 'A place to read' prepares the child for blending sounds themselves as part of the process of learning to read. You will model the dynamic blending technique for the child who will then tell you what word they can hear forming. Refer to the full explanation of the 'A place to read' activity in the 'Working through the programme' section.

Segmenting, the ability to split words up into their component sounds in sequence, is a key skill in spelling. The child needs to isolate each sound and match a sound spelling to successfully spell a word.

Activity 28 'A place to listen' prepares the child for segmenting words as part of the process of learning to spell. Refer to the full explanation of the 'A place to listen' activity in the 'Working through the programme' section.

Below is a list of words to use for both activities. At this early stage in the programme there are very few meaningful words which can be generated from the sounds studied in set 1.

Activity 22 A place to read Set 3
Activity 28 A place to listen

on

cab can cap cat cop cot

dig dog dot

gap got

kid kit

mop

nod not

pop pot

tig top

This set of cards is made up of words containing the target sounds for set 3. Copy onto card and cut out. Practise dynamic blending for reading, as described in the 'Working through the programme' section, using these cards. Notice that the letters get gradually darker as the child works through the word, a visual signal that they are pushing together the sounds and preparing them to listen to the word forming. Model this process for the child if necessary.

Activity 23 Dynamic blending Set 3

on	can
cot	dog
got	kid
mop	pot

Print out onto card and cut out.
Stack them with the biggest (the complete word) on the bottom and in decreasing size so that the smallest is on the top.
Make sure the left-hand edge of the cards are flush. Staple the cards together on the left-hand side.
When the child runs a finger over the cards the sound spellings flip up. Ask the child to say the sounds and match to the flips.

Flippies — Set 3 - a

c	c a	c a n
d	d o	d o g
n	n o	n o t

Print out onto card and cut out.
Stack them with the biggest (the complete word) on the bottom and in decreasing size so that the smallest is on the top.
Make sure the left-hand edge of the cards are flush. Staple the cards together on the left-hand side.
When the child runs a finger over the cards the sound spellings flip up. Ask the child to say the sounds and match to the flips.

Flippies

Set 3 - b

t	t o	t o p
g	g o	g o t
c	c a	c a t

Read the clue on the left for the child.
Use the clue to work out what the answer word is.
Encourage the child to think about the sounds in the word and write a sound spelling for each sound in the boxes on the right, one by one.
The first one is done as an example for you.
Explain that they may not need to use all the boxes and so some are shaded in.
Break this task into a number of shorter tasks over a number of lessons if necessary.

Activity 30 Sound boxes Set 3

Clue	Sound boxes		
Sam _________ a present for his birthday.	g	o	t
Babies sleep in a _________.			
The cat sat _________ the mat.			(shaded)
I wear a _________ in the sun.			
A guide _________ helps people.			

Support the child to read the words on the left one by one.
For each word support the child to work out what sounds are in the word and count them.
Then support the child to cross out any boxes that are not needed.
In each of the boxes in the middle, have the child write the sound spelling to match each sound.
In the last column the child writes how many sounds there are in the word.
Break this task into a number of shorter tasks over a number of lessons if necessary.

Activity 31 How many sounds? Set 3

Word	Sound spellings					How many sounds?
kit	k	i	t			3
on						
cat						
not						
top						
am						
cop						
dot						
nod						

During this activity the child will get the chance to slide sounds in and out of words, i.e. practise phoneme manipulation. Sounds will be swapped, added or taken away. Print the sound spellings on card and cut out.

Build a starting word from the prompt list, demonstrating dynamic blending as you move the sound spelling cards into place.

Repeat the word, running your finger along the cards so that it corresponds with the sounds within the word.

Ask the child to change the word to the next word on the prompt list. As you say the new word run your finger under the cards so that it corresponds with the sounds within the word and gives the child the chance to hear and see what is different.

The child can then swap the appropriate sound spelling cards.

Activity 33 Sound swap Set 3

Sound swap g o c k

List 1	List 2	List 3
kid	tig	cod
kit	dig	cop
sit	dog	mop
sat	dot	top
cat	not	tip
cot	nod	tap

g	o	c
k	i	a
d	t	s
n	m	p

Support the child to read the word in the first column. Then, referring to the second column, ask the child what sound they are going to take away.
Then ask the child to think about what word would be made if the sound in the second column was taken out of the word, in this case from the beginning of it.
Remind the child to think about the sounds, blend dynamically and listen to the word forming.
Have the child write out the new word on the line at the end, sounding out the word as they write each sound spelling. Remind the child that the sound 'k' can be written using the **c** or the **k** sound spelling

Break this task into a number of shorter tasks over a number of lessons if necessary.

Activity 34 Read – Delete – Spell Set 3

Read	Read without this sound	Spell the new word
can	'k'	____________
kit	'k'	____________
con	'k'	____________
cat	'k'	____________

Support the child to read the word in the first column. Then, referring to the second column, ask the child to think about what word would be made if the sound in the second column was added in front of the word. Remind the child to think about the sounds, blend dynamically and listen to the word forming.
Have the child write out the new word on the line at the end, sounding out the word as they write each sound spelling. Remind the child that the sound 'k' can be written using the **c** or the **k** sound spelling.

Break this task into a number of shorter tasks over a number of lessons if necessary.

Activity 35 Read – Add – Spell Set 3

Read	Read with this sound at the beginning	Spell the new word
an	'k'	can
it	'k'	______
at	'k'	______
op	'k'	______
in	't'	______

Support the child to read the words on the left, one by one.
For each word read the clue to the child and work out what the answer word is.
Explain to the child that they will need to either: add a sound, take away a sound or change a sound to make the answer word
e.g. sip > slip > lip > lap.
Have the child write out the new word on the line on the right, saying each sound as they write each sound spelling.
An example is done for you.

Break this task into a number of shorter tasks over a number of lessons if necessary.

Activity 36 Sound exchange Set 3

Starting word	Clue	New word
dog	Turn over soil	*dig*
can	Furry pet	
pot	Burst like a balloon	
got	Small spot	
kid	Football outfit	
not	Move your head up and down	
gap	Hat with a peak	

This set of cards is made up of words containing the target sounds for set 3. Copy onto card and cut out. Practise dynamic blending for reading, as described in the 'Working through the programme' section, using these cards. Model this process for the child if necessary.

Activity 37 Reading words with target sounds Set 3

cap	cop
dig	gap
kid	kit
mop	nod
pop	pot

This set of cards is made up of the high frequency words containing the target sounds for set 3. Copy onto card and cut out.

Practise dynamic blending for reading, as described in the 'Working through the programme' section, using these cards. Model this process for the child if necessary.

Activity 38 Reading high frequency words Set 3

on	can
cat	dog
got	not
top	

Starting at 'not' have the child read each of the words as quickly as possible tracking along the line one by one until they get to 'cop'.
Support the child to read the words by giving information about sounds and supporting dynamic blending but do not supply the whole word.
Time how long it takes to read all the words and record the time at the bottom of the page.
Repeat at a later point, e.g. at the end of the lesson or the following day, and see if the child can beat their *own* previous time.

Activity 39 Reading race — Set 3

not dog kid on cop

1 _____ minutes ____ seconds
2 _____ minutes ____ seconds
3 _____ minutes ____ seconds

Starting at cat have the child read each of the words as quickly as possible tracking along the line one by one until they get to 'can'.
Support the child to read the words by giving information about sounds and supporting dynamic blending but do not supply the whole word.
Time how long it takes to read all the words to and record the time at the bottom of the page.
Repeat at a later point, e.g. at the end of the lesson or the following day, and see if the child can beat their *own* previous time.

Activity 39 Reading race — Set 3 Words with a 'k' sound

cat kid cot cap kit can

1 ____ minutes ___ seconds
2 ____ minutes ___ seconds
3 ____ minutes ___ seconds

Visual discrimination is the ability to see differences between objects that are similar. Good visual discrimination helps keep us from getting confused when looking at shapes and forms in the environment. Children with poor visual discrimination may find it difficult to recognise letters, may confuse letters such as b and d and may find it difficult to identify mathematical symbols.

Ask the child to look at the word in the pink box then track along the row looking at the other words. The child indicates or puts a ring around the word that is the same as the one in the pink box.

Break this task into a number of shorter tasks over a number of lessons if necessary.

Activity 40 Spot the word Set 3

cab	can	cat	cab
top	top	pot	dot
dig	dog	dot	dig
kid	kit	kid	kip
got	got	pot	gap

Visual memory is the ability to remember and identify a shape or picture that we have previously seen. Children with poor visual memory may struggle to remember pictures, figures, shapes, letters and numbers and may have difficulties with reading, writing and number work.

Ask the child to look at the word in the yellow box for at least five seconds, covering the white box underneath. Then cover the yellow box so that the letter cannot be seen and reveal the choice of words in the white box below. Ask the child to select the matching word from the white box.

Break this task into a number of shorter tasks over a number of lessons if necessary.

Activity 41 Remembering words Set 3

on
on an

cot
got cot

kid
kit kid

pop
pot pop

cat
can cat cap

got
gap cot got

Form constancy is the ability to generalise forms and figures and identify them even if they are slightly different from that usually seen. This skill helps us distinguish differences in size, shape, and orientation or position. Children with poor form constancy may frequently reverse letters and numbers.

Ask the child to look at the word in the orange box then track along the row looking at the other words. The child indicates or puts a ring around the word that is the same as the one in the orange box.

Break this task into a number of shorter tasks over a number of lessons if necessary.

Activity 42 Which is the word? Set 3

on	on	an	in
cat	cap	cat	can
dig	did	dip	dig
kid	kid	kit	ken
got	gap	got	dog

Visual closure is the ability to identify an object, shape or symbol from a visually incomplete or disorganised presentation and to see where different parts of a whole fit together, i.e. to recognise something when seeing only part of it. This skill helps us understand things quickly because our visual system doesn't have to process every detail to recognise what we're seeing.

Ask the child to look at the large word and then at the choice of smaller words underneath. The child indicates or puts a ring around the word that is the same as the big word.

Break this task into a number of shorter tasks over a number of lessons if necessary.

Activity 43 Word splits Set 3

can

cat	can

dig

dog	dig

pop

pot	pop

kid

kit	kid

Figure ground is the ability to find patterns or shapes when hidden within a busy background without getting confused by surrounding images. This skill keeps children from getting lost in the details, for example when looking at pictures in books or reading. Children with poor figure ground become easily confused with too much print on the page, affecting their concentration and attention.

Ask the child to look at the words, which are overlapping. Ask the child to first find all the words. Some words are written more than once. How many of each word are there?

Break this task into a number of shorter tasks over a number of lessons if necessary.

Activity 44 Busy words Set 3

kid dig can on
can

kid dog kid dog
can

on
can

got can dig kid
dog

dig dig
got dog on kid
got got
kid

Visual sequential memory is the ability to remember sequences of figures, symbols and shapes. Children with poor visual sequencing struggle to remember a sequence of letters and follow visual patterns. They may have difficulties writing a sequence of letters to form a word and a sequence of words to form a sentence.

Ask the child to look at the words in the yellow box for at least five seconds, covering the white box underneath. Then cover the yellow box so that the words cannot be seen and reveal the sequence of words in the white box below. Ask the child to remember the missing word and write it in the space.

Break this task into a number of shorter tasks over a number of lessons if necessary.

Activity 45 Remembering lots of words Set 3

on got
____ got

dog dig
dog ____

pop	kid
____	kid

cap	top
cap	____

not	got	kit
____	got	kit

pot	can	dot
pot	____	dot

Tracking is the ability to follow a sequence of letters, figures or symbols. The eyes need to focus on the symbols in order and not look randomly at the symbols on the page. This is an important skill for reading and writing where letters and words are written from left to right and the reader is required to work down a page from the top to the bottom.

Ask the child to look at the symbols and sound spellings and track from left to right. When the child finds a group of sound spellings then they indicate or put a circle around them all. The child then reads the word.

Break this task into a number of shorter tasks over a number of lessons if necessary.

Activity 46 Hidden words Set 3

↘⇨⇨↘kid→↔▷cop⇦▽⇨top⇨→↘⇦got⇦
▷▽↘▽pop⇦▷↓▽⇦↘⇦⇨can⇨↙⇨⇦dig⇨

↙⇦cat▷⇦⇨mop←↙▷↔dog↗▽⇦↘↕↱▽⇨
⇨▷kit⇦▷↕↔⇦▽↕↔gap▷←↕↗nod⇨⇦↕⇦

θ σ μ c a p δ ω ν σ ψ o n π ω p ω α d o t φ π λ
ω ω ν t o p λ μ δ φ υ τ g o t ω φ κ ν ε k i d ε δ ω κ φ

γ η κ ε m o p δ ω κ δ σ φ p o t π ω ρ ω α t o p φ π
λ ω ω ν g a p λ κ δ φ υ τ k i t ω φ κ ρ ε n o d ε ω φ

Prior to working with the child, read through the instructions in the 'Working through the programme' section.

Activity 47 Word build **Set 3**

o	n		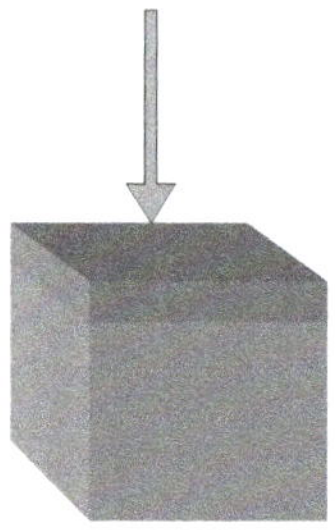
c	a	n	
d	i	g	
k	i	d	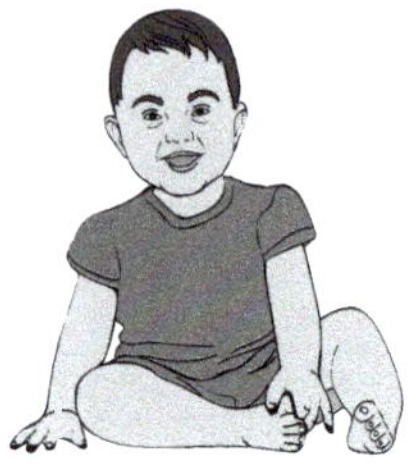

m	o	p	
p	o	t	
t	o	p	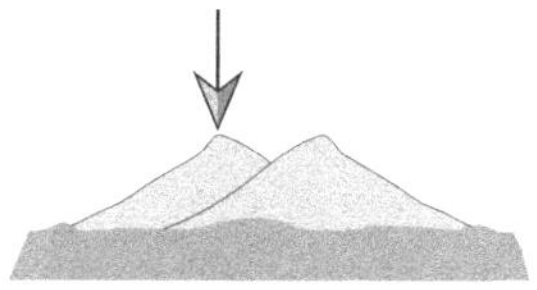

Support the child to look at the picture and work out what the word is.
Then support the child to work out the initial sound in the word and match a sound spelling in the gap provided.
The 'Place to listen' technique should be used to support this.
Read through the 'Place to listen' instructions in the 'Working through the programme' section of this book prior to working with the child.
Ask the child to read the completed word using the dynamic blending technique.

Activity 48 Finish the word 1 — Set 3

____ a p

____ o p

____ o g

____ i t

____ a n

____ i g

____ o p
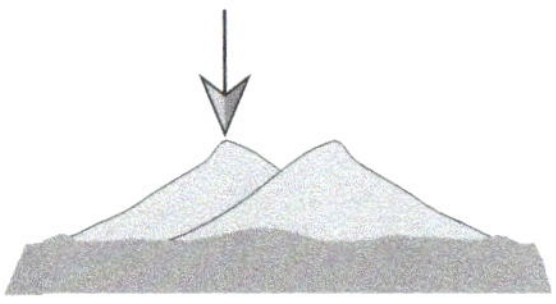

Support the child to look at the picture and work out what the word is.
Then support the child to work out the middle sound in the word and match a sound spelling in the gap provided.
The 'Place to listen' technique should be used to support this.
Read through the 'Place to listen' instructions in the 'Working through the programme' section of this book prior to working with the child.
Ask the child to read the completed word using the dynamic blending technique.

Activity 49 Finish the word 2 Set 3

c ____ n

c ____ t

d ____ g

k ____ d

p ____ t

t ____ p

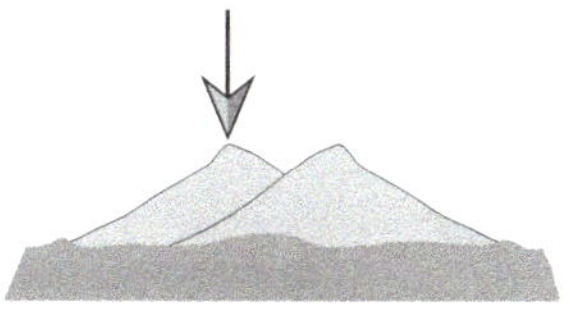

d ____ t

Support the child to look at the picture and work out what the word is.
Then support the child to work out the final sound in the word and match a sound spelling in the gap provided.
The 'Place to listen' technique should be used to support this.
Read through the 'Place to listen' instructions in the 'Working through the programme' section of this book prior to working with the child.
Ask the child to read the completed word using the dynamic blending technique.

Activity 50 Finish the word 3 — Set 3

c a ____

m o ____

d i ____

k i ____

c o ____

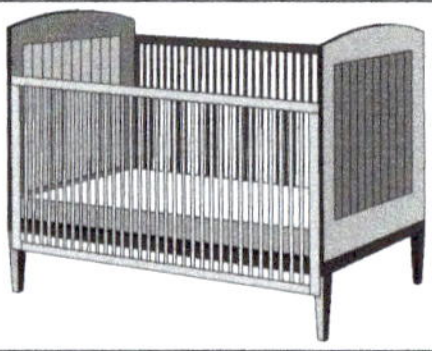

n o ____

c o ____

Read the instructions in the introduction of this book to guide you on how to work through this spelling practise sheet with the child.

Activity 52 Spelling challenge — Set 3

on	o n	o n	__ __	__________
can	c a n	c a n	__ __ __	__________
dog	d o g	d o g	__ __ __	__________
got	g o t	g o t	__ __ __	__________
not	n o t	n o t	__ __ __	__________

Support the child to read the sentences. Have the child look at the pictures and find the picture that matches the sentence.
Have the child draw a line from the sentence to the matching picture.
Break this task into a number of shorter tasks over a number of lessons if necessary.

Activity 53 Read the sentence and match to a picture — Set 3

Dan sat in a pan.

Sam got a dog.

Tim on a tap.

Pam pat a dog.

A cat sat on Tom.

Support the child to read the sentences. Have the child look at the pictures and find the picture that matches the sentence.
Have the child draw a line from the sentence to the matching picture.
Remind the child that there are two sound spellings for the sound 'k', **c** and **k**.
Break this task into a number of shorter tasks over a number of lessons if necessary.

Activity 53a Read the sentence and match to a picture — Set 3 'k' sound words

Cod in a can.

Ken in a cap.

A man in a kit.

A kid in a cot.

A cat on a cap.

Support the child to read the sentence.
For each sentence, support the child to spot the spelling mistake.
Have the child underline or highlight the mistake and then write out the sentence correcting the mistake.
Encourage the child to say the sounds in each word at the same time as writing the sound spellings.
Break this task into a number of shorter tasks over a number of lessons if necessary.

Activity 54 Oops! Correct the spelling — Set 3

1. Dan sat in a man.

2. Sam got a dot.

3. Tim on a cap.

4. A cat sad on Tom.

5. Pam pat a cog.

Support the child to read the sentences.
There is a missing word with a choice of two words to fill the gap.
For each sentence support the child to identify the missing word which makes sense in the sentence.
Have the child write the word on the line within the sentence.
Break this task into a number of shorter tasks over a number of lessons if necessary.

Activity 55 Spot the spelling Set 3

1. Kim sat on a ____________.
   mat cat

2. Sam had a ____________.
   nap it

3. Pat ____________ a dog.
   did got

4. Tom can ____________ on a mat.
   sip sit

5. Dad got Dan a ____________.
   cap pip

6. Pam can pat a ____________.
   dig dog

Support the child to read each sentence.
Ask the child to re-read the sentence, several times if necessary, and try to remember it.
Cover the sentence and ask the child to recall it verbally from memory.
Once they can do this, ask the child to write out the sentence from memory.
The child might find it helpful to say the sounds as they write and say individual words once written.
When the sentence is complete, the child reads out their sentence and then compares it to the original.
Alternatively, using the text to speech function on a laptop or similar software, the child could type the sentence with the computer reading back each word and then the completed sentence.

Activity 56 Writing challenge Set 3

A sad man got a cat.

Nap on a mat, Dan.

A mad cat sat in a cot.

Sam, sit in a can.

Answers Set 3: g o c k

Page 120

Activity 8a Investigating the sound 'k'

c can cap cat cod cot

k kit keg kid Kim

Page 127

Activity 12 Spot the sound spelling

g 7
o 7
c 4
k 7

Page 133

Activity 17 Busy sound spellings

g 6
o 4
c 8
k 7

Page 144

Activity 30 Sound boxes

cot
on
hat
dog

Page 145

Activity 31 How many sounds?

on	2	cat	3
not	3	top	3
am	2	cop	3
dot	3	nod	3

Page 148

Activity 34 Read – Delete – Spell

an
it
on
at

Page 149

Activity 35 Read – Add – Spell

kit
cat
cop
tin

Page 150

Activity 36 Sound exchange

cat	pop
dot	kit
nod	cap

Page 160

Activity 44 Busy words

on	3
can	5
kid	6
got	4
dog	4
dig	4

Page 166

Activity 48 Finish the word 1

cap
mop
dog
kit
can
dig
top

Page 167

Activity 48 Finish the word 2

can
cat
dog
kid
pot
top
dot

Page 168

Activity 50 Finish the word 3

can	mop
dig	kit
cot	nod
cop	

Page 172

Activity 54 Oops! Correct the spelling

pan
dog
tap
sat
dog

Page 173

Activity 55 Spot the spelling

mat
nap
got
sit
cap
dog

SECTION 4

SET 4 SOUNDS AND SOUND SPELLINGS

eur

Auditory discrimination is the ability to hear differences between sounds. Good auditory discrimination helps us to recognise and identify the sounds in words and so interpret them correctly. Children with poor auditory discrimination may confuse sounds and misinterpret things they have heard. Their spelling and writing may reflect their confusion over what sounds they heard in a word. **Auditory attention and tracking** is the ability to actively listen and follow auditory information from beginning to end. Good auditory attention and tracking helps us to follow a conversation, a story read out loud or a set of instructions, being able to focus on key information. Children with poor auditory attention and tracking may find it difficult to follow and respond appropriately to what is being said to them.

This story contains lots of words that start with the sounds 'e' and 'r', but you will focus on just one 'target' sound. Read the story out loud. Encourage the child to listen carefully and spot any word that starts with the 'target' sound. When a target word has been read, the child indicates that they have heard and spotted it by tapping the table, putting up a hand or any other agreed signal, but without shouting out. Stop reading and discuss the word, making any error correction necessary. If a word is missed, re-read the sentence. Do not show the story to the children. The target words are highlighted below for you: 'e' and 'r'. Repeat on another occasion focusing on a different target sound.

Activity 1 Sound target – Story sheet Set 4

A rat is an example of an animal called a rodent. Rats live in the wild and can also be raised as pets.
Rats are really clever and enjoy learning tricks. Pet rats can be trained to come when called, just like dogs.
Every rat has soft fur and a long tail at the end of their body.
Rats eat almost anything. They like meat, eggs, seeds, fruits and vegetables.
They have razor sharp teeth which grow all the time so they need to keep chewing to rub them down.
Wild rats are pests as they can enter houses and spread illnesses.
Unfortunately, because of their bad reputation it is rather unlikely that rats will ever become really popular as pets.

Please Note: The focus of activity is the *sound* in the word, NOT what *letter* is in the word.

Auditory discrimination is the ability to hear differences between sounds. Good auditory discrimination helps us to recognise and identify the sounds in words and so interpret them correctly. Children with poor auditory discrimination may confuse sounds and misinterpret things they have heard. Their spelling and writing may reflect their confusion over what sounds they heard in a word. **Auditory sequential memory** is the ability to remember and recall a series of things that they have heard. Children with poor auditory sequential memory may find it difficult to remember information given earlier in a conversation or set of instructions and may struggle to recall the sequence of sounds in a word.

The sentences contain lots of words beginning with one of the target sounds 'e', 'u' or 'r'.
Read the sentence to the child several times, invite them to join in as you say it and gradually recall it on their own.
Ask them to say it as quickly as they can and have some fun with it. After some practise, ask the child if they can identify which sound they hear a lot in the tongue twister. Perhaps they can make up their own?
Note that the vocabulary included in these tongue twisters may be unfamiliar to the child, especially the adjectives. If appropriate, talk about unfamiliar words and discuss their meaning.
Break this task into a number of shorter tasks over a number of lessons if necessary.

Activity 2 Sound target – Tongue twister fun Set 4

Every elephant eats extra eggs.

Excited Ellie experiments on engines.

Uncle unfolds ugly umbrellas.

Raging rivers run rapidly.

Ravi races red rabbits.

Auditory discrimination is the ability to hear differences between sounds. Good auditory discrimination helps us to recognise and identify the sounds in words and so interpret them correctly. Children with poor auditory discrimination may confuse sounds and misinterpret things they have heard. Their spelling and writing may reflect their confusion over what sounds they heard in a word. **Auditory attention and tracking** is the ability to actively listen and follow auditory information from beginning to end. Good auditory attention and tracking helps us to follow a conversation, a story read out loud or a set of instructions, being able to focus on key information. Children with poor auditory attention and tracking may find it difficult to follow and respond appropriately to what is being said to them.

This activity focuses the child on listening to short lists of words starting with the sounds 'e', 'u' and 'r'. The words get increasingly complex as does the number of words the child has to listen to. Later items include words starting with sounds from previous sets.

Read out the words and ask the child to identify the odd one out, the word that *does not* start with the same sound as the others. Do not show the words to the child. The odd one out is highlighted for you.
Break this task into a number of shorter tasks over a number of lessons if necessary.

Activity 3 Odd one out Set 4

1.	red	up	rat
2.	mum	ran	rip
3.	run	rag	nut
4.	end	elf	ink
5.	rust	pink	rest
6.	desk	ramp	rink

Auditory attention and tracking is the ability to actively listen and follow auditory information from beginning to end. Good auditory attention and tracking helps us to follow a conversation, a story read out loud or a set of instructions, being able to focus on key information. Children with poor auditory attention and tracking may find it difficult to follow and respond appropriately to what is being said to them. **Auditory sequential memory** is the ability to remember and recall a series of things that they have heard. Children with poor auditory sequential memory may find it difficult to remember information given earlier in a conversation or a set of instructions and may struggle to recall the sequence of sounds in a word.

In this activity the child has to process the auditory information but also respond by working out the pattern and stating the next sound in the sequence. Read out the list of sounds with a clear space between each. Ask the child to listen and work out what sound would come next. Answers are in red.

Break this task into a number of shorter tasks over a number of lessons if necessary.

Activity 7 What comes next? Set 4

1. e u e u e u …… e
2. r e r e r e …… e
3. u r u r u r …… u
4. e e r e e r …… r
5. u r r u r r …… u
6. u u e u u e …… e
7. r r e r r e …… r
8. u u e e u u e e …… u
9. r r e e r r e e …… r
10. r r u u r r u u …… r
11. e u r e u r e u r …… g
12. r u e r u e r u e …… r
13. r u e e r u e e …… r
14. u e r r u e r r …… u
15. e r u u e r u u …… e
16. e e r r u u e e r r u u …… e
17. r r e e u u r r e e u u …… r
18. r e e e u r e e e u …… r
19. e r r r u e r r r u …… e
20. r u u u e r u u u e …… r
21. e r e u e r e u …… e
22. r e r u r e r u …… r
23. r r u u e r r u u e …… r
24. e e u u r e e u u r …… e

Print out the cards below to use when introducing the sounds and the sound spellings.

Activity 8 Sound spelling cards Set 4

e	u
r	

There are six different bingo cards and a set of individual sound spelling cards which can be copied and cut out. Each child is given their own bingo card. Shuffle the sound spelling cards, select and 'call' the sound spellings, one by one, from the top of the pile. There are a number of ways to do this, depending on the focus for the pupils:

- show the selected sound spelling and say the sound – child matches visual figures with auditory reinforcement
- show the selected sound spelling only – child matches visual figures without auditory reinforcement
- say the sound for the selected sound spelling but do not show it to the children – child processes the auditory information and matches to a visual figure.

When a child has a sound spelling on their card they can cover it with a counter or write over the sound spelling on the bingo card, writing in between the lines as a guide, saying the sound as they write. If they have more than one of a sound spelling on the card then they must only cover one and wait for that sound spelling to be called again. The first person to cover all their sound spellings is the winner.

Activity 9 Sound spelling bingo Set 4

e	e
u	u

e	e
r	r

u	u
r	r

e	u
r	r

e	e
u	r

u	u
r	e

e	e	e	e	e
e	e	e	u	u
u	u	u	u	u
u	r	r	r	r
r	r	r	r	

Visual discrimination is the ability to see differences between objects that are similar. Good visual discrimination helps keep us from getting confused when looking at shapes and forms in the environment. Children with poor visual discrimination may find it difficult to recognise letters, may confuse letters such as b and d and may find it difficult to identify mathematical symbols.

Ask the child to look at the letter in the yellow box then track along the row looking at the other letters. The child indicates or puts a ring around the letter that is the same as the one in the yellow box.

Break this task into a number of shorter tasks over a number of lessons if necessary.

Activity 11 Sound spelling tracker Set 4

e	o	e	a	u
r	a	o	r	c
e	e	a	u	o
u	n	u	m	a
r	c	r	a	e
e	a	u	e	o
u	m	a	n	u

Visual discrimination is the ability to see differences between objects that are similar. Good visual discrimination helps keep us from getting confused when looking at shapes and forms in the environment. Children with poor visual discrimination may find it difficult to recognise letters, may confuse letters such as b and d and may find it difficult to identify mathematical symbols.

Focus on one sound spelling e.g. **r** (say the sound 'r' and point to the matching sound spelling rather than using the letter name when talking to the child).

Ask the child to look at all the sound spellings and indicate or put a ring round all the letters matching the target.

Break this task into a number of shorter tasks over a number of lessons if necessary.

Activity 12 Spot the sound spelling — Set 4

e u r u r e r

e r u r e

u e u

r e u

r u

u r e e r

Visual memory is the ability to remember and identify a shape or picture that we have previously seen. Children with poor visual memory may struggle to remember pictures, figures, shapes, letters and numbers and may have difficulties with reading, writing and number work.

Ask the child to look at the sound spelling in the yellow box for at least five seconds, covering the white box underneath. Then cover the yellow box so that the sound spelling cannot be seen and reveal the choice of sound spellings in the white box below. Ask the child to select the matching sound spelling from the white box.

Break this task into a number of shorter tasks over a number of lessons if necessary.

Activity 13 Remembering sound spellings Set 4

e
e u

u
e u

r
r u

e
r e

r
u r e

u
u e r

Visual discrimination is the ability to see differences between objects that are similar. Good visual discrimination helps keep us from getting confused when looking at shapes and forms in the environment. Children with poor visual discrimination may find it difficult to recognise letters, may confuse letters such as b and d and may find it difficult to identify mathematical symbols.

Ask the child to colour in the shapes according to the sound spelling colour key at the bottom.

Activity 14 Colour the picture Set 4

Colour r red e yellow u blue

Form constancy is the ability to generalise forms and figures and identify them even if they are slightly different from that usually seen. This skill helps us distinguish differences in size, shape, and orientation or position. Children with poor form constancy may frequently reverse letters and numbers.

Ask the child to look at the letter on the left and match to a letter on the right (written differently), drawing a line to connect each.

Activity 15 Which is the same? Set 4

r	e
e	u
u	r
r	e
u	r
e	u

Visual closure is the ability to identify an object, shape or symbol from a visually incomplete or disorganised presentation and to see where the different parts of a whole fit together, i.e. to recognise something when seeing only part of it. This skill helps us understand things quickly because our visual system doesn't have to process every detail to recognise what we're seeing.

Ask the child to look at the sound spelling in the white box then track left to right along the row.
Ask the child to indicate or put a ring around the sound spelling that is the same as the sound spelling in the white box.

Break this task into a number of shorter tasks over a number of lessons if necessary.

Activity 16 Bits missing Set 4

e	c	e	a
u	u	a	c
r	c	a	r
u	c	u	a
e	a	e	c
r	r	a	c
u	a	c	u
e	c	e	a

Figure ground is the ability to find patterns or shapes when hidden within a busy background without getting confused by surrounding images. This skill keeps children from getting lost in the details, for example when looking at pictures in books or reading. Children with poor figure ground become easily confused with too much print on the page, affecting their concentration and attention.

Ask the child to look at the sound spellings, which are overlapping. Ask the child to first find and count all the **e** sound spellings (refer to the sound not the letter name), then the **u** etc. Ask the child to write down how many of each sound spelling they found.

Break this task into a number of shorter tasks over a number of lessons if necessary.

Activity 17 Busy sound spellings — Set 4

Spatial relations is the ability to perceive the position of objects in relation to ourselves and to each other. This skill helps children to understand relationships between symbols and letters. Children with poor spatial relations may find it difficult to write letters in the correct orientation, write consistently starting at the margin and write letters of the same size.

In the first part, ask the child to copy the sound spellings on the line underneath in exactly the same places as they appear above.
In the second part, ask the child to copy the words on the line underneath in exactly the same places, saying the matching sound as they write each sound spellings.
Break this task into a number of shorter tasks over a number of lessons if necessary.

Activity 18 Where am I? Set 4

r e u

e r u

get run up

sun men

Visual sequential memory is the ability to remember sequences of figures, symbols and shapes. Children with poor visual sequencing struggle to remember a sequence of letters and follow visual patterns. They may have difficulties writing a sequence of letters to form a word and a sequence of words to form a sentence.

Ask the child to look at the sound spellings in the yellow box for at least five seconds, covering the white box underneath. Then cover the yellow box so that the sound spellings cannot be seen and reveal the sequence of sound spellings in the white box below. Ask the child to remember the missing sound spelling and write it in the space.

Break this task into a number of shorter tasks over a number of lessons if necessary.

Activity 19 Remembering lots of sound spellings Set 4

e u
e _

r u
_ u

e r
_ r

u e
u _

e u r
e u _

u e r
u r _

Tracking is the ability to follow a sequence of symbols. The eyes need to focus on the symbols in order and not look randomly at the symbols on the page. This is an important skill for reading and writing where letters and words are written from left to right and the reader is required to work down a page from the top to the bottom.

Choose a target sound spelling for the child to find. Ask the child to look at the sound spellings, tracking from left to right and down the page.
When they find the target sound spelling the child indicates or puts a ring around it. Repeat with a different sound spelling.

Break this task into a number of shorter tasks over a number of lessons if necessary.

Activity 20 Tracking sound spellings Set 4

r e u e u r r e u e

e r r u e u e r e u

r e r u e u r r u e e r u

u e r e u r e e r u e u r

e r u r r e u u e r u e e

r e u r e e r u e u r e r u r r e u u

e r u e r e r u e u r e r u r r e u u

r e r u u r e r u u r r e u e u r e r

r u e r e r u e u r e r u r r e u e r

e r u u r e r r e u r e e r u e r u r

r e u e u r e r u r e r u r u r e r u

Having introduced the sounds and their corresponding sound spellings it is important that the child is given the opportunity to practise forming the sound spellings. As discussed in the introductory chapter, the child should be provided with lots of sensory and kinaesthetic experiences of forming the sound spellings in a variety of media as well as writing on conventional paper.

In this activity the child can practise forming the sound spellings by copying over the grey sound spellings which act as a guide. Encourage the child to say the sound at the same time as writing the sound spelling. The child can then practise writing the sound spellings within the boxes underneath which focuses the child on the spatial relationship between the sound spelling as it forms and the surrounding visual environment.

Activity 21 Writing sound spellings Set 4

e e e e e

e e e e e e e

e						

u u u u u

u u u u u u u

r r r r r

r r r r r r r

Blending is the ability to push sounds together to make a word and is a key skill in reading. Blending is a dynamic activity where the child actively pushes the sounds together and listens to the word forming.

Activity 22 'A place to read' prepares the child for blending sounds themselves as part of the process of learning to read. You will model the dynamic blending technique for the child who will then tell you what word they can hear forming. Refer to the full explanation of the 'A place to read' activity in the 'Working through the programme' section.

Segmenting, the ability to split words up into their component sounds in sequence, is a key skill in spelling. The child needs to isolate each sound and match a sound spelling to successfully spell a word.

Activity 28 'A place to listen' activity prepares the child for segmenting words as part of the process of learning to spell. Refer to the full explanation of the 'A place to listen' activity in the 'Working through the programme' section.

Below is a list of words to use for both activities. Use words from previous sets if required.

Activity 22 A place to read — Set 4
Activity 28 A place to listen

up

cup cut

den

get

men met mug mum

net nut

peg pen pet put

ran rat red rip run

set sun

ten

This set of cards is made up of words containing the target sounds for set 4. Copy onto card and cut out. Practise dynamic blending for reading, as described in the 'Working through the programme' section, using these cards. Notice that the letters get gradually darker as the child works through the word, a visual signal that they are pushing together the sounds and preparing them to listen to the word forming. Model this process for the child if necessary.

Activity 23 Dynamic blending Set 4

up	cup
get	men
mum	pen
ran	ten

Print out onto card and cut out.
Stack them with the biggest (the complete word) on the bottom and in decreasing size so that the smallest is on the top.
Make sure the left-hand edge of the cards are flush. Staple the cards together on the left-hand side.
When the child runs a finger over the cards the sound spellings flip up. Ask the child to say the sounds and match to the flips.

Flippies Set 4 - a

r	r a	r a n
r	r e	r e d
t	t e	t e n

Print out onto card and cut out.
Stack them with the biggest (the complete word) on the bottom and in decreasing size so that the smallest is on the top.
Make sure the left-hand edge of the cards are flush. Staple the cards together on the left-hand side.
When the child runs a finger over the cards the sound spellings flip up. Ask the child to say the sounds and match to the flips.

Flippies Set 4 - b

m	m e	m e n
g	g e	g e t
m	m e	m e t

Print out onto card and cut out.
Stack them with the biggest (the complete word) on the bottom and in decreasing size so that the smallest is on the top.
Make sure the left-hand edge of the cards are flush. Staple the cards together on the left-hand side.
When the child runs a finger over the cards the sound spellings flip up. Ask the child to say the sounds and match to the flips.

Flippies

Set 4 - c

m	m	u	m	u	m
p	p	u	p	u	t
r	r	u	r	u	n

Read the clue on the left for the child.
Use the clue to work out what the answer word is.
Encourage the child to think about the sounds in the word and write a sound spelling for each sound in the boxes on the right, one by one.
The first one is done as an example for you.
Explain that they may not need to use all the boxes and so some are shaded in.
Break this task into a number of shorter tasks over a number of lessons if necessary.

Activity 30 Sound boxes Set 4

Clue	Sound boxes		
Sam _________ in a race.	r	a	n
We write with a ________.			
Look __________ to the sky.			
Another word for mother is __________.			
Blood is __________.			

Support the child to read the words on the left one by one.
For each word support the child to work out what sounds are in the word and count them.
Then support the child to cross out any boxes that are not needed.
In each of the boxes in the middle, have the child write the sound spelling to match each sound.
In the last column the child writes how many sounds there are in the word.
Break this task into a number of shorter tasks over a number of lessons if necessary.

Activity 31 How many sounds? Set 4

Word	Sound spellings					How many sounds?
ran	r	a	n			3
up						
get						
mum						
red						
on						
ten						
sun						
net						

During this activity the child will get the chance to slide sounds in and out of words, i.e. practise phoneme manipulation. Sounds will be swapped, added or taken away. Print the sound spellings on card and cut out.

Build a starting word from the prompt list, demonstrating dynamic blending as you move the sound spelling cards into place.

Repeat the word, running your finger along the cards so that it corresponds with the sounds within the word.

Ask the child to change the word to the next word on the prompt list. As you say the new word run your finger under the cards so that it corresponds with the sounds within the word and gives the child the chance to hear and see what is different.

The child can then swap the appropriate sound spelling cards.

Activity 33 Sound swap Set 4

Sound swap e u r

List 1	List 2	List 3
cup	men	run
cut	ten	rug
put	tin	mug
pet	pin	mum
net	pen	mud
not	den	mad

c	p	t
n	d	r
g	m	m
a	e	i
o	u	

Support the child to read the word in the first column. Then, referring to the second column, ask the child what sound they are going to take away.

Then ask the child to think about what word would be made if the sound in the second column was taken out of the word, in this case from the beginning of it.

Remind the child to think about the sounds, blend dynamically and listen to the word forming.

Have the child write out the new word on the line at the end, sounding out the word as they write each sound spelling. Remind the child that the sound 'k' can be written using the **c** or the **k** sound spelling.

Break this task into a number of shorter tasks over a number of lessons if necessary.

Activity 34 Read – Delete – Spell Set 4

Read	Read without this sound	Spell the new word
ram	'r'	________________
cup	'k'	________________
rat	'r'	________________
ran	'r'	________________
sup	's'	________________

Support the child to read the word in the first column. Then, referring to the second column, ask the child to think about what word would be made if the sound in the second column was added in front of the word. Remind the child to think about the sounds, blend dynamically and listen to the word forming.
Have the child write out the new word on the line at the end, sounding out the word as they write each sound spelling. Remind the child that the sound 'k' can be written using the **c** or the **k** sound spelling.

Break this task into a number of shorter tasks over a number of lessons if necessary.

Activity 35 Read – Add – Spell Set 4

Read	Read with this sound at the beginning	Spell the new word
am	'r'	ram
up	'k'	______
at	'r	______
an	'r'	______
up	's'	______

Support the child to read the words on the left, one by one.
For each word read the clue to the child and work out what the answer word is.
Explain to the child that they will need to either: add a sound, take away a sound or change a sound to make the answer word
e.g. sip > slip > lip > lap.
Have the child write out the new word on the line on the right, saying each sound as they write each sound spelling.
An example is done for you.

Break this task into a number of shorter tasks over a number of lessons if necessary.

Activity 36 Sound exchange — Set 4

Starting word	Clue	New word
up	Drink out of this	cup
rat	We look __ things	______
rid	United's colour	______
get	Animal that lives with us	______
an	Moved very fast	______
sup	We look ___ to the sky	______
pin	Write with this	______

This set of cards is made up of words containing the target sounds for set 4. Copy onto card and cut out. Practise dynamic blending for reading, as described in the 'Working through the programme' section, using these cards. Model this process for the child if necessary.

Activity 37 Reading words with target sounds Set 4

cup	cut
den	men
met	net
pen	rat
set	ten

This set of cards is made up of the high frequency words containing the target sounds for set 4. Copy onto card and cut out.
Practise dynamic blending for reading, as described in the 'Working through the programme' section, using these cards. Model this process for the child if necessary.

Activity 38 Reading high frequency words Set 4

up	get
mum	put
ran	red
run	sun

Starting at 'men' have the child read each of the words as quickly as possible tracking along the line one by one until they get to 'up'.
Support the child to read the words by giving information about sounds and supporting dynamic blending but do not supply the whole word.
Time how long it takes to read all the words and record the time at the bottom of the page.
Repeat at a later point, e.g. at the end of the lesson or the following day, and see if the child can beat their *own* previous time.

Activity 39 Reading race — Set 4

men run put red up

1 _____ minutes ___ seconds
2 _____ minutes ___ seconds
3 _____ minutes ___ seconds

Visual discrimination is the ability to see differences between objects that are similar. Good visual discrimination helps keep us from getting confused when looking at shapes and forms in the environment. Children with poor visual discrimination may find it difficult to recognise letters, may confuse letters such as b and d and may find it difficult to identify mathematical symbols.

Ask the child to look at the word in the pink box then track along the row looking at the other words. The child indicates or puts a ring around the word that is the same as the one in the pink box.

Break this task into a number of shorter tasks over a number of lessons if necessary.

Activity 40 Spot the word Set 4

run	ran	run	red
net	ten	net	met
cup	cut	cup	cop
men	man	men	mum
pet	pot	pet	get

Visual memory is the ability to remember and identify a shape or picture that we have previously seen. Children with poor visual memory may struggle to remember pictures, figures, shapes, letters and numbers and may have difficulties with reading, writing and number work.

Ask the child to look at the word in the yellow box for at least five seconds, covering the white box underneath. Then cover the yellow box so that the letter cannot be seen and reveal the choice of words in the white box below. Ask the child to select the matching word from the white box.

Break this task into a number of shorter tasks over a number of lessons if necessary.

Activity 41 Remembering words Set 4

up
on up

red
rid red

get		
get	got	

mum		
mug	mum	

run		
ran	run	rug

pen		
pet	peg	pen

Form constancy is the ability to generalise forms and figures and identify them even if they are slightly different from that usually seen. This skill helps us distinguish differences in size, shape, and orientation or position. Children with poor form constancy may frequently reverse letters and numbers.

Ask the child to look at the word in the orange box then track along the row looking at the other words. The child indicates or puts a ring around the word that is the same as the one in the orange box.

Break this task into a number of shorter tasks over a number of lessons if necessary.

Activity 42 Which is the word? Set 4

cup	cut	cup	cot
get	gap	got	get
red	red	ran	rat
sun	sad	sun	set
pen	pen	peg	pet

Visual closure is the ability to identify an object, shape or symbol from a visually incomplete or disorganised presentation and to see where different parts of a whole fit together, i.e. to recognise something when seeing only part of it. This skill helps us understand things quickly because our visual system doesn't have to process every detail to recognise what we're seeing.

Ask the child to look at the large word and then at the choice of smaller words underneath. The child indicates or puts a ring around the word that is the same as the big word.

Break this task into a number of shorter tasks over a number of lessons if necessary.

Activity 43 Word splits — Set 4

run

ran   run

put

put   pet

men

man   men

cup

cup   cut

Figure ground is the ability to find patterns or shapes when hidden within a busy background without getting confused by surrounding images. This skill keeps children from getting lost in the details, for example when looking at pictures in books or reading. Children with poor figure ground become easily confused with too much print on the page, affecting their concentration and attention.

Ask the child to look at the words, which are overlapping. Ask the child to first find all the words. Some words are written more than once. How many of each word are there?

Break this task into a number of shorter tasks over a number of lessons if necessary.

Activity 44 Busy words Set 4

sun peg red run peg red

run net mum up

net peg sun run sun

mum red

peg run net up

mum red sun

Visual sequential memory is the ability to remember sequences of figures, symbols and shapes. Children with poor visual sequencing struggle to remember a sequence of letters and follow visual patterns. They may have difficulties writing a sequence of letters to form a word and a sequence of words to form a sentence.

Ask the child to look at the words in the yellow box for at least five seconds, covering the white box underneath. Then cover the yellow box so that the words cannot be seen and reveal the sequence of words in the white box below. Ask the child to remember the missing word and write it in the space.

Break this task into a number of shorter tasks over a number of lessons if necessary.

Activity 45 Remembering lots of words Set 4

red up
____ up

men set
men ____

rip get
___ get

den rug
den ___

pen set ten
___ set ten

put rag net
put ___ net

Tracking is the ability to follow a sequence of letters, figures or symbols. The eyes need to focus on the symbols in order and not look randomly at the symbols on the page. This is an important skill for reading and writing where letters and words are written from left to right and the reader is required to work down a page from the top to the bottom.

Ask the child to look at the symbols and sound spellings and track from left to right. When the child finds a group of sound spellings then they indicate or put a circle around them all. The child then reads the word.

Break this task into a number of shorter tasks over a number of lessons if necessary.

Activity 46 Hidden words — Set 4

↘⇨⇨↘ran→↔▷cup⇦▽⇨sun⇨→↘⇦ten⇦
▷▽↘▽men⇦▷↓▽⇦↘⇦⇨get⇨↙⇨⇦nut⇨

↙⇦set▷⇦⇨pen←↙▷↔net↗▽⇦↘⇕↦▽⇨⇨▷
mum⇦▷⇕⇦▽⇕↔met▷←⇕↗cut⇨⇦⇕⇦

θσκμrunδωνσdenπωρωαupφπλωκτωνputμμδ
φυτragωφνεgetεδωφ

γηκεredδωκδσπratπωρωαnetφπλτωνpegλκδ
φυτcupωφκρεrigεωφ

Prior to working with the child, read through the instructions in the 'Working through the programme' section.

Activity 47 Word build Set 4

u	p		
m	e	n	
m	u	m	
p	e	t	

r	u	g	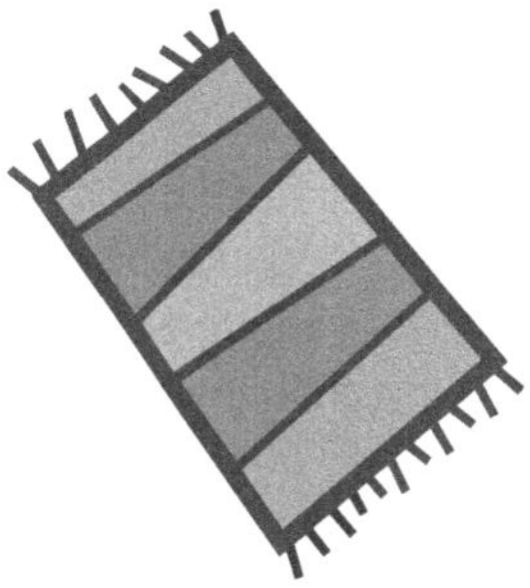
t	e	n	10
s	u	n	

Support the child to look at the picture and work out what the word is.
Then support the child to work out the initial sound in the word and match a sound spelling in the gap provided.
The 'Place to listen' technique should be used to support this.
Read through the 'Place to listen' instructions in the 'Working through the programme' section of this book prior to working with the child.
Ask the child to read the completed word using the dynamic blending technique.

Activity 48 Finish the word 1 Set 4

_____ up 

_____ et 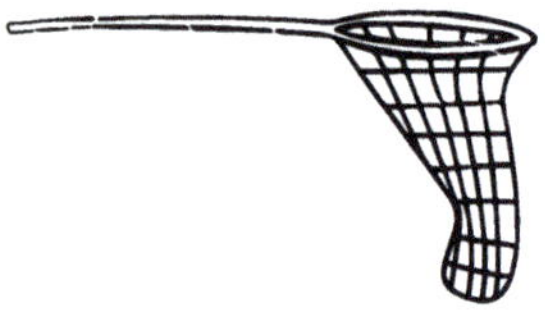

_____ ug 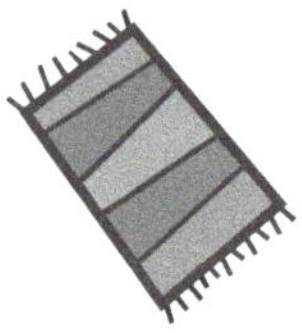

_____ un 

_____ um 

_____ ut 

_____ en 10

Support the child to look at the picture and work out what the word is.
Then support the child to work out the initial sound in the word and match a sound spelling in the gap provided.
The 'Place to listen' technique could be used to support this.
Ask the child to read the completed word using the dynamic blending technique.

Activity 49 Finish the word 2 — Set 4

c ____ p

m ____ n

r ____ d

p ____ n

n ____ t

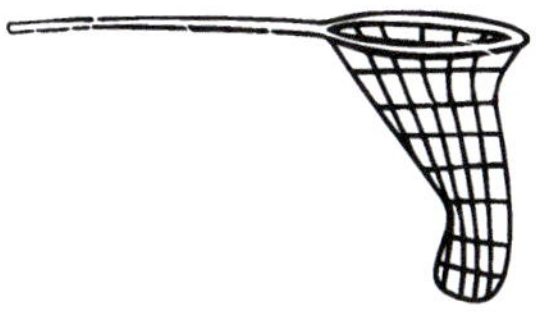

r ____ n

t ____ n

10

Support the child to look at the picture and work out what the word is.
Support the child to look at the picture and work out what the word is.
Then support the child to work out the final sound in the word and match a sound spelling in the gap provided.
The 'Place to listen' technique should be used to support this.
Read through the 'Place to listen' instructions in the 'Working through the programme' section of this book prior to working with the child.
Ask the child to read the completed word using the dynamic blending technique.

Activity 50 Finish the word 3 Set 4

p e ____

r u ____

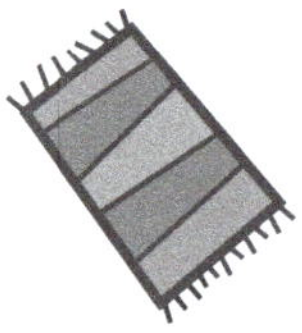

t e ____

10

m u ____

d e ____

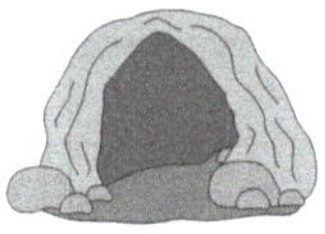

m e ____

r i ____

Read the instructions in the introduction of this book to guide you on how to work through this spelling practise sheet with the child.

Activity 52 Spelling challenge — Set 4

up	u p	u p	__ __	________
get	g e t	g e t	__ __ __	________
mum	m u m	m u m	__ __ __	________
put	p u t	p u t	__ __ __	________
ran	r a n	r a n	__ __ __	________
red	r e d	r e d	__ __ __	________

Support the child to read the sentences. Have the child look at the pictures and find the picture that matches the sentence.
Have the child draw a line from the sentence to the matching picture.
Break this task into a number of shorter tasks over a number of lessons if necessary.

Activity 53 Read the sentence and match to a picture — Set 4

Pat sat in the sun.

Ted got a red pen.

A dog can run on a rug.

Sam in a den.

Sid got a pet rat.

Support the child to read the sentence.
For each sentence, support the child to spot the spelling mistake.
Have the child underline or highlight the mistake and then write out the sentence correcting the mistake.
Encourage the child to say the sounds in each word at the same time as writing the sound spellings.
Break this task into a number of shorter tasks over a number of lessons if necessary.

Activity 54 Oops! Correct the spelling Set 4

1. Ted got a met.

2. Sid set up ten meg.

3. Tom got a red pan.

4. Dan met Ted it a den.

5. Kim got a pod.

Support the child to read the sentences.
There is a missing word with a choice of two words to fill the gap.
For each sentence support the child to identify the missing word which makes sense in the sentence.
Have the child write the word on the line within the sentence.
Break this task into a number of shorter tasks over a number of lessons if necessary.

Activity 55 Spot the spelling Set 4

1. Ted sat on a ____________.

   rat rug

2. Kim got a red ____________.

   pen peg

3. Dan ____________ up ten men.

   set sad

4. Pat ____________ in the sun.

   sat sit

5. Tom can run on a ____________.

   mat man

6. A rat can ____________ it up.

   dig big

Support the child to read each sentence.
Ask the child to re-read the sentence, several times if necessary, and try to remember it.
Cover the sentence and ask the child to recall it verbally from memory.
Once they can do this, ask the child to write out the sentence from memory.
The child might find it helpful to say the sounds as they write and say individual words once written.
When the sentence is complete, the child reads out their sentence and then compares it to the original.
Alternatively, using the text to speech function on a laptop or similar software, the child could type the sentence with the computer reading back each word and then the completed sentence.

Activity 56 Writing challenge — Set 4

Put a cat on a rug.

Pat a red dog.

Tim put on a red rag.

Did Pam get it?

Answers Set 4: e u r

Page 187
Activity 12 Spot the sound spelling

e 8
u 8
r 9

Page 193
Activity 17 Busy sound spellings

e 8
u 8
r 9

Page 205
Activity 30 Sound boxes

pen
up
mum
red

Page 206
Activity 31 How many sounds?

up	2	get	3
mum	3	red	3
on	2	ten	3
sun	3	net	3

Page 209
Activity 34 Read – Delete – Spell

am
up
at
an
up

Page 210
Activity 35 Read – Add – Spell

cup
rat
ran
sup

Page 211
Activity 36 Sound exchange

at	red
pet	ran
up	pen

Page 220
Activity 44 Busy words

sun	4
run	4
red	4
mum	3
net	3
up	2
peg	4

Page 226
Activity 48 Finish the word 1

cup	net
rug	sun
mum	nut
ten	

Page 227
Activity 49 Finish the word 2

cup	men
red	pen
net	run
ten	

Page 228
Activity 50 Finish the word 3

peg	rug
ten	mug
den	men
rip	

Page 232
Activity 55 Spot the spelling

rug	pen
set	sat
mat	dig

SECTION 5

SET 5 SOUNDS AND SOUND SPELLINGS

h b f l

Auditory discrimination is the ability to hear differences between sounds. Good auditory discrimination helps us to recognise and identify the sounds in words and so interpret them correctly. Children with poor auditory discrimination may confuse sounds and misinterpret things they have heard. Their spelling and writing may reflect their confusion over what sounds they heard in a word. **Auditory attention and tracking** is the ability to actively listen and follow auditory information from beginning to end. Good auditory attention and tracking helps us to follow a conversation, a story read out loud or a set of instructions, being able to focus on key information. Children with poor auditory attention and tracking may find it difficult to follow and respond appropriately to what is being said to them.

This story contains lots of words that start with the sounds 'h', 'b', 'f' and 'l', but you will focus on just one 'target' sound.
Read the story out loud. Encourage the child to listen carefully and spot any word that starts with the 'target' sound.
When a target word has been read, the child indicates that they have heard and spotted it by tapping the table, putting up a hand or any other agreed signal, but without shouting out. Stop reading and discuss the word, making any error correction necessary. If a word is missed, re-read the sentence. Do not show the story to the children. The target words are highlighted below for you: 'h', 'b', 'f' and 'l'. Repeat on another occasion focusing on a different target sound.

Activity 1 Sound target – Story sheet Set 5

Hasim and Ben are best friends. They both love to play football. They play football at breaktime, football at lunchtime and football after school. They both have a place on the school team. They even play football together on their games consoles at home.
But there is one thing that is different. Hasim supports Liverpool FC and Ben supports West Ham.
When the teams play a match Hasim hopes Liverpool will win and Ben longs for West Ham to win.
They each wear their favourite team's kit and have scarves and flags to wave.
During the match they shout and bawl at each other. They leap about and play fight. Both hope the other team loses. But once the game has finished they are hearty best friends again.

Please Note: The focus of activity is the *sound* in the word, NOT what *letter* is in the word.

Auditory discrimination is the ability to hear differences between sounds. Good auditory discrimination helps us to recognise and identify the sounds in words and so interpret them correctly. Children with poor auditory discrimination may confuse sounds and misinterpret things they have heard. Their spelling and writing may reflect their confusion over what sounds they heard in a word. **Auditory sequential memory** is the ability to remember and recall a series of things that they have heard. Children with poor auditory sequential memory may find it difficult to remember information given earlier in a conversation or set of instructions and may struggle to recall the sequence of sounds in a word.

The sentences contain lots of words beginning with one of the target sounds 'h', 'b', 'f' or 'l'.
Read the sentence to the child several times, invite them to join in as you say it and gradually recall it on their own.
Ask them to say it as quickly as they can and have some fun with it. After some practise, ask the child if they can identify which sound they hear a lot in the tongue twister. Perhaps they can make up their own?
Note that the vocabulary included in these tongue twisters may be unfamiliar to the child, especially the adjectives. If appropriate, talk about unfamiliar words and discuss their meaning.
Break this task into a number of shorter tasks over a number of lessons if necessary.

Activity 2 Sound target – Tongue twister fun Set 5

Happy horses hug hairy hippos.

Harry hears hedgehog howls.

Busy bees buzz on blossoms.

Bald babbling babies balance on baskets.

Fearless Freddie finds forty faded feathers.

In father's field fifty flowers flourish.

Lonely leopards love lemon loaves.

Lovely Lin likes licking lilac lollies.

Auditory discrimination is the ability to hear differences between sounds. Good auditory discrimination helps us to recognise and identify the sounds in words and so interpret them correctly. Children with poor auditory discrimination may confuse sounds and misinterpret things they have heard. Their spelling and writing may reflect their confusion over what sounds they heard in a word. **Auditory attention and tracking** is the ability to actively listen and follow auditory information from beginning to end. Good auditory attention and tracking helps us to follow a conversation, a story read out loud or a set of instructions, being able to focus on key information. Children with poor auditory attention and tracking may find it difficult to follow and respond appropriately to what is being said to them.

This activity focuses the child on listening to short lists of words starting with the sounds 'h', 'b', 'f' and 'l'. The words get increasingly complex as does the number of words the child has to listen to. Later items include words starting with sounds from previous sets.

Read out the words and ask the child to identify the odd one out, the word that *does not* start with the same sound as the others. Do not show the words to the child. The odd one out is highlighted for you.
Break this task into a number of shorter tasks over a number of lessons if necessary.

Activity 3 Odd one out — Set 5

1.	hit	hat	**fan**	2.	bob	**lad**	bad
3.	leg	let	**bug**	4.	**fan**	lit	let
5.	hop	hot	**ban**	6.	lap	**him**	led
7.	hand	help	**end**	8.	**bump**	lift	last
9.	fast	**elf**	felt	10.	bend	best	**lamp**
11.	**brag**	flag	flap	12.	from	frog	**brim**
13.	flask	**drink**	flint	14.	blink	blank	**plant**
15.	bet	bed	**fun**	bin			
16.	him	**fog**	hen	hop			
17.	**fib**	lid	let	lad			

Auditory discrimination is the ability to hear differences between sounds. Good auditory discrimination helps us to recognise and identify the sounds in words and so interpret them correctly. Children with poor auditory discrimination may confuse sounds and misinterpret things they have heard. Their spelling and writing may reflect their confusion over what sounds they heard in a word. **Auditory recall memory** is the ability to remember and recall something that they have just heard. Children with poor auditory recall memory may find it difficult to remember sounds and words and respond appropriately.

Read the list of words below clearly, asking the child to listen carefully. All the words start with an 'e', 'u' or 'r' from set 4 or 'h', 'b', 'f' and 'l' from set 5 and get increasingly complex.
At random points, tap the table and stop reading, asking the child to remember and say the last word you said. Then ask them to tell you what the first sound in the word is.

Break this task into a number of shorter tasks over a number of lessons if necessary.

Activity 4 What sound am I? Set 4 & 5

1.	leg	red	bad	rug	lad	bet	lit
2.	fan	rip	bed	fog	let	hop	bug
3.	lap	fed	lip	hut	bun	beg	lot
4.	rust	lend	fast	left	last	help	band
5.	ramp	bump	lost	lamp	hand	rest	best
6.	flap	brag	flag	from	frog	brim	flip
7.	boot	food	loop	rude	fool	boom	loot
8.	foam	boat	hole	road	loaf	bone	rope
9.	blame	fame	late	rain	flame	lake	lane
10.	found	loud	brown	round	how	foul	howl

Auditory discrimination is the ability to hear differences between sounds. Good auditory discrimination helps us to recognise and identify the sounds in words and so interpret them correctly. Children with poor auditory discrimination may confuse sounds and misinterpret things they have heard. Their spelling and writing may reflect their confusion over what sounds they heard in a word.

Read out the pairs of words. Ask the child to tell you whether or not they start with the same sound. The words get increasingly complex. Word pairs that start with the same sound are highlighted.

Break this task into a number of shorter tasks over a number of lessons if necessary.

Activity 5 Same or different? Set 4 & 5

1. up - if
2. fed - fun
3. run - red
4. leg - bad
5. let - hop
6. bet - bud
7. rat - ran
8. bob - him
9. lot - lad
10. fog - bin
11. rip - bug
12. hug - hid
13. left - last
14. help - bank
15. best - bump
16. lend - land
17. fast - hand
18. brag - brim
19. hope - hole
20. bowl - loan
21. late - lake
22. brain - hate
23. leap - beak
24. heat - feet

Auditory fusion is the ability to hear the subtle gaps between sounds and words. Children with poor auditory fusion may get lost in conversations and when following a list of instructions given verbally.

Say the sounds or read the words in the list one after another at a brisk pace so that there are no obvious gaps between the sounds or words. Ask the child to listen carefully and then tell you how many sounds or words you have said. All the words start with the sound 'e', 'u', or 'r' from set 4 or 'h', 'b', 'f' or 'l' from set 5 and get increasingly complex.

Break this task into a number of shorter tasks over a number of lessons if necessary.

Activity 6 How many did you hear? Set 4 & 5

1. u - e - r - u
2. r - u - r - e - r
3. h - b - f - h - f - b
4. l - b - f - l - b
5. u - f - l - b - u
6. r - b - l - u - h - r - h
7. f - r - h - l - f - r
8. b - l - r - e - b - f
9. run - bad - hug
10. red - fan - bin - hat - him
11. bob - leg - hat - up - rat
12. fed - hen - fog - lip
13. lit - bus - rap - hot
14. bed - rip - fat - lap - hit
15. end - elf
16. rust - hand - help
17. left - lamp - held - bank
18. lamp - last - bend
19. brag - brim
20. lane - bake - hate - lake
21. rain - late - flake
22. flea - heat - bean - leap
23. read - beat - leak - heel
24. bowl - hole - load

Auditory attention and tracking is the ability to actively listen and follow auditory information from beginning to end. Good auditory attention and tracking helps us to follow a conversation, a story read out loud or a set of instructions, being able to focus on key information. Children with poor auditory attention and tracking may find it difficult to follow and respond appropriately to what is being said to them. **Auditory sequential memory** is the ability to remember and recall a series of things that they have heard. Children with poor auditory sequential memory may find it difficult to remember information given earlier in a conversation or a set of instructions and may struggle to recall the sequence of sounds in a word.

In this activity the child has to process the auditory information but also respond by working out the pattern and stating the next sound in the sequence. Read out the list of sounds with a clear space between each. Ask the child to listen and work out what sound would come next. Answers are in red.

Break this task into a number of shorter tasks over a number of lessons if necessary.

Activity 7 What comes next? Set 5

1. h b h b h b ...... h
2. f l f l f l ...... f
3. b f b f b f ...... b
4. l h l h l h l
5. b b h b b h b b h ...... b
6. l l f l l f l l f l
7. f f b f f b f f b ...... f
8. h h l h h l h h l ...... h
9. b b h h b b h h b b ...... h
10. l l f f l l f f l l ...... f
11. f f b b f f b b f f ...... b
12. h h l l h h l l h h l
13. h h f f h h f f h h ...... f
14. l l b b l l b b l l ...... b
15. b b b h b b b h b b h ...... b
16. l l l f l l l f l l l f l
17. f f f b f f f b f f f b ...... f
18. h h h l h h h l h h h l ...... h
19. b f l b f l b f l ...... b
20. h f b h f b h f b ...... h
21. f h l f h l f h l ...... f
22. h b l h b l h b l ...... h
23. h h b b l h h b b l ...... h
24. l l f f b l l f f b l

Print out the cards below to use when introducing the sounds and the sound spellings.

Activity 8 Sound spelling cards Set 5

h	b
f	l

There are six different bingo cards and a set of individual sound spelling cards which can be copied and cut out.

Each child is given their own bingo card. Shuffle the sound spelling cards, select and 'call' the sound spellings, one by one, from the top of the pile. There are a number of ways to do this, depending on the focus for the pupils:

- show the selected sound spelling and say the sound – child matches visual figures with auditory reinforcement
- show the selected sound spelling only – child matches visual figures without auditory reinforcement
- say the sound for the selected sound spelling but do not show it to the children – child processes the auditory information and matches to a visual figure.

When a child has a sound spelling on their card they can cover it with a counter or write over the sound spelling on the bingo card, writing in between the lines as a guide, saying the sound as they write. If they have more than one of a sound spelling on the card then they must only cover one and wait for that sound spelling to be called again. The first person to cover all their sound spellings is the winner.

Activity 9 Sound spelling bingo Set 5

h	h
b	f

b	h
l	f

f	b
h	b

f	f
b	l

l	l
h	b

f	l
h	l

h	h	h	h	h
h	b	b	b	b
b	b	f	f	f
f	f	f	l	l
l	l	l	l	

Visual discrimination is the ability to see differences between objects that are similar. Good visual discrimination helps keep us from getting confused when looking at shapes and forms in the environment. Children with poor visual discrimination may find it difficult to recognise letters, may confuse letters such as b and d and may find it difficult to identify mathematical symbols.

Ask the child to look at the sound spelling in the yellow box then track along the row looking at the other sound spellings. The child indicates or puts a ring around the sound spelling that is the same as the one in the yellow box.

Break this task into a number of shorter tasks over a number of lessons if necessary.

Activity 11 Sound spelling tracker Set 5

h	b	d	h	t
f	f	t	h	k
b	d	p	h	b
h	b	h	d	p
l	t	h	l	b
f	k	t	f	l
b	b	d	h	p

Visual discrimination is the ability to see differences between objects that are similar. Good visual discrimination helps keep us from getting confused when looking at shapes and forms in the environment. Children with poor visual discrimination may find it difficult to recognise letters, may confuse letters such as b and d.

It is important that the child is given the opportunity to visually explore these two letters in the same activity so they are able to compare and contrast. Ask the child to look at the letter in the yellow box then track along the row looking at the other letters. The child indicates or puts a ring around the letter that is the same as the one in the yellow box.

Break this task into a number of shorter tasks over a number of lessons if necessary.

Activity 11 Sound spelling tracker — Focus on b & d

b	d	b	p	d
d	d	b	b	p
d	b	p	d	b
b	d	b	d	p
b	p	d	p	b
d	b	p	d	b
d	b	d	p	d

Visual discrimination is the ability to see differences between objects that are similar. Good visual discrimination helps keep us from getting confused when looking at shapes and forms in the environment. Children with poor visual discrimination may find it difficult to recognise letters, may confuse letters such as b and d and may find it difficult to identify mathematical symbols.

Focus on one sound spelling e.g. **f** (say the sound 'f' and point to the matching sound spelling rather than using the letter name when talking to the child).
Ask the child to look at all the sound spellings and indicate or put a ring round all the letters matching the target.

Break this task into a number of shorter tasks over a number of lessons if necessary.

Activity 12 Spot the sound spelling Set 5

h l f f b l

b f l b f b

h f l l h

h b h f l

h b b l

l r l f b

Visual discrimination is the ability to see differences between objects that are similar. Good visual discrimination helps keep us from getting confused when looking at shapes and forms in the environment. Children with poor visual discrimination may find it difficult to recognise letters, may confuse letters such as b and d and may find it difficult to identify mathematical symbols.

Focus on one sound spelling e.g. **b** (say the sound 'b' and point to a matching sound spelling rather than using the letter name when talking to the child).
Ask the child to look at all the sound spellings and indicate or put a ring round all the letters matching the target.

Break this task into a number of shorter tasks over a number of lessons if necessary.

Activity 12 Spot the sound spelling Focus on b & d

b b b bd

d d

d

d d

d

b

d b b b

b

d

bd d b

b b

Visual memory is the ability to remember and identify a shape or picture that we have previously seen. Children with poor visual memory may struggle to remember pictures, figures, shapes, letters and numbers and may have difficulties with reading, writing and number work.

Ask the child to look at the sound spelling in the yellow box for at least five seconds, covering the white box underneath. Then cover the yellow box so that the sound spelling cannot be seen and reveal the choice of sound spellings in the white box below. Ask the child to select the matching sound spelling from the white box.

Break this task into a number of shorter tasks over a number of lessons if necessary.

Activity 13 Remembering sound spellings Set 5

b
b h

h
b h

l
h l

f
b f

b
h b f

f
b h f

Visual memory is the ability to remember and identify a shape or picture that we have previously seen. Children with poor visual memory may struggle to remember pictures, figures, shapes, letters and numbers and may have difficulties with reading, writing and number work.

Ask the child to look at the sound spelling in the yellow box for at least five seconds, covering the white box underneath. Then cover the yellow box so that the sound spelling cannot be seen and reveal the choice of sound spellings in the white box below. Ask the child to select the matching sound spelling from the white box.

Break this task into a number of shorter tasks over a number of lessons if necessary.

Activity 13 Remembering sound spellings — Focus on b & d

b
b d

d
d b

b
d b

d
b d

d
p d b

b
d p b

Visual discrimination is the ability to see differences between objects that are similar. Good visual discrimination helps keep us from getting confused when looking at shapes and forms in the environment. Children with poor visual discrimination may find it difficult to recognise letters, may confuse letters such as b and d and may find it difficult to identify mathematical symbols.

Ask the child to colour in the shapes according to the sound spelling colour key at the bottom.

Activity 14 Colour the picture Set 5

Colour h brown b grey f red l green

Form constancy is the ability to generalise forms and figures and identify them even if they are slightly different from that usually seen. This skill helps us distinguish differences in size, shape, and orientation or position. Children with poor form constancy may frequently reverse letters and numbers.

Ask the child to look at the letter on the left and match to a letter on the right (written differently), drawing a line to connect each.

Activity 15 Which is the same? Set 5

b	*f*
l	*b*
h	l
f	h
b	*h*
f	b
l	f
h	*l*

Visual closure is the ability to identify an object, shape or symbol from a visually incomplete or disorganised presentation and to see where the different parts of a whole fit together, i.e. to recognise something when seeing only part of it. This skill helps us understand things quickly because our visual system doesn't have to process every detail to recognise what we're seeing.

Ask the child to look at the sound spelling in the white box then track left to right along the row.
Ask the child to indicate or put a ring around the sound spelling that is the same as the sound spelling in the white box.

Break this task into a number of shorter tasks over a number of lessons if necessary.

Activity 16 Bits missing Set 5

f	t	j	f
l	t	l	i
b	d	b	p
h	b	d	h
l	l	i	t
f	j	f	t
b	p	d	b
h	d	h	b

Visual closure is the ability to identify an object, shape or symbol from a visually incomplete or disorganised presentation and to see where the different parts of a whole fit together, i.e. to recognise something when seeing only part of it. This skill helps us understand things quickly because our visual system doesn't have to process every detail to recognise what we're seeing.

Ask the child to look at the sound spelling in the white box then track left to right along the row.
Ask the child to indicate or put a ring around the sound spelling that is the same as the sound spelling in the white box.

Break this task into a number of shorter tasks over a number of lessons if necessary.

Activity 16 Bits missing Focus on b & d

b	d	b	p
d	b	p	d
d	d	b	p
b	p	d	b
d	b	d	p
b	p	d	b
d	b	p	d
b	b	p	d

Figure ground is the ability to find patterns or shapes when hidden within a busy background without getting confused by surrounding images. This skill keeps children from getting lost in the details, for example when looking at pictures in books or reading. Children with poor figure ground become easily confused with too much print on the page, affecting their concentration and attention.

Ask the child to look at the sound spellings, which are overlapping. Ask the child to first find and count all the **b** sound spellings (refer to the sound not the letter name), then the **h** etc. Ask the child to write down how many of each sound spelling they found.

Break this task into a number of shorter tasks over a number of lessons if necessary.

Activity 17 Busy sound spellings Set 5

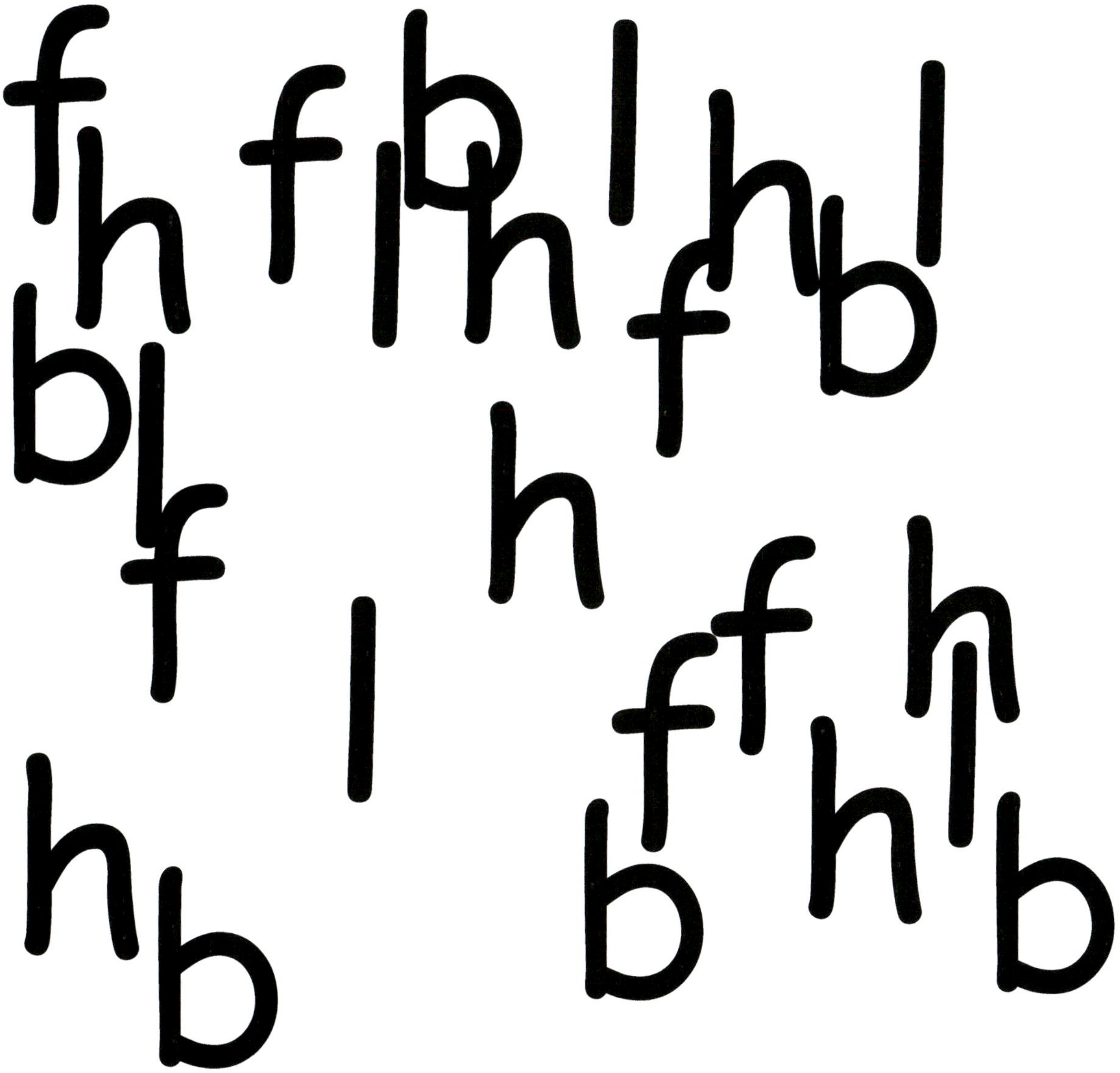

Figure ground is the ability to find patterns or shapes when hidden within a busy background without getting confused by surrounding images. This skill keeps children from getting lost in the details, for example when looking at pictures in books or reading. Children with poor figure ground become easily confused with too much print on the page, affecting their concentration and attention.

Ask the child to look at the sound spellings, which are overlapping. Ask the child to first find and count all the **b** sound spellings (refer to the sound not the letter name), then the **d** etc. Ask the child to write down how many of each sound spelling they found.

Break this task into a number of shorter tasks over a number of lessons if necessary.

Activity 17 Busy sound spellings Focus on b & d

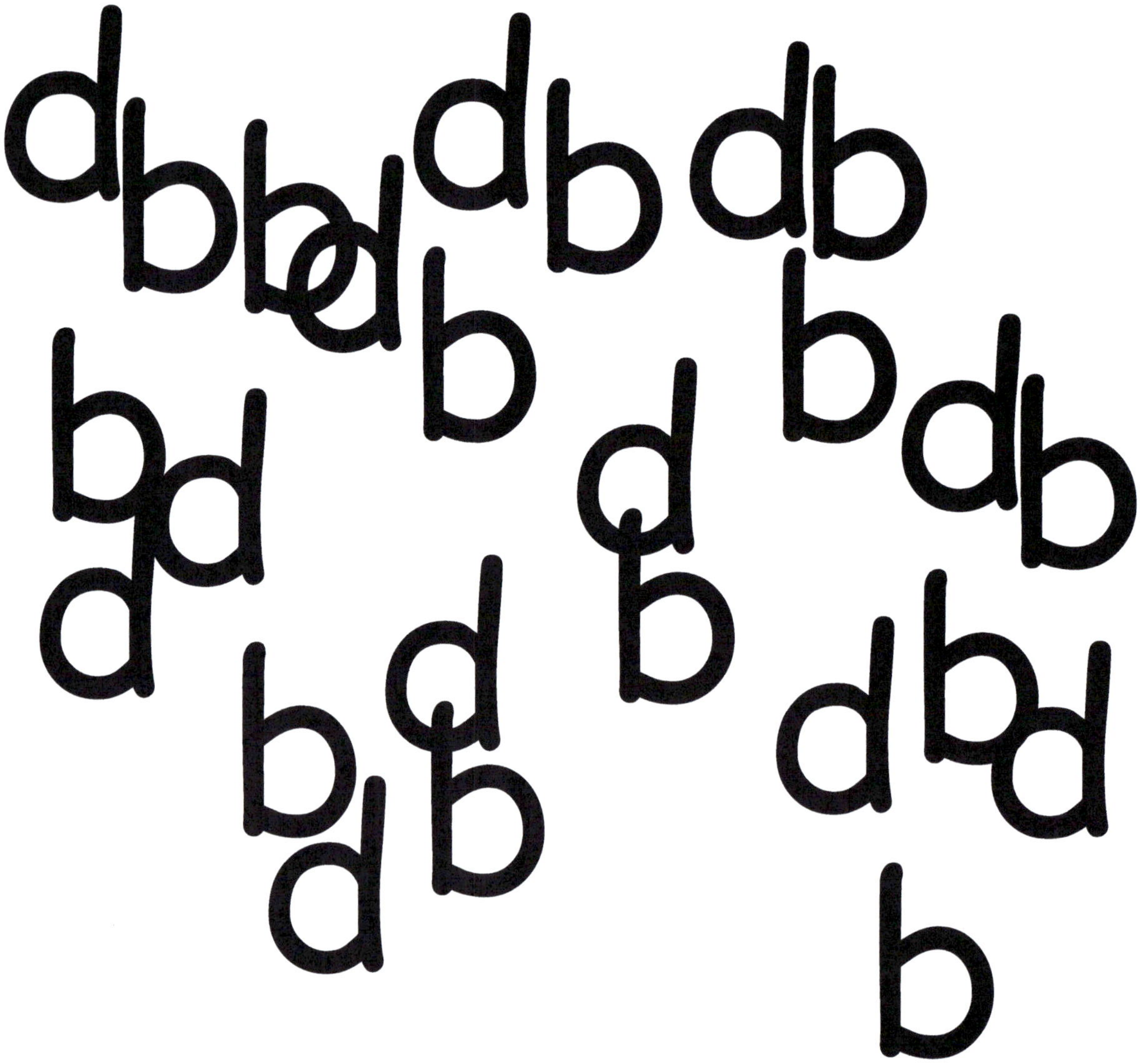

Spatial relations is the ability to perceive the position of objects in relation to ourselves and to each other. This skill helps children to understand relationships between symbols and letters. Children with poor spatial relations may find it difficult to write letters in the correct orientation, write consistently starting at the margin and write letters of the same size.

In the first part, ask the child to copy the sound spellings on the line underneath in exactly the same places as they appear above.
In the second part, ask the child to copy the words on the line underneath in exactly the same places, saying the matching sound as they write each sound spellings.
Break this task into a number of shorter tasks over a number of lessons if necessary.

Activity 18 Where am I? Set 5

b h f l

l h b f

cab if lot

bag fan

Spatial relations is the ability to perceive the position of objects in relation to ourselves and to each other. This skill helps children to understand relationships between symbols and letters. Children with poor spatial relations may find it difficult to write letters in the correct orientation, write consistently starting at the margin and write letters of the same size.

In the first part, ask the child to copy the sound spellings on the line underneath in exactly the same places as they appear above.
In the second part, ask the child to copy the words on the line underneath in exactly the same places, saying the matching sound as they write each sound spellings.
Break this task into a number of shorter tasks over a number of lessons if necessary.

Activity 18 Where am I? Focus on b & d

b d b d

b d b b d

bib did

dad bid bad

Visual sequential memory is the ability to remember sequences of figures, symbols and shapes. Children with poor visual sequencing struggle to remember a sequence of letters and follow visual patterns. They may have difficulties writing a sequence of letters to form a word and a sequence of words to form a sentence.

Ask the child to look at the sound spellings in the yellow box for at least five seconds, covering the white box underneath. Then cover the yellow box so that the sound spellings cannot be seen and reveal the sequence of sound spellings in the white box below. Ask the child to remember the missing sound spelling and write it in the space.

Break this task into a number of shorter tasks over a number of lessons if necessary.

Activity 19 Remembering lots of sound spellings — Set 5

b l
b _

h b
_ b

f l
f _

b f
b _

b f l
b _ l

u e r
_ e r

Visual sequential memory is the ability to remember sequences of figures, symbols and shapes. Children with poor visual sequencing struggle to remember a sequence of letters and follow visual patterns. They may have difficulties writing a sequence of letters to form a word and a sequence of words to form a sentence.

Ask the child to look at the sound spellings in the yellow box for at least five seconds, covering the white box underneath. Then cover the yellow box so that the sound spellings cannot be seen and reveal the sequence of sound spellings in the white box below. Ask the child to remember the missing sound spelling and write it in the space.

Break this task into a number of shorter tasks over a number of lessons if necessary.

Activity 19 Remembering lots of sound spellings — Focus on b & d

b p
_ p

d p
d _

d p
_ p

d b
_ b

p b d
p b _

d p b
d _ b

Tracking is the ability to follow a sequence of symbols. The eyes need to focus on the symbols in order and not look randomly at the symbols on the page. This is an important skill for reading and writing where letters and words are written from left to right and the reader is required to work down a page from the top to the bottom.

Choose a target sound spelling for the child to find. Ask the child to look at the sound spellings, tracking from left to right and down the page.
When they find the target sound spelling the child indicates or puts a ring around it. Repeat with a different sound spelling.

Break this task into a number of shorter tasks over a number of lessons if necessary.

Activity 20 Tracking sound spellings Set 5

h l b l f h b l h f
f b l h b l f h b l

b f l f l h b f l h b f h
l f b h f l b h f l h b f
f l h b f b h f l b b h f

f b h f l b h f l f b h f l b f l f l h
b h f l b b h b f l f l h b h f l f b h
h l b f l f l h f l b h h f l b h f l b

h f l b b h b f l f l h b h f l f l h f
l b h h f l f l h f l b h h h f l b h f
l f b h f l b f l f l h f l b b h b f h

Tracking is the ability to follow a sequence of symbols. The eyes need to focus on the symbols in order and not look randomly at the symbols on the page. This is an important skill for reading and writing where letters and words are written from left to right and the reader is required to work down a page from the top to the bottom.

Choose a target sound spelling for the child to find. Ask the child to look at the sound spellings, tracking from left to right and down the page.
When they find the target sound spelling the child indicates or puts a ring around it. Repeat with a different sound spelling.

Break this task into a number of shorter tasks over a number of lessons if necessary.

Activity 20 Tracking sound spellings Focus on b & d

p b d h b d p h d
b p p d b h p d b

b h d b p h b b d h p b
p h b h d d p b h b p h
b d h b d p h p b d d b

b p d p b d d p b h d b h p b d d b
d p b h b b d p h h b d d p b b h p
h b d b d p b b d p h d b p b d p b

d p b h d b h d b p b d p b h b b d
p h d b d b d p b b d b h p b p b h
p b h h h b d d p p d p b b d p h d

Having introduced the sounds and their corresponding sound spellings it is important that the child is given the opportunity to practise forming the sound spellings. As discussed in the introductory chapter, the child should be provided with lots of sensory and kinaesthetic experiences of forming the sound spellings in a variety of media as well as writing on conventional paper.

In this activity the child can practise forming the sound spellings by copying over the grey sound spellings which act as a guide. Encourage the child to say the sound at the same time as writing the sound spelling. The child can then practise writing the sound spellings within the boxes underneath which focuses the child on the spatial relationship between the sound spelling as it forms and the surrounding visual environment.

Activity 21 Writing sound spellings Set 5

h h h h h

h h h h h h h

h						

b b b b b

b b b b b b b

f f f f f

f f f f f f f

l l l l l

l l l l l l l

Many children confuse and reverse the letters b and d. It is important that the child is given the opportunity to practise forming these letters in the same activity so they are able to compare and notice the different kinaesthetic experience of writing each. As discussed in the introductory chapter, the child should be provided with lots of sensory and kinaesthetic experiences of forming these letters in a variety of media as well as writing on paper.

In this activity the child can practise forming these letters by copying over the grey letters which act as a guide. Encourage the child to say the sound at the same time as writing the letter. The child can then practise writing the letter within the boxes underneath which focuses the child on the spatial relationship between the letter as it forms and the surrounding visual environment.

Activity 21 Writing sound spellings — Focus on b & d

b b b

b b b b

d d d

d d d d

Copy the letters into the boxes underneath, saying the sounds at the same time.

b	b	d	d	b

d	b	d	b	b	d	b

b	b	d	b	d	d	b

b	d	d	b	d	b	b

b	b	d	b	d	b	d

Blending is the ability to push sounds together to make a word and is a key skill in reading.Blending is a dynamic activity where the child actively pushes the sounds together and listens to the word forming.

Activity 22 'A place to read' prepares the child for blending sounds themselves as part of the process of learning to read. You will model the dynamic blending technique for the child who will then tell you what word they can hear forming. Refer to the full explanation of the 'A place to read' activity in the 'Working through the programme' section.

Segmenting, the ability to split words up into their component sounds in sequence, is a key skill in spelling. The child needs to isolate each sound and match a sound spelling to successfully spell a word.

Activity 28 'A place to listen' activity prepares the child for segmenting words as part of the process of learning to spell. Refer to the full explanation of the 'A place to listen' activity in the 'Working through the programme' section.

Below is a list of words to use for both activities. Use words from previous sets if required.

Activity 22 A place to read — Set 5
Activity 28 A place to listen

if

bad bag bat bed big bin bit

fan fat fed fog

had hat hen hid him hit hop hot

led leg let lit lot

peg

This set of cards is made up of words containing the target sounds for set 5. Copy onto card and cut out. Practise dynamic blending for reading, as described in the 'Working through the programme' section, using these cards. Notice that the letters get gradually darker as the child works through the word, a visual signal that they are pushing together the sounds and preparing them to listen to the word forming. Model this process for the child if necessary.

Activity 23 Dynamic blending Set 5

if	bag
bit	fan
him	hop
leg	lot

Print out onto card and cut out.
Stack them with the biggest (the complete word) on the bottom and in decreasing size so that the smallest is on the top.
Make sure the left-hand edge of the cards are flush. Staple the cards together on the left-hand side.
When the child runs a finger over the cards the sound spellings flip up. Ask the child to say the sounds and match to the flips.

Flippies

Set 5 - a

b	b a	b a d
h	h a	h a d
b	b e	b e d

Print out onto card and cut out.
Stack them with the biggest (the complete word) on the bottom and in decreasing size so that the smallest is on the top.
Make sure the left-hand edge of the cards are flush. Staple the cards together on the left-hand side.
When the child runs a finger over the cards the sound spellings flip up. Ask the child to say the sounds and match to the flips.

Flippies — Set 5 - b

l	l e	l e t
h	h i	h i d
b	b i	b i g

Print out onto card and cut out.
Stack them with the biggest (the complete word) on the bottom and in decreasing size so that the smallest is on the top.
Make sure the left-hand edge of the cards are flush. Staple the cards together on the left-hand side.
When the child runs a finger over the cards the sound spellings flip up. Ask the child to say the sounds and match to the flips.

Flippies   Set 5 - c

h	h i	h i m
h	h i	h i t
l	l o	l o t

Read the clue on the left for the child.
Use the clue to work out what the answer word is.
Encourage the child to think about the sounds in the word and write a sound spelling for each sound in the boxes on the right, one by one.
The first one is done as an example for you.
Explain that they may not need to use all the boxes and so some are shaded in.
Break this task into a number of shorter tasks over a number of lessons if necessary

Activity 30 Sound boxes Set 5

Clue	Sound boxes		
We had ________ at the party.	f	u	n
Rav plays cricket with a ________ and ball.			
________ I finish my work, I can play.			
Write 10 in a word.			
In summer the ________ shines brightly.			

Support the child to read the words on the left one by one.
For each word support the child to work out what sounds are in the word and count them.
Then support the child to cross out any boxes that are not needed.
In each of the boxes in the middle, have the child write the sound spelling to match each sound.
In the last column the child writes how many sounds there are in the word.
Break this task into a number of shorter tasks over a number of lessons if necessary.

Activity 31 How many sounds? Set 5

Word	Sound spellings					How many sounds?
bad	b	a	d			3
big						
if						
hit						
leg						
up						
him						
fun						
hot						

During this activity the child will get the chance to slide sounds in and out of words, i.e. practise phoneme manipulation. Sounds will be swapped, added or taken away. Print the sound spellings on card and cut out.

Build a starting word from the prompt list, demonstrating dynamic blending as you move the sound spelling cards into place.

Repeat the word, running your finger along the cards so that it corresponds with the sounds within the word.

Ask the child to change the word to the next word on the prompt list. As you say the new word run your finger under the cards so that it corresponds with the sounds within the word and gives the child the chance to hear and see what is different.

The child can then swap the appropriate sound spelling cards.

Activity 33 Sound swap Set 5

Sound swap h b f l

List 1	List 2	List 3
him	bed	fed
hit	bad	led
bit	had	leg
bet	hid	log
let	hip	fog
lot	lip	fig

h	m	t
b	l	d
p	f	g
a	e	i
o	u	

Support the child to read the word in the first column. Then, referring to the second column, ask the child what sound they are going to take away.
Then ask the child to think about what word would be made if the sound in the second column was taken out of the word, in this case from the beginning of it.
Remind the child to think about the sounds, blend dynamically and listen to the word forming.
Have the child write out the new word on the line at the end, sounding out the word as they write each sound spelling.

Break this task into a number of shorter tasks over a number of lessons if necessary.

Activity 34 Read – Delete – Spell Set 5

Read	Read without this sound	Spell the new word
fan	'f'	________________
hat	'h'	________________
ban	'b'	________________
bin	'b'	________________
fat	'f'	________________

Support the child to read the word in the first column. Then, referring to the second column, ask the child to think about what word would be made if the sound in the second column was added in front of the word. Remind the child to think about the sounds, blend dynamically and listen to the word forming.
Have the child write out the new word on the line at the end, sounding out the word as they write each sound spelling.

Break this task into a number of shorter tasks over a number of lessons if necessary.

Activity 35 Read – Add – Spell Set 5

Read	Read with this sound at the beginning	Spell the new word
an	'b'	ban
in	'b'	________
an	'f'	________
at	'h'	________
it	'l'	________

Support the child to read the words on the left, one by one.
For each word read the clue to the child and work out what the answer word is.
Explain to the child that they will need to either: add a sound, take away a sound or change a sound to make the answer word
e.g. sip > slip > lip > lap.
Have the child write out the new word on the line on the right, saying each sound as they write each sound spelling.
An example is done for you.
Break this task into a number of shorter tasks over a number of lessons if necessary.

Activity 36 Sound exchange Set 5

Starting word	Clue	New word
in	Put rubbish in this	*bin*
hit	Which one? Point to ____	____________
log	Misty weather	____________
bug	A cuddle	____________
lit	Allow	____________
at	Play cricket with this	____________
fan	We say 'a' cat ... but ____ elephant	____________
beg	Large	____________

This set of cards is made up of words containing the target sounds for set 5. Copy onto card and cut out. Practise dynamic blending for reading, as described in the 'Working through the programme' section, using these cards. Model this process for the child if necessary.

Activity 37 Reading words with target sounds Set 5

bag	bat
bin	fan
fog	hen
hit	leg
lot	peg

This set of cards is made up of the high frequency words containing the target sounds for set 5. Copy onto card and cut out.
Practise dynamic blending for reading, as described in the 'Working through the programme' section, using these cards. Model this process for the child if necessary.

Activity 38 Reading high frequency words Set 5

if	bad
bed	big
but	fun
had	him
hot	let

Starting at 'him' have the child read each of the words as quickly as possible tracking along the line one by one until they get to 'let'.
Support the child to read the words by giving information about sounds and supporting dynamic blending but do not supply the whole word.
Time how long it takes to read all the words and record the time at the bottom of the page.
Repeat at a later point, e.g. at the end of the lesson or the following day, and see if the child can beat their *own* previous time.

Activity 39 Reading race — Set 5

him big fan if let

1 _____ minutes ____ seconds
2 _____ minutes ____ seconds
3 _____ minutes ____ seconds

Starting at 'bid' have the child read each of the words as quickly as possible tracking along the line one by one until they get to 'bad'.
Support the child to read the words by giving information about sounds and supporting dynamic blending but do not supply the whole word.
Time how long it takes to read all the words and record the time at the bottom of the page.
Repeat at a later point, e.g. at the end of the lesson or the following day, and see if the child can beat their *own* previous time.

Activity 39 Reading race — Focus on b & d

bid dad bed bud did dab bad

1 _____ minutes ____ seconds
2 _____ minutes ____ seconds
3 _____ minutes ____ seconds

Visual discrimination is the ability to see differences between objects that are similar. Good visual discrimination helps keep us from getting confused when looking at shapes and forms in the environment. Children with poor visual discrimination may find it difficult to recognise letters, may confuse letters such as b and d and may find it difficult to identify mathematical symbols.

Ask the child to look at the word in the pink box then track along the row looking at the other words. The child indicates or puts a ring around the word that is the same as the one in the pink box.

Break this task into a number of shorter tasks over a number of lessons if necessary.

Activity 40 Spot the word Set 5

bad	bed	bad	bib
fan	fun	fin	fan
him	him	hit	hip
leg	log	leg	led
big	bin	bun	big

Visual discrimination is the ability to see differences between objects that are similar. Good visual discrimination helps keep us from getting confused when looking at shapes and forms in the environment. Children with poor visual discrimination may find it difficult to recognise letters, may confuse letters such as b and d and may find it difficult to identify mathematical symbols.

Ask the child to look at the word in the pink box then track along the row looking at the other words. The child indicates or puts a ring around the word that is the same as the one in the pink box.

Break this task into a number of shorter tasks over a number of lessons if necessary.

Activity 40 Spot the word — Focus on b & d

dab	bad	bed	dab
bid	bib	bid	did
bud	bud	bad	bed
did	bib	bid	did
bib	did	bib	bid

Visual memory is the ability to remember and identify a shape or picture that we have previously seen. Children with poor visual memory may struggle to remember pictures, figures, shapes, letters and numbers and may have difficulties with reading, writing and number work.

Ask the child to look at the word in the yellow box for at least five seconds, covering the white box underneath. Then cover the yellow box so that the letter cannot be seen and reveal the choice of words in the white box below. Ask the child to select the matching word from the white box.

Break this task into a number of shorter tasks over a number of lessons if necessary.

Activity 41 Remembering words Set 5

fix
fox fix

jug
jug jog

web
wet web

vet
van vet

fox
fix box fox

wet
wet web win

Visual memory is the ability to remember and identify a shape or picture that we have previously seen. Children with poor visual memory may struggle to remember pictures, figures, shapes, letters and numbers and may have difficulties with reading, writing and number work.

Ask the child to look at the word in the yellow box for at least five seconds, covering the white box underneath. Then cover the yellow box so that the letter cannot be seen and reveal the choice of words in the white box below. Ask the child to select the matching word from the white box.

Break this task into a number of shorter tasks over a number of lessons if necessary.

Activity 41 Remembering words — Focus on b & d

bed
bed bad

did
bid did

dad
did dad

bud
bud bad

bib
did bid bib

bob
bob bib did

Form constancy is the ability to generalise forms and figures and identify them even if they are slightly different from that usually seen. This skill helps us distinguish differences in size, shape, and orientation or position. Children with poor form constancy may frequently reverse letters and numbers.

Ask the child to look at the word in the orange box then track along the row looking at the other words. The child indicates or puts a ring around the word that is the same as the one in the orange box.

Break this task into a number of shorter tasks over a number of lessons if necessary.

Activity 42 Which is the word? Set 5

if	in	it	if
bad	bed	bad	bag
hen	hat	had	hen
fan	fan	fat	fed
leg	let	leg	lap

Form constancy is the ability to generalise forms and figures and identify them even if they are slightly different from that usually seen. This skill helps us distinguish differences in size, shape, and orientation or position. Children with poor form constancy may frequently reverse letters and numbers.

Ask the child to look at the word in the orange box then track along the row looking at the other words. The child indicates or puts a ring around the word that is the same as the one in the orange box.

Break this task into a number of shorter tasks over a number of lessons if necessary.

Activity 42 Which is the word? Focus on b & d

bib	bib	did	bid
dab	dad	dab	bad
bad	bed	bid	bad
bid	dib	bid	bib
bud	bud	bad	bed

Visual closure is the ability to identify an object, shape or symbol from a visually incomplete or disorganised presentation and to see where different parts of a whole fit together, i.e. to recognise something when seeing only part of it. This skill helps us understand things quickly because our visual system doesn't have to process every detail to recognise what we're seeing.

Ask the child to look at the large word and then at the choice of smaller words underneath. The child indicates or puts a ring around the word that is the same as the big word.

Break this task into a number of shorter tasks over a number of lessons if necessary.

Activity 43 Word splits Set 5

bed bad

let led

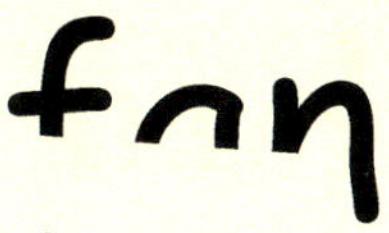

fan fun

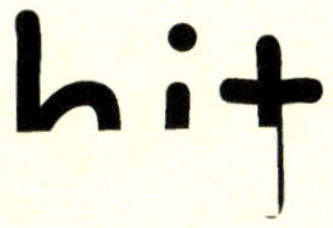

hid hit

Visual closure is the ability to identify an object, shape or symbol from a visually incomplete or disorganised presentation and to see where different parts of a whole fit together, i.e. to recognise something when seeing only part of it. This skill helps us understand things quickly because our visual system doesn't have to process every detail to recognise what we're seeing.

Ask the child to look at the large word and then at the choice of smaller words underneath. The child indicates or puts a ring around the word that is the same as the big word.

Break this task into a number of shorter tasks over a number of lessons if necessary.

Activity 43 Word splits — Focus on b & d

bib
bib did
dad
dad bad
bud
bed bud
did
dad did

Figure ground is the ability to find patterns or shapes when hidden within a busy background without getting confused by surrounding images. This skill keeps children from getting lost in the details, for example when looking at pictures in books or reading. Children with poor figure ground become easily confused with too much print on the page, affecting their concentration and attention.

Ask the child to look at the words, which are overlapping. Ask the child to first find all the words. Some words are written more than once. How many of each word are there?

Break this task into a number of shorter tasks over a number of lessons if necessary.

Activity 44 Busy words Set 5

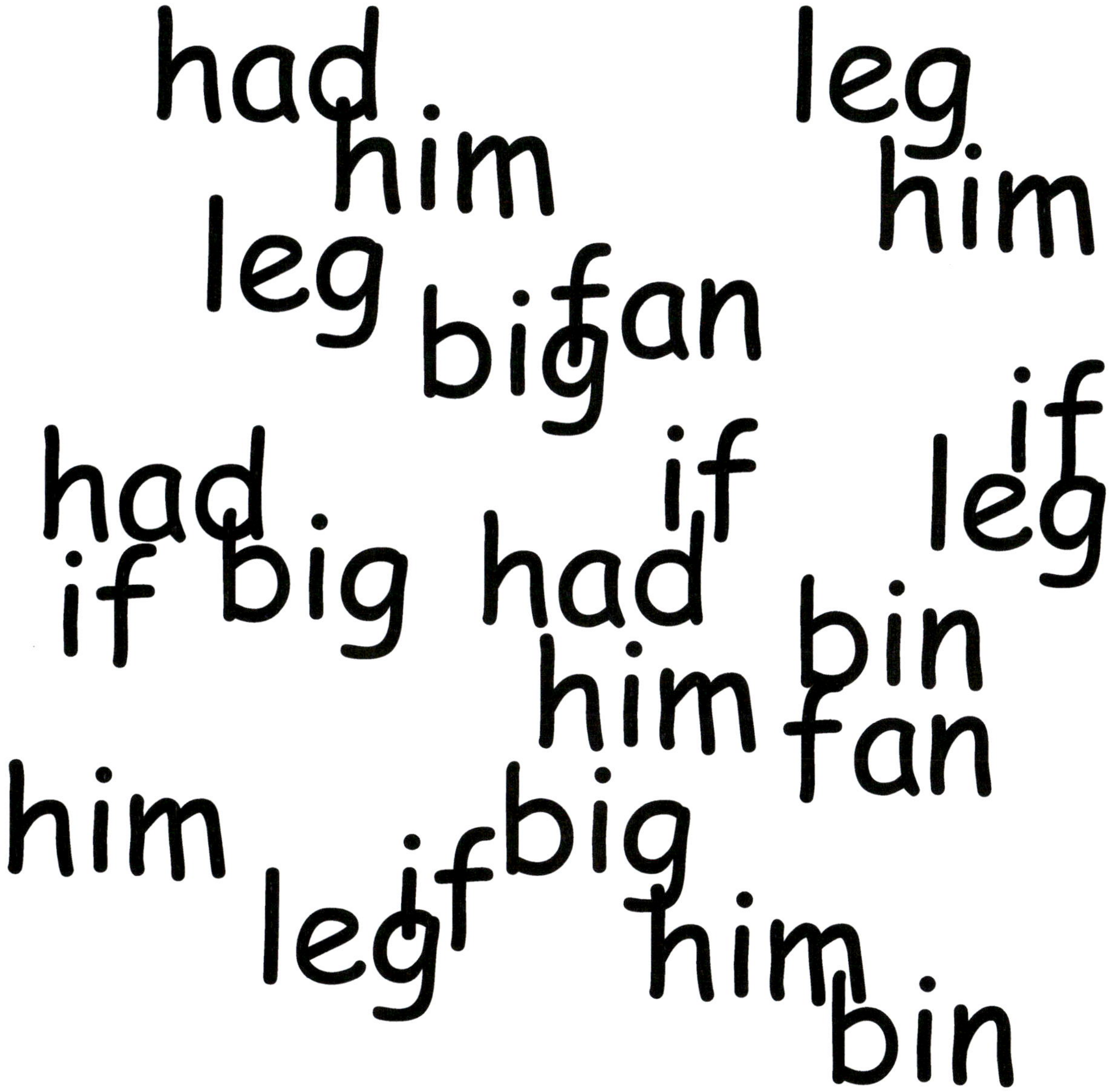

Figure ground is the ability to find patterns or shapes when hidden within a busy background without getting confused by surrounding images. This skill keeps children from getting lost in the details, for example when looking at pictures in books or reading. Children with poor figure ground become easily confused with too much print on the page, affecting their concentration and attention.

Ask the child to look at the words, which are overlapping. Ask the child to first find all the words. Some words are written more than once. How many of each word are there?

Break this task into a number of shorter tasks over a number of lessons if necessary.

Activity 44 Busy words — Focus on b & d

bed dad

dab bad

dad bud

dab dad bad

bud

bid bed

bad bad bid bed

dad

dab

bad

Visual sequential memory is the ability to remember sequences of figures, symbols and shapes. Children with poor visual sequencing struggle to remember a sequence of letters and follow visual patterns. They may have difficulties writing a sequence of letters to form a word and a sequence of words to form a sentence.

Ask the child to look at the words in the yellow box for at least five seconds, covering the white box underneath. Then cover the yellow box so that the words cannot be seen and reveal the sequence of words in the white box below. Ask the child to remember the missing word and write it in the space.

Break this task into a number of shorter tasks over a number of lessons if necessary.

Activity 45 Remembering lots of words Set 5

hid leg
____ leg

bat hot
bat ____

lot fog
____ fog

cab hen
cab ____

him	lad	bun
____	lad	bun

bob	fun	bed
bob	____	bed

Visual sequential memory is the ability to remember sequences of figures, symbols and shapes. Children with poor visual sequencing struggle to remember a sequence of letters and follow visual patterns. They may have difficulties writing a sequence of letters to form a word and a sequence of words to form a sentence.

Ask the child to look at the words in the yellow box for at least five seconds, covering the white box underneath. Then cover the yellow box so that the words cannot be seen and reveal the sequence of words in the white box below. Ask the child to remember the missing word and write it in the space.

Break this task into a number of shorter tasks over a number of lessons if necessary.

Activity 45 Remembering lots of words — Focus on b & d

bad	bid
____	bid

bib	bob
bib	____

bed did
____ did

dad dab
dad ____

bud	bad	bed
____	bad	bed

did	dad	bid
did	____	bid

Tracking is the ability to follow a sequence of letters, figures or symbols. The eyes need to focus on the symbols in order and not look randomly at the symbols on the page. This is an important skill for reading and writing where letters and words are written from left to right and the reader is required to work down a page from the top to the bottom.

Ask the child to look at the symbols and sound spellings and track from left to right. When the child finds a group of sound spellings then they indicate or put a circle around them all. The child then reads the word.

Break this task into a number of shorter tasks over a number of lessons if necessary.

Activity 46 Hidden words Set 5

◁↘⇨↘if→↔▷bad⇦↙▽cab⇨→↘⇦led⇦▷↙
▽↑⇦↘lot⇦▷↓↘⇦⇨hen⇨↓↙⇦fan⇨↓⇨⇨↓

↙→↓⇦bad▷⇦⇨bib←↙▷↔let↗▽⇦↘▽⇨⇨
▷↙↖⇕bob⇦▷⇕▽⇕↔lip▷↖←⇕↗him⇨⇦⇕⇦

θσυμbinδσδχfedπωρλαifφπλωμετρμσδbug
μμδφυτhitωφνεhadεδω

γηκεbatδωκδσbusπωρωαlegφπλωηδνbudλδφ
υτfanωφκρεpegεωφ

Prior to working with the child, read through the instructions in the 'Working through the programme' section.

Activity 47 Word build Set 5

i	f		
b	a	d	
b	i	g	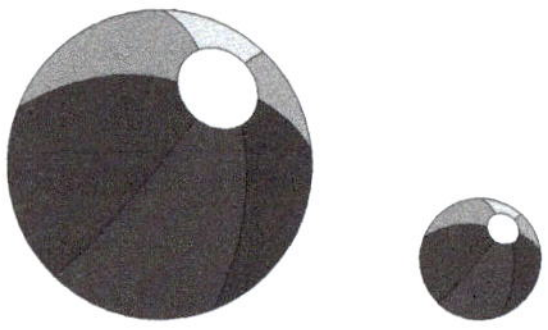
f	a	n	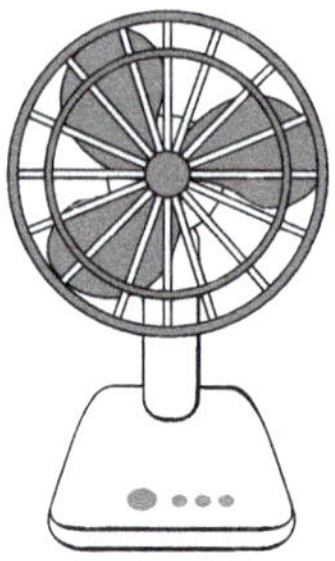

f	o	g	
h	a	t	
l	e	g	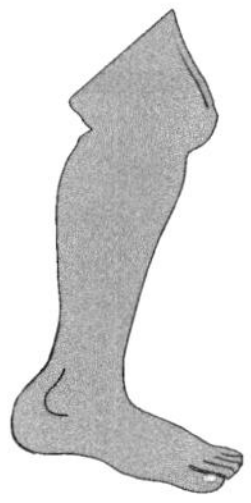

Support the child to look at the picture and work out what the word is.
Then support the child to work out the initial sound in the word and match a sound spelling in the gap provided.
The 'Place to listen' technique should be used to support this.
Read through the 'Place to listen' instructions in the 'Working through the programme' section of this book prior to working with the child.
Ask the child to read the completed word using the dynamic blending technique.

Activity 48 Finish the word 1 — Set 5

____ i m

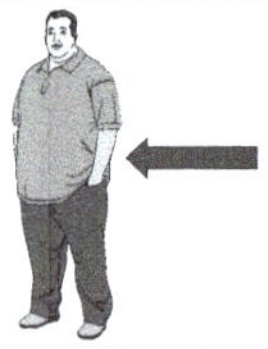

____ i d

____ e g

____ a b

____ u g

____ e n

____ e g

Support the child to look at the picture and work out what the word is.
Then support the child to work out the middle sound in the word and match a sound spelling in the gap provided.
The 'Place to listen' technique should be used to support this.
Read through the 'Place to listen' instructions in the 'Working through the programme' section of this book prior to working with the child.
Ask the child to read the completed word using the dynamic blending technique.

Activity 49 Finish the word 2 Set 5

b ___ g

h ___ t

l ___ d

b ___ t

l ___ g

h ___ t

b ___ d

Support the child to look at the picture and work out what the word is.
Then support the child to work out the final sound in the word and match a sound spelling in the gap provided.
The 'Place to listen' technique should be used to support this.
Read through the 'Place to listen' instructions in the 'Working through the programme' section of this book prior to working with the child.
Ask the child to read the completed word using the dynamic blending technique.

Activity 50 Finish the word 3 Set 5

c a ____

f o ____

h i ____

l i ____

h o ____

b a ____

b i ____

Read the instructions in the introduction of this book to guide you on how to work through this spelling practise sheet with the child.

Activity 52 Spelling challenge — Set 5

if	i f	i f	__ __	________
bad	b a d	b a d	__ __ __	________
bed	b e d	b e d	__ __ __	________
big	b i g	b i g	__ __ __	________
but	b u t	b u t	__ __ __	________
fun	f u n	f u n	__ __ __	________
let	l e t	l e t	__ __ __	________

Support the child to read the sentences. Have the child look at the pictures and find the picture that matches the sentence.
Have the child draw a line from the sentence to the matching picture.
Break this task into a number of shorter tasks over a number of lessons if necessary.

Activity 53 Read the sentence and match to a picture Set 5

Sam got hot in the sun.

Kim can hop on a log.

Ben had a nap in bed.

Pat had a big hug.

Sid fed a pet rat.

Support the child to read the sentence.
For each sentence, support the child to spot the spelling mistake.
Have the child underline or highlight the mistake and then write out the sentence correcting the mistake.
Encourage the child to say the sounds in each word at the same time as writing the sound spellings.
Break this task into a number of shorter tasks over a number of lessons if necessary.

Activity 54 Oops! Correct the spelling — Set 5

1. A bun can hop on a bud.

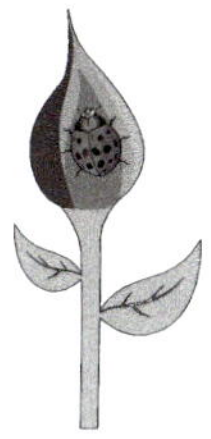

2. A cat can hug a dot.

3. Ben had a bit, fat hen.

4. Kim hid in a bag den.

5. Tom got hot in the bun.

Support the child to read the sentences.
There is a missing word with a choice of two words to fill the gap.
For each sentence support the child to identify the missing word which makes sense in the sentence.
Have the child write the word on the line within the sentence.
Break this task into a number of shorter tasks over a number of lessons if necessary.

Activity 55 Spot the spelling — Set 5

1. Ben hid in a ____________.
   den dad

2. Kim got a ____________ bun.
   big dig

3. Tom fed a fat ____________.
   hat hen

4. Pam got ____________ in the sun.
   hot had

5. Mum put a hat on ____________.
   did dad

6. Tom can ____________ a big cat.
   hug rug

Support the child to read each sentence.
Ask the child to re-read the sentence, several times if necessary, and try to remember it.
Cover the sentence and ask the child to recall it verbally from memory.
Once they can do this, ask the child to write out the sentence from memory.
The child might find it helpful to say the sounds as they write and say individual words once written.
When the sentence is complete, the child reads out their sentence and then compares it to the original.
Alternatively, using the text to speech function on a laptop or similar software, the child could type the sentence with the computer reading back each word and then the completed sentence.

Activity 56 Writing challenge Set 5

Ben had a red leg.

A fat dog sat on a log.

Dan fed ten men.

Mum sat in mud.

Answers Set 5: h b f l

Page 249
Activity 12 Spot the sound spelling

h 5
b 8
f 6
l 8

Page 250
Activity 12 Spot the sound spelling b & d

b 12

d 11

Page 259
Activity 17 Busy sound spellings

h 7
b 6
f 6
l 6

Page 260
Activity 17 Busy sound spellings b & d

b 13

d 12

Page 278
Activity 30 Sound boxes

bat
if
ten
sun

Page 279
Activity 31 How many sounds?

big	3	if	2
hit	3	leg	3
up	2	him	3
fun	3	hot	3

Page 282
Activity 34 Read – Delete – Spell

an
at
an
in
at

Page 283
Activity 35 Read – Add – Spell

ban
bin
fan
hat
lit

Page 284
Activity 36 Sound exchange

it	fog
hug	let
bat	an
big	

Page 308
Activity 48 Finish the word 1

him	lid
peg	cab
bug	hen
leg	

Page 309
Activity 49 Finish the word 2

bag	hit
lad	bat
log	hot
bud	

Page 310
Activity 50 Finish the word 3

cab	fog
hid	lip
hot	bag
bin	

Page 313
Activity 54 Oops! Correct the spelling

bug	dog
big	big
sun	

Page 314
Activity 55 Spot the spelling

den	big
hen	hot
dad	hug

SECTION 6

SET 6 SOUNDS AND SOUND SPELLINGS

j v w x

Auditory discrimination is the ability to hear differences between sounds. Good auditory discrimination helps us to recognise and identify the sounds in words and so interpret them correctly. Children with poor auditory discrimination may confuse sounds and misinterpret things they have heard. Their spelling and writing may reflect their confusion over what sounds they heard in a word. **Auditory attention and tracking** is the ability to actively listen and follow auditory information from beginning to end. Good auditory attention and tracking helps us to follow a conversation, a story read out loud or a set of instructions, being able to focus on key information. Children with poor auditory attention and tracking may find it difficult to follow and respond appropriately to what is being said to them.

This story contains lots of words that start with the sounds 'j', 'v' and 'w' in but you will focus on just one 'target' sound. Read the story out loud. Encourage the child to listen carefully and spot any word that starts with the 'target' sound. When a target word has been read, the child indicates that they have heard and spotted it by tapping the table, putting up a hand or any other agreed signal, but without shouting out. Stop reading and discuss the word, making any error correction necessary. If a word is missed, re-read the sentence. Do not show the story to the children. The target words are highlighted below for you: 'j', 'v' and 'w'. Repeat on another occasion focusing on a different target sound.

Activity 1 Sound target – Story sheet Set 6

Victor was a proud and noble animal. He guarded his house and protected his wonderful family. He was very fierce and brave.

When the jolly postman came in his van to make a delivery he would be very vocal and bark and jump at the letters as they came through the door. "That dog is vicious!" the not-so-jolly postman would shout.

Victor thought he was a wild wolf but really he was just a small Jack Russell dog.

When Victor went to the see the vet it was a different story. Victor whimpered all the way there and would just sit sadly in his carrier. Jenny the vet could do anything she wanted without him even growling.

Even wolves know who is boss - Jenny the Vet!

Please Note: The focus of activity is the *sound* in the word, NOT what *letter* is in the word.

Auditory discrimination is the ability to hear differences between sounds. Good auditory discrimination helps us to recognise and identify the sounds in words and so interpret them correctly. Children with poor auditory discrimination may confuse sounds and misinterpret things they have heard. Their spelling and writing may reflect their confusion over what sounds they heard in a word. **Auditory sequential memory** is the ability to remember and recall a series of things that they have heard. Children with poor auditory sequential memory may find it difficult to remember information given earlier in a conversation or set of instructions and may struggle to recall the sequence of sounds in a word.

The sentences contain lots of words beginning with one of the target sounds 'j', 'v' or 'w'.
Read the sentence to the child several times, invite them to join in as you say it and gradually recall it on their own.
Ask them to say it as quickly as they can and have some fun with it. After some practise, ask the child if they can identify which sound they hear a lot in the tongue twister. Perhaps they can make up their own?
Note that the vocabulary included in these tongue twisters may be unfamiliar to the child, especially the adjectives. If appropriate, talk about unfamiliar words and discuss their meaning.
Break this task into a number of shorter tasks over a number of lessons if necessary.

Activity 2 Sound target – Tongue twister fun Set 6

Jolly jesters juggle jiggling jelly.

Jordan jokes with jumping jaguars.

Vet Vicky views visiting vipers.

William weighs wobbling whales.

Wild wolves wander with woolly weasels.

Auditory attention and tracking is the ability to actively listen and follow auditory information from beginning to end. Good auditory attention and tracking helps us to follow a conversation, a story read out loud or a set of instructions, being able to focus on key information. Children with poor auditory attention and tracking may find it difficult to follow and respond appropriately to what is being said to them. **Auditory sequential memory** is the ability to remember and recall a series of things that they have heard. Children with poor auditory sequential memory may find it difficult to remember information given earlier in a conversation or a set of instructions and may struggle to recall the sequence of sounds in a word.

In this activity the child has to process the auditory information but also respond by working out the pattern and stating the next sound in the sequence. Read out the list of sounds with a clear space between each. Ask the child to listen and work out what sound would come next. Answers are in red.

Break this task into a number of shorter tasks over a number of lessons if necessary.

Activity 7 What comes next? Set 6

1. j v j v j v j v ...... j
2. w x w x w x w x ...... w
3. w v w v w v w v ...... w
4. j x j x j x j x ...... j
5. j j v j j v j j v ...... j
6. x x w x x w x x w x
7. v v w v v w v v w v
8. w w j w w j w w j ...... w
9. v v j j v v j j v v j j v
10. x x w w x x w w x x w w x
11. w w v v w w v v w w v v ...... w
12. j j w w j j w w j j w w ...... j
13. v v x x v v x x v v x x v
14. x x j j x x j j x x j j x
15. j j j w j j j w j j j w ...... j
16. x x x v x x x v x x x v x
17. w w w x w w w x w w w x ...... w
18. v v v j v v v j v v v j v
19. j v x j v x j v x ...... j
20. w x j w x j w x j ...... w
21. x v j x v j x v j x
22. w v j w v j w v j ...... w
23. v v j j x v v j j x v
24. x x w w j x x w w j x

Print out the cards below to use when introducing the sounds and the sound spellings.

Activity 8 Sound spelling cards Set 6

j	v
w	x

There are six different bingo cards and a set of individual sound spelling cards which can be copied and cut out.

Each child is given their own bingo card. Shuffle the sound spelling cards, select and 'call' the sound spellings, one by one, from the top of the pile. There are a number of ways to do this, depending on the focus for the pupils:

- show the selected sound spelling and say the sound – child matches visual figures with auditory reinforcement
- show the selected sound spelling only – child matches visual figures without auditory reinforcement
- say the sound for the selected sound spelling but do not show it to the children – child processes the auditory information and matches to a visual figure.

When a child has a sound spelling on their card they can cover it with a counter or write over the sound spelling on the bingo card, writing in between the lines as a guide, saying the sound as they write. If they have more than one of a sound spelling on the card then they must only cover one and wait for that sound spelling to be called again. The first person to cover all their sound spellings is the winner.

Activity 9 Sound spelling bingo Set 6

j	v
w	x

v	w
w	x

j	j
x	w

v	w
v	j

v	x
j	v

j	w
x	x

j	j	j	j	j
j	v	v	v	v
v	v	w	w	w
w	w	w	x	x
x	x	x	x	

Visual discrimination is the ability to see differences between objects that are similar. Good visual discrimination helps keep us from getting confused when looking at shapes and forms in the environment. Children with poor visual discrimination may find it difficult to recognise letters, may confuse letters such as b and d and may find it difficult to identify mathematical symbols.

Ask the child to look at the sound spelling in the yellow box then track along the row looking at the other sound spellings. The child indicates or puts a ring around the sound spelling that is the same as the one in the yellow box.

Break this task into a number of shorter tasks over a number of lessons if necessary.

Activity 11 Sound spelling tracker Set 6

v	u	v	w	m
j	g	p	y	j
w	m	n	w	u
v	u	n	y	v
x	x	s	z	w
j	y	g	j	p
w	v	w	m	u

Visual discrimination is the ability to see differences between objects that are similar. Good visual discrimination helps keep us from getting confused when looking at shapes and forms in the environment. Children with poor visual discrimination may find it difficult to recognise letters, may confuse letters such as b and d and may find it difficult to identify mathematical symbols.

Focus on one sound spelling e.g. **v** (say the sound 'v' and point to the matching sound spelling rather than using the letter name when talking to the child).
Ask the child to look at all the sound spellings and indicate or put a ring round all the letters matching the target.

Break this task into a number of shorter tasks over a number of lessons if necessary.

Activity 12 Spot the sound spelling Set 6

j v j w v j v

w j x j x

v j v w j

x w x

w w v

v

j v x j v j

Visual memory is the ability to remember and identify a shape or picture that we have previously seen. Children with poor visual memory may struggle to remember pictures, figures, shapes, letters and numbers and may have difficulties with reading, writing and number work.

Ask the child to look at the sound spelling in the yellow box for at least five seconds, covering the white box underneath. Then cover the yellow box so that the sound spelling cannot be seen and reveal the choice of sound spellings in the white box below. Ask the child to select the matching sound spelling from the white box.

Break this task into a number of shorter tasks over a number of lessons if necessary.

Activity 13 Remembering sound spellings Set 6

w
v w

j
j x

x
v x

w
w v

x
v x w

j
j f w

Form constancy is the ability to generalise forms and figures and identify them even if they are slightly different from that usually seen. This skill helps us distinguish differences in size, shape, and orientation or position. Children with poor form constancy may frequently reverse letters and numbers.

Ask the child to look at the letter on the left and match to a letter on the right (written differently), drawing a line to connect each.

Activity 15 Which is the same? Set 6

w	j
v	w
j	x
x	v
v	j
j	v
x	W
w	x

Visual closure is the ability to identify an object, shape or symbol from a visually incomplete or disorganised presentation and to see where the different parts of a whole fit together, i.e. to recognise something when seeing only part of it. This skill helps us understand things quickly because our visual system doesn't have to process every detail to recognise what we're seeing.

Ask the child to look at the sound spelling in the white box then track left to right along the row.
Ask the child to indicate or put a ring around the sound spelling that is the same as the sound spelling in the white box.

Break this task into a number of shorter tasks over a number of lessons if necessary.

Activity 16 Bits missing Set 6

v	w	v	k
x	x	k	y
w	m	v	w
i	y	g	j
v	w	k	v
j	g	j	y
x	k	y	x
w	w	v	k

Figure ground is the ability to find patterns or shapes when hidden within a busy background without getting confused by surrounding images. This skill keeps children from getting lost in the details, for example when looking at pictures in books or reading. Children with poor figure ground become easily confused with too much print on the page, affecting their concentration and attention.

Ask the child to look at the sound spellings, which are overlapping. Ask the child to first find and count all the **w** sound spellings (refer to the sound not the letter name), then the **v** etc. Ask the child to write down how many of each sound spelling they found.

Break this task into a number of shorter tasks over a number of lessons if necessary.

Activity 17 Busy sound spellings Set 6

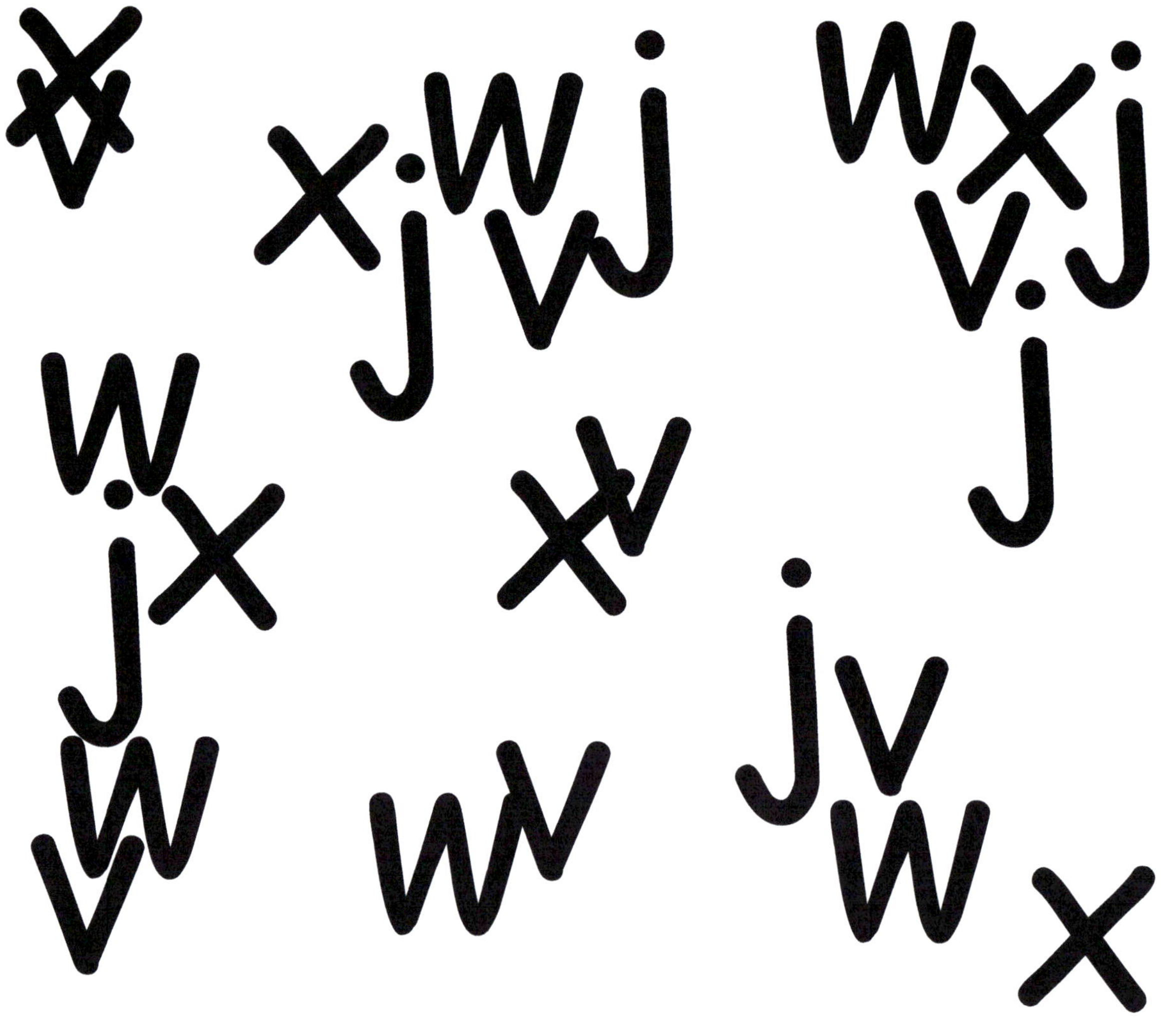

Spatial relations is the ability to perceive the position of objects in relation to ourselves and to each other. This skill helps children to understand relationships between symbols and letters. Children with poor spatial relations may find it difficult to write letters in the correct orientation, write consistently starting at the margin and write letters of the same size.

In the first part, ask the child to copy the sound spellings on the line underneath in exactly the same places as they appear above.
In the second part, ask the child to copy the words on the line underneath in exactly the same places, saying the matching sound as they write each sound spellings.
Break this task into a number of shorter tasks over a number of lessons if necessary.

Activity 18 Where am I? Set 6

x v j w

w x j v

fix van web

jet box

Visual sequential memory is the ability to remember sequences of figures, symbols and shapes. Children with poor visual sequencing struggle to remember a sequence of letters and follow visual patterns. They may have difficulties writing a sequence of letters to form a word and a sequence of words to form a sentence.

Ask the child to look at the sound spellings in the yellow box for at least five seconds, covering the white box underneath. Then cover the yellow box so that the sound spellings cannot be seen and reveal the sequence of sound spellings in the white box below. Ask the child to remember the missing sound spelling and write it in the space.

Break this task into a number of shorter tasks over a number of lessons if necessary.

Activity 19 Remembering lots of sound spellings Set 6

v	w
_	w

j	x
j	_

x v
x _

w j
_ j

x j w
x _ w

v x j
_ x j

Tracking is the ability to follow a sequence of symbols. The eyes need to focus on the symbols in order and not look randomly at the symbols on the page. This is an important skill for reading and writing where letters and words are written from left to right and the reader is required to work down a page from the top to the bottom.

Choose a target sound spelling for the child to find. Ask the child to look at the sound spellings, tracking from left to right and down the page.
When they find the target sound spelling the child indicates or puts a ring around it. Repeat with a different sound spelling.

Break this task into a number of shorter tasks over a number of lessons if necessary.

Activity 20 Tracking sound spellings Set 6

j v w x j v x w x j

w j x v j x w v j v

v w x v j v w x j v x w x

j w j x v j x w v j v v w

x j v w w x v j x w j v j

v j v w x j v x w x j w j x v j x v j

x w j v w x v j v w x v j x w x v j x

w v w x v x j w j x j x w x v j x w j

w x v j v w x v j x w x v j x w v w j

x v x j w j x v w x j v x w x j w j x

v j x v j x w j v v w x j v x w x j v

Having introduced the sounds and their corresponding sound spellings it is important that the child is given the opportunity to practise forming the sound spellings. As discussed in the introductory chapter, the child should be provided with lots of sensory and kinaesthetic experiences of forming the sound spellings in a variety of media as well as writing on conventional paper.

In this activity the child can practise forming the sound spellings by copying over the grey sound spellings which act as a guide. Encourage the child to say the sound at the same time as writing the sound spelling. The child can then practise writing the sound spellings within the boxes underneath which focuses the child on the spatial relationship between the sound spelling as it forms and the surrounding visual environment.

Activity 21 Writing sound spellings Set 6

j j j j j

j j j j j j j

j						

v v v v v

v v v v v v v

W W W W W

w w w w w w w

X X X X X

x x x x x x x

Blending is the ability to push sounds together to make a word and is a key skill in reading. Blending is a dynamic activity where the child actively pushes the sounds together and listens to the word forming.

Activity 22 'A place to read' prepares the child for blending sounds themselves as part of the process of learning to read. You will model the dynamic blending technique for the child who will then tell you what word they can hear forming. Refer to the full explanation of the 'A place to read' activity in the 'Working through the programme' section.

Segmenting, the ability to split words up into their component sounds in sequence, is a key skill in spelling. The child needs to isolate each sound and match a sound spelling to successfully spell a word.

Activity 28 'A place to listen' activity prepares the child for segmenting words as part of the process of learning to spell. Refer to the full explanation of the 'A place to listen' activity in the 'Working through the programme' section.

Below is a list of words to use for both activities. Use words from previous sets if required.

Activity 22 A place to read Set 6
Activity 28 A place to listen

box

fox

jam jet jog

van vet

wax web wet wig win

This set of cards is made up of words containing the target sounds for set 6. Copy onto card and cut out. Practise dynamic blending for reading, as described in the 'Working through the programme' section, using these cards. Notice that the letters get gradually darker as the child works through the word, a visual signal that they are pushing together the sounds and preparing them to listen to the word forming. Model this process for the child if necessary.

Activity 23 Dynamic blending — Set 6

box	fix
jam	jet
van	wag
wet	win

Print out onto card and cut out.
Stack them with the biggest (the complete word) on the bottom and in decreasing size so that the smallest is on the top.
Make sure the left-hand edge of the cards are flush. Staple the cards together on the left-hand side.
When the child runs a finger over the cards the sound spellings flip up. Ask the child to say the sounds and match to the flips.

Flippies — Set 6

w	w e	w e t
f	f o	f o x
w	w i	w i n

Read the clue on the left for the child.
Use the clue to work out what the answer word is.
Encourage the child to think about the sounds in the word and write a sound spelling for each sound in the boxes on the right, one by one.
The first one is done as an example for you.
Explain that they may not need to use all the boxes and so some are shaded in.
Break this task into a number of shorter tasks over a number of lessons if necessary.

Activity 30 Sound boxes Set 6

Clue	Sound boxes		
A __________ has a bushy tail.	f	o	x
A dog can __________ its tail.			
We will __________ the prize.			
A __________ helps sick animals.			
I like strawberry __________ on my toast.			

Support the child to read the words on the left one by one.
For each word support the child to work out what sounds are in the word and count them.
Then support the child to cross out any boxes that are not needed.
In each of the boxes in the middle, have the child write the sound spelling to match each sound.
In the last column the child writes how many sounds there are in the word.
Break this task into a number of shorter tasks over a number of lessons if necessary.

Activity 31 How many sounds? Set 6

Word	Sound spellings					How many sounds?
vet	v	e	t			3
box						
van						
web						
if						
up						
wag						
fox						
wet						

During this activity the child will get the chance to slide sounds in and out of words, i.e. practise phoneme manipulation. Sounds will be swapped, added or taken away. Print the sound spellings on card and cut out.

Build a starting word from the prompt list, demonstrating dynamic blending as you move the sound spelling cards into place.

Repeat the word, running your finger along the cards so that it corresponds with the sounds within the word.

Ask the child to change the word to the next word on the prompt list. As you say the new word run your finger under the cards so that it corresponds with the sounds within the word and gives the child the chance to hear and see what is different.

The child can then swap the appropriate sound spelling cards.

Activity 33 Sound swap Set 6

Sound swap j v w x

List 1	List 2	List 3
jet	web	jug
vet	wet	jog
met	bet	fog
men	bit	fox
man	bin	box
van	win	

e	a	i
o	u	t
v	m	n
w	b	j
g	x	f

Support the child to read the words on the left, one by one.
For each word read the clue to the child and work out what the answer word is.
Explain to the child that they will need to either: add a sound, take away a sound or change a sound to make the answer word
e.g. sip > slip > lip > lap.
Have the child write out the new word on the line on the right, saying each sound as they write each sound spelling.
An example is done for you.

Break this task into a number of shorter tasks over a number of lessons if necessary.

Activity 36 Sound exchange Set 6

Starting word	Clue	New word
in	Be the best	win
fox	Like a cow or bull	
jet	Animal doctor	
yet	Covered in water	
am	Nice on toast	
zap	Closes my coat	
jig	Wear like hair	
bag	Dogs' tails do this	

This set of cards is made up of words containing the target sounds for set 6. Copy onto card and cut out. Practise dynamic blending for reading, as described in the 'Working through the programme' section, using these cards. Model this process for the child if necessary.

Activity 37 Reading words with target sounds Set 6

box	fix
fox	jam
jug	van
vet	web
wet	win

This set of cards is made up of the high frequency words containing the target sounds for set 6. Copy onto card and cut out.

Practise dynamic blending for reading, as described in the 'Working through the programme' section, using this card. Model this process for the child if necessary.

Activity 38 Reading high frequency words Set 6

fox	

Starting at 'jam' have the child read each of the words as quickly as possible tracking along the line one by one until they get to 'van'.
Support the child to read the words by giving information about sounds and supporting dynamic blending but do not supply the whole word.
Time how long it takes to read all the words and record the time at the bottom of the page.
Repeat at a later point, e.g. at the end of the lesson or the following day, and see if the child can beat their *own* previous time.

Activity 39 Reading race — Set 6

jam wet win fox van

1 _____ minutes ____ seconds
2 _____ minutes ____ seconds
3 _____ minutes ____ seconds

Visual discrimination is the ability to see differences between objects that are similar. Good visual discrimination helps keep us from getting confused when looking at shapes and forms in the environment. Children with poor visual discrimination may find it difficult to recognise letters, may confuse letters such as b and d and may find it difficult to identify mathematical symbols.

Ask the child to look at the word in the pink box then track along the row looking at the other words. The child indicates or puts a ring around the word that is the same as the one in the pink box.

Break this task into a number of shorter tasks over a number of lessons if necessary.

Activity 40 Spot the word Set 6

fix	fox	box	fix
jog	jug	jog	jig
web	web	wet	met
van	win	van	man
jam	him	jet	jam

Visual memory is the ability to remember and identify a shape or picture that we have previously seen. Children with poor visual memory may struggle to remember pictures, figures, shapes, letters and numbers and may have difficulties with reading, writing and number work.

Ask the child to look at the word in the yellow box for at least five seconds, covering the white box underneath. Then cover the yellow box so that the letter cannot be seen and reveal the choice of words in the white box below. Ask the child to select the matching word from the white box.

Break this task into a number of shorter tasks over a number of lessons if necessary.

Activity 41 Remembering words Set 6

fix
fox fix

jug
jug jog

web
wet web

vet
van vet

fox
fix box fox

wet
wet web win

Form constancy is the ability to generalise forms and figures and identify them even if they are slightly different from that usually seen. This skill helps us distinguish differences in size, shape, and orientation or position. Children with poor form constancy may frequently reverse letters and numbers.

Ask the child to look at the word in the orange box then track along the row looking at the other words. The child indicates or puts a ring around the word that is the same as the one in the orange box.

Break this task into a number of shorter tasks over a number of lessons if necessary.

Activity 42 Which is the word? Set 6

box	fox	box	fix
fix	fix	fox	box
jam	jog	jet	jam
van	vet	van	wet
web	wet	web	wag

Visual closure is the ability to identify an object, shape or symbol from a visually incomplete or disorganised presentation and to see where different parts of a whole fit together, i.e. to recognise something when seeing only part of it. This skill helps us understand things quickly because our visual system doesn't have to process every detail to recognise what we're seeing.

Ask the child to look at the large word and then at the choice of smaller words underneath. The child indicates or puts a ring around the word that is the same as the big word.

Break this task into a number of shorter tasks over a number of lessons if necessary.

Activity 43 Word splits Set 6

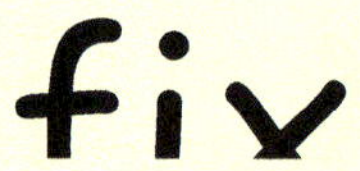

fox fix

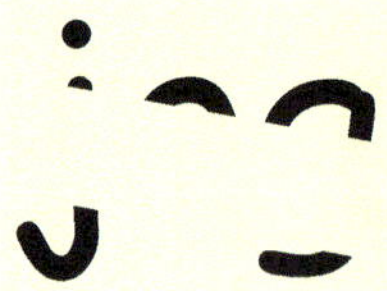

jog jug

wet vet

wet web

Figure ground is the ability to find patterns or shapes when hidden within a busy background without getting confused by surrounding images. This skill keeps children from getting lost in the details, for example when looking at pictures in books or reading. Children with poor figure ground become easily confused with too much print on the page, affecting their concentration and attention.

Ask the child to look at the words, which are overlapping. Ask the child to first find all the words. Some words are written more than once. How many of each word are there?

Break this task into a number of shorter tasks over a number of lessons if necessary.

Activity 44 Busy words Set 6

box fox fix

wet jam

van fix fox

win van

wet wet

fix fox

win

wet jam win

win wet wet

jam

van

box

Visual sequential memory is the ability to remember sequences of figures, symbols and shapes. Children with poor visual sequencing struggle to remember a sequence of letters and follow visual patterns. They may have difficulties writing a sequence of letters to form a word and a sequence of words to form a sentence.

Ask the child to look at the words in the yellow box for at least five seconds, covering the white box underneath. Then cover the yellow box so that the words cannot be seen and reveal the sequence of words in the white box below. Ask the child to remember the missing word and write it in the space.

Break this task into a number of shorter tasks over a number of lessons if necessary.

Activity 45 Remembering lots of words Set 6

web	van
____	van

win	box
win	____

fox vet
___ vet

wet fix
wet ___

jug box jet
___ box jet

wag jog jam
wag ___ jam

Tracking is the ability to follow a sequence of letters, figures or symbols. The eyes need to focus on the symbols in order and not look randomly at the symbols on the page. This is an important skill for reading and writing where letters and words are written from left to right and the reader is required to work down a page from the top to the bottom.

Ask the child to look at the symbols and sound spellings and track from left to right. When the child finds a group of sound spellings then they indicate or put a circle around them all. The child then reads the word.

Break this task into a number of shorter tasks over a number of lessons if necessary.

Activity 46 Hidden words — Set 6

◁↘⇨↘fox→↔▷jam⇦↙▽jug⇨→↘⇦wag⇦
▷↙▽↘wet⇦▷↘⇦⇨fix⇨↓↙⇦jet⇨↓⇨⇨↓

⇦↖↗↓⇦van▷⇦⇨wax←↙▷↔wig↗▽⇦↘▽⇨
⇨▷↕box⇦▷↕→▽↕↔jog▷→↖←↕↗vet⇨⇦↕

θσμwebδσχwinπωρλαboxφπλωμεβδja
mμβδφυτvetωφvεwinεδωβρ

γηκρεvanδωκδσjogπωρωαfixφπλωφwetλδ
φυτjetωφκρεwagερωφψ

Prior to working with the child, read through the instructions in the 'Working through the programme' section.

Activity 47 Word build Set 6

b	o	x	
f	o	x	
j	a	m	
j	e	t	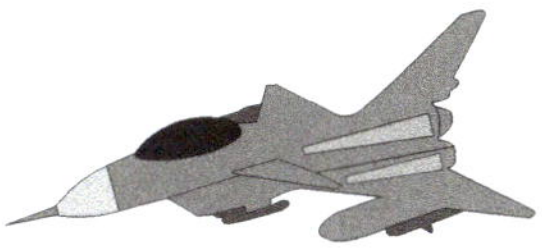

v	a	n	
v	e	t	
w	e	b	

Support the child to look at the picture and work out what the word is.
Then support the child to work out the initial sound in the word and match a sound spelling in the gap provided.
The 'Place to listen' technique should be used to support this.
Read through the 'Place to listen' instructions in the 'Working through the programme' section of this book prior to working with the child.
Ask the child to read the completed word using the dynamic blending technique.

Activity 48 Finish the word 1 Set 6

____ o x

____ a m

____ o x

____ e t

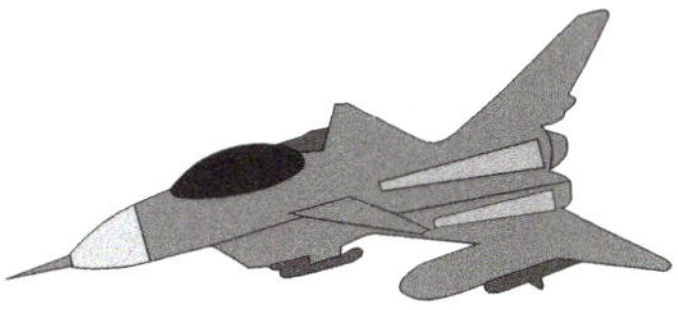

____ a n

____ e t

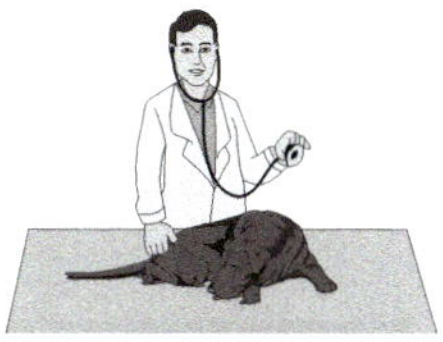

____ i n

Support the child to look at the picture and work out what the word is.
Then support the child to work out the middle sound in the word and match a sound spelling in the gap provided.
The 'Place to listen' technique should be used to support this.
Read through the 'Place to listen' instructions in the 'Working through the programme' section of this book prior to working with the child.
Ask the child to read the completed word using the dynamic blending technique.

Activity 49 Finish the word 2 Set 6

j ____ g

v ____ n

j ____ g

w ____ b

w ____ n

f ____ x

j ____ m

Support the child to look at the picture and work out what the word is.
Then support the child to work out the final sound in the word and match a sound spelling in the gap provided.
The 'Place to listen' technique should be used to support this.
Read through the 'Place to listen' instructions in the 'Working through the programme' section of this book prior to working with the child.
Ask the child to read the completed word using the dynamic blending technique.

Activity 50 Finish the word 3 — Set 6

j e ____

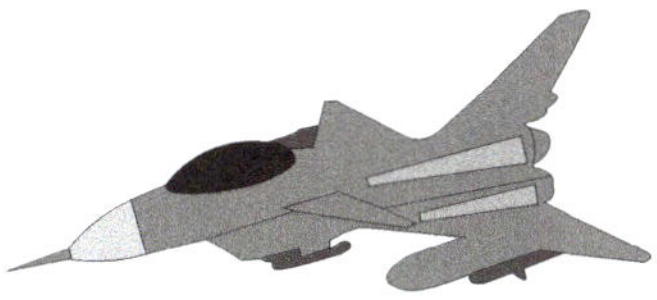

b o ____

v e ____

w e ____

f i ____

j o ____

w i ____

Read the instructions in the introduction of this book to guide you on how to work through this spelling practise sheet with the child.

Activity 52 Spelling challenge — Set 6

box	b o x	b o x	___ ___ ___	____________
fox	f o x	f o x	___ ___ ___	____________
had	h a d	h a d	___ ___ ___	____________
hot	h o t	h o t	___ ___ ___	____________
wet	w e t	w e t	___ ___ ___	____________
win	w i n	w i n	___ ___ ___	____________

Support the child to read the sentences. Have the child look at the pictures and find the picture that matches the sentence.
Have the child draw a line from the sentence to the matching picture.
Break this task into a number of shorter tasks over a number of lessons if necessary.

Activity 53 Read the sentence and match to a picture — Set 6

Jim bit a big bun.

Jon can win a big cup.

Max had a bug in a net.

Jan put on the fun wig.

Sam had red jam in a pot.

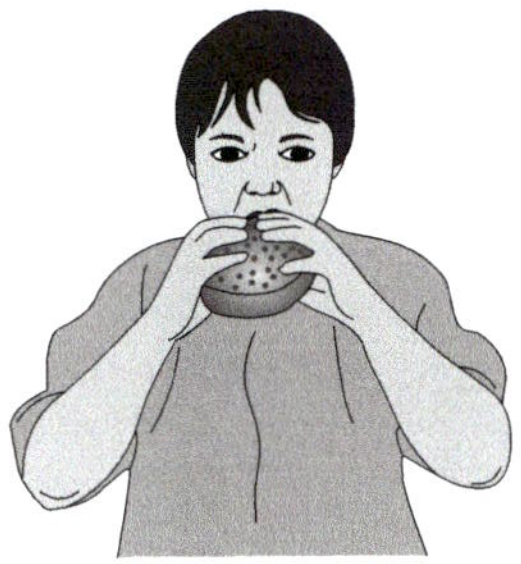

Support the child to read the sentence.
For each sentence, support the child to spot the spelling mistake.
Have the child underline or highlight the mistake and then write out the sentence correcting the mistake.
Encourage the child to say the sounds in each word at the same time as writing the sound spellings.
Break this task into a number of shorter tasks over a number of lessons if necessary.

Activity 54 Oops! Correct the spelling — Set 6

1. Jan put a hen in a fox.

____

2. A vet can hum a cat.

____

3. Jim fed a sat fox.

____

4. Tom had a red jam pit.

____

5. Kim hat a big bun.

____

Support the child to read the sentences.
There is a missing word with a choice of two words to fill the gap.
For each sentence support the child to identify the missing word which makes sense in the sentence.
Have the child write the word on the line within the sentence.
Break this task into a number of shorter tasks over a number of lessons if necessary.

Activity 55 Spot the spelling — Set 6

1. A ____________ can hug a cat.
   jet vet

2. Jim had red ____________.
   jam jog

3. Jan can ____________ the cup.
   win bin

4. The fox got ___________.
   wet pet

5. Tom put a rat in a ____________.
   box fox

6. Dad did not ____________ the big rat.
   hug mug

Support the child to read each sentence.
Ask the child to re-read the sentence, several times if necessary, and try to remember it.
Cover the sentence and ask the child to recall it verbally from memory.
Once they can do this, ask the child to write out the sentence from memory.
The child might find it helpful to say the sounds as they write and say individual words once written.
When the sentence is complete, the child reads out their sentence and then compares it to the original.
Alternatively, using the text to speech function on a laptop or similar software, the child could type the sentence with the computer reading back each word and then the completed sentence.

Activity 56 Writing challenge Set 6

Fit a wig on him.

A pet hen got wet.

Red fox hid in a van.

Ted had a big jog.

Answers Set 6: j v w x

Page 327
Activity 12 Spot the sound spelling

j 9
v 9
w 6
x 5

Page 332
Activity 17 Busy sound spellings

j 6
v 7
w 6
x 6

Page 342
Activity 30 Sound boxes

wag
win
vet
jam

Page 343
Activity 31 How many sounds?

box	3	van	3
web	3	if	2
up	2	wag	3
fox	3	wet	3

Page 346
Activity 36 Sound exchange

ox	vet
wet	jam
zip	wig
wag	

Page 355
Activity 44 Busy words

jam 3
wet 6
box 2

fix 3	fox 3
win 4	van 3

Page 361
Activity 48 Finish the word 1

box	jam
fox	jet
van	vet
win	

Page 362
Activity 49 Finish the word 2

jog	van
jug	web
win	fox
jam	

Page 363
Activity 50 Finish the word 3

jet	box
vet	web
fix	jog
win	

Page 366
Activity 54 Oops! Correct the spelling

box
hug
sad
pot
had

Page 367
Activity 55 Spot the spelling

vet
jam
win
wet
box
hug

SECTION 7

SET 7 SOUNDS AND SOUND SPELLINGS

y z

Auditory discrimination is the ability to hear differences between sounds. Good auditory discrimination helps us to recognise and identify the sounds in words and so interpret them correctly. Children with poor auditory discrimination may confuse sounds and misinterpret things they have heard. Their spelling and writing may reflect their confusion over what sounds they heard in a word. **Auditory attention and tracking** is the ability to actively listen and follow auditory information from beginning to end. Good auditory attention and tracking helps us to follow a conversation, a story read out loud or a set of instructions, being able to focus on key information. Children with poor auditory attention and tracking may find it difficult to follow and respond appropriately to what is being said to them.

This story contains lots of words that start with the sounds 'y' and 'z', but you will focus on just one 'target' sound.
Read the story out loud. Encourage the child to listen carefully and spot any word that starts with the 'target' sound.
When a target word has been read, the child indicates that they have heard and spotted it by tapping the table, putting up a hand or any other agreed signal, but without shouting out. Stop reading and discuss the word, making any error correction necessary. If a word is missed, re-read the sentence. Do not show the story to the children. The target words are highlighted below for you: 'y' and 'z'. Repeat on another occasion focusing on a different target sound.

Activity 1 Sound target – Story sheet Set 7

Yesterday Yasin went to the zoo. He saw lots of interesting things:

- young lions,
- kicking zebras,
- yawning tigers,
- zooming cheetahs,
- woolly yaks,
- zigzag crabs,
- yellow parrots,

- cool zebrafish,
- yacking monkeys and
- zany penguins.

Yesterday was a busy day for Yasin and a busy day for the zookeepers.

Please Note: The focus of activity is the *sound* in the word, NOT what *letter* is in the word.

Auditory discrimination is the ability to hear differences between sounds. Good auditory discrimination helps us to recognise and identify the sounds in words and so interpret them correctly. Children with poor auditory discrimination may confuse sounds and misinterpret things they have heard. Their spelling and writing may reflect their confusion over what sounds they heard in a word. **Auditory sequential memory** is the ability to remember and recall a series of things that they have heard. Children with poor auditory sequential memory may find it difficult to remember information given earlier in a conversation or set of instructions and may struggle to recall the sequence of sounds in a word.

The sentences contain lots of words beginning with one of the target sounds 'y' or 'z'.
Read the sentence to the child several times, invite them to join in as you say it and gradually recall it on their own.
Ask them to say it as quickly as they can and have some fun with it. After some practise, ask the child if they can identify which sound they hear a lot in the tongue twister. Perhaps they can make up their own?
Note that the vocabulary included in these tongue twisters may be unfamiliar to the child, especially the adjectives. If appropriate, talk about unfamiliar words and discuss their meaning.
Break this task into a number of shorter tasks over a number of lessons if necessary.

Activity 2 Sound target – Tongue twister fun Set 7

Yes, yellow yams are yuck!

You yodel at yogurts.

Zigzag zebras zoom in zoos.

Auditory discrimination is the ability to hear differences between sounds. Good auditory discrimination helps us to recognise and identify the sounds in words and so interpret them correctly. Children with poor auditory discrimination may confuse sounds and misinterpret things they have heard. Their spelling and writing may reflect their confusion over what sounds they heard in a word. **Auditory attention and tracking** is the ability to actively listen and follow auditory information from beginning to end. Good auditory attention and tracking helps us to follow a conversation, a story read out loud or a set of instructions, being able to focus on key information. Children with poor auditory attention and tracking may find it difficult to follow and respond appropriately to what is being said to them.

This activity focuses the child on listening to short lists of words starting with the sounds 'j', 'v', 'w' and 'x' of set 6 and 'y' and 'z' from set 7. The words get increasingly complex as does the number of words the child has to listen to. Later items include words starting with sounds from previous sets.

Read out the words and ask the child to identify the odd one out, the word that *does not* start with the same sound as the others. Do not show the words to the child. The odd one out is highlighted for you.
Break this task into a number of shorter tasks over a number of lessons if necessary.

Activity 3 Odd one out — Set 6 & 7

1.	jam	jet	**win**
2.	web	**jog**	wet
3.	**jug**	van	vet
4.	fox	fix	**box**
5.	yes	yet	**zap**
6.	zip	**yap**	zig
7.	just	**went**	jump
8.	west	**next**	wink

Auditory discrimination is the ability to hear differences between sounds. Good auditory discrimination helps us to recognise and identify the sounds in words and so interpret them correctly. Children with poor auditory discrimination may confuse sounds and misinterpret things they have heard. Their spelling and writing may reflect their confusion over what sounds they heard in a word. **Auditory recall memory** is the ability to remember and recall something that they have just heard. Children with poor auditory recall memory may find it difficult to remember sounds and words and respond appropriately.

Read the list of words below clearly, asking the child to listen carefully. All the words start with a 'j', 'v', or 'w' from set 6 and 'y' and 'z' from set 7. At random points, tap the table and stop reading, asking the child to remember and say the last word you said. Then ask them to tell you what the first sound in the word is.

Break this task into a number of shorter tasks over a number of lessons if necessary.

Activity 4 What sound am I? Set 6 & 7

1.	jet	yes	web	jog	wax	yet
2.	zip	wet	zig	zag	win	yam
3.	jam	vet	van	yap	zap	jug
4.	jump	west	went	just	zinc	
5.	woke	zone	joke	vote	vole	
6.	whale	jail	vain	wait	jade	
7.	word	verb	work	world	jerk	
8.	wheel	jeans	weed	jeep	wheat	
9.	why	jive	vibe	wise	wipe	
10.	war	jaw	worn	ward	yawn	

Auditory discrimination is the ability to hear differences between sounds. Good auditory discrimination helps us to recognise and identify the sounds in words and so interpret them correctly. Children with poor auditory discrimination may confuse sounds and misinterpret things they have heard. Their spelling and writing may reflect their confusion over what sounds they heard in a word.

Read out the pairs of words. Ask the child to tell you whether or not they start with the same sound. The words get increasingly complex. Word pairs that start with the same sound are highlighted.

Break this task into a number of shorter tasks over a number of lessons if necessary.

Activity 5 Same or different? Set 6 & 7

1. jam - jet
2. van - web
3. wet - win
4. vet - jog
5. zip - yap
6. yes - yet
7. west - went
8. just - vest
9. jump - wink
10. jail - vain
11. wait - wake
12. joke - vote
13. weep - weak
14. yawn - worn
15. word - world
16. join - joy

Auditory fusion is the ability to hear the subtle gaps between sounds and words. Children with poor auditory fusion may get lost in conversations and when following a list of instructions given verbally.

Say the sounds or read the words in the list one after another at a brisk pace so that there are no obvious gaps between the sounds or words. Ask the child to listen carefully and then tell you how many sounds or words you have said. All the words start with the sound 'j', 'v', 'w' or 'x' from set 6 or 'y' or 'z' from set 7 and get increasingly complex.

Break this task into a number of shorter tasks over a number of lessons if necessary.

Activity 6 How many did you hear? Set 6 & 7

1. j - v - j - w
2. w - x - w - v j - v
3. y - z - z - y
4. w - y - z - j
5. w - v - j - y - z - w
6. z - j - v - j - w
7. z - j - z - v - w - v - j
8. v - w - j - v
9. jam - vet - win
10. van - wet - jog - jet
11. wag - web - jet
12. zip - yes - wig - yet
13. zig - yam - jam - yap
14. wax - wet - jam
15. went - just - wink
16. vest - wind - jest
17. woke - vote - zone - joke
18. weed - week - jeans
19. wade - vein
20. yawn - worn - ward - jaws
21. join - joy
22. zoom - june - youth

Auditory attention and tracking is the ability to actively listen and follow auditory information from beginning to end. Good auditory attention and tracking helps us to follow a conversation, a story read out loud or a set of instructions, being able to focus on key information. Children with poor auditory attention and tracking may find it difficult to follow and respond appropriately to what is being said to them. **Auditory sequential memory** is the ability to remember and recall a series of things that they have heard. Children with poor auditory sequential memory may find it difficult to remember information given earlier in a conversation or a set of instructions and may struggle to recall the sequence of sounds in a word.

In this activity the child has to process the auditory information but also respond by working out the pattern and stating the next sound in the sequence. Read out the list of sounds with a clear space between each. Ask the child to listen and work out what sound would come next. Answers are in red. This activity focuses on the sounds 'y' and 'z' from set 7 and sounds previously encountered in other sets.

Break this task into a number of shorter tasks over a number of lessons if necessary.

Activity 7 What comes next? Set 7

1. y z y z y z y z ...... y
2. y x y x y x y x ...... y
3. z m z m z m z m ...... z
4. y y z y y z y y z ...... y
5. z z y z z y z z y ...... z
6. p z z p z z p z z ...... p
7. f y y f y y f y y ...... f
8. t z z t z z t z z ...... t
9. y y z z y y z z y y z z ...... y
10. z z s s z z s s z z s s...... z
11. y y t t y y t t y y t t ...... y
12. y z t t y z t t y z t t ...... y
13. z y s s z y s s z y s s ...... z
14. z z z y z z z y z z z y ...... z
15. y y y t y y y t y y y t ...... y
16. z y t z y t z y t ...... z
17. y t z y t z y t z ...... y
18. s s s y s s s y s s s y ...... s
19. p p p z p p p z p p p z ...... p
20. z y t p z y t p z y t p ...... z
21. y p z t y p z t y p z t ...... y
22. y y p z y y p z y y p z ...... y
23. z z t y z z t y z z t y ...... z
24. y z t t y z t t y z t t ...... y

Print out the cards below to use when introducing the sounds and the sound spellings.

Activity 8 Sound spelling cards Set 7

y	z

There are six different bingo cards and a set of individual sound spelling cards which can be copied and cut out.

Each child is given their own bingo card. Shuffle the sound spelling cards, select and 'call' the sound spellings, one by one, from the top of the pile. There are a number of ways to do this, depending on the focus for the pupils:

- show the selected sound spelling and say the sound – child matches visual figures with auditory reinforcement
- show the selected sound spelling only – child matches visual figures without auditory reinforcement
- say the sound for the selected sound spelling but do not show it to the children – child processes the auditory information and matches to a visual figure.

When a child has a sound spelling on their card they can cover it with a counter or write over the sound spelling on the bingo card, writing in between the lines as a guide, saying the sound as they write. If they have more than one of a sound spelling on the card then they must only cover one and wait for that sound spelling to be called again. The first person to cover all their sound spellings is the winner.

Activity 9 Sound spelling bingo Set 7

z	w
x	y

z	w
y	x

x	y
z	w

z	y
w	y

x	z
x	y

w	y
z	z

y	y	y	y	y
y	y	z	z	z
z	z	z	z	w
w	w	w	w	x
x	x	x	x	

Visual discrimination is the ability to see differences between objects that are similar. Good visual discrimination helps keep us from getting confused when looking at shapes and forms in the environment. Children with poor visual discrimination may find it difficult to recognise letters, may confuse letters such as b and d and may find it difficult to identify mathematical symbols.

Ask the child to look at the sound spelling in the yellow box then track along the row looking at the other sound spellings. The child indicates or puts a ring around the sound spelling that is the same as the one in the yellow box.

Break this task into a number of shorter tasks over a number of lessons if necessary.

Activity 11 Sound spelling tracker Set 7

y	y	v	g	j
z	s	x	z	e
y	g	y	j	v
b	d	p	g	b
d	b	d	g	p
z	s	z	e	c
b	d	g	b	p

Visual discrimination is the ability to see differences between objects that are similar. Good visual discrimination helps keep us from getting confused when looking at shapes and forms in the environment. Children with poor visual discrimination may find it difficult to recognise letters, may confuse letters such as b and d and may find it difficult to identify mathematical symbols.

Focus on one sound spelling e.g. **y** (say the sound 'y' and point to the matching sound spelling rather than using the letter name when talking to the child).
Ask the child to look at all the sound spellings and indicate or put a ring round all the letters matching the target.

Break this task into a number of shorter tasks over a number of lessons if necessary.

Activity 12 Spot the sound spelling — Set 7

y y z y z

z z z y z y

z z y y z

y z y z z z y y

Visual memory is the ability to remember and identify a shape or picture that we have previously seen. Children with poor visual memory may struggle to remember pictures, figures, shapes, letters and numbers and may have difficulties with reading, writing and number work.

Ask the child to look at the sound spelling in the yellow box for at least five seconds, covering the white box underneath. Then cover the yellow box so that the sound spelling cannot be seen and reveal the choice of sound spellings in the white box below. Ask the child to select the matching sound spelling from the white box.

Break this task into a number of shorter tasks over a number of lessons if necessary.

Activity 13 Remembering sound spellings Set 7

y
y z

z
z y

z		
y	z	

y		
z	y	

y		
z	x	y

z		
y	s	z

Form constancy is the ability to generalise forms and figures and identify them even if they are slightly different from that usually seen. This skill helps us distinguish differences in size, shape, and orientation or position. Children with poor form constancy may frequently reverse letters and numbers.

Ask the child to look at the letter on the left and match to a letter on the right (written differently), drawing a line to connect each.

Activity 15 Which is the same? Set 7

y	z
z	y
b	d
d	b
z	y
y	z
p	g
p	g

Visual closure is the ability to identify an object, shape or symbol from a visually incomplete or disorganised presentation and to see where the different parts of a whole fit together, i.e. to recognise something when seeing only part of it. This skill helps us understand things quickly because our visual system doesn't have to process every detail to recognise what we're seeing.

Ask the child to look at the sound spelling in the white box then track left to right along the row.
Ask the child to indicate or put a ring around the sound spelling that is the same as the sound spelling in the white box.

Break this task into a number of shorter tasks over a number of lessons if necessary.

Activity 16 Bits missing Set 7

y	x	v	y
z	z	x	s
y	v	y	x
b	d	p	b
d	b	p	d
z	s	z	x
b	b	p	d
d	b	d	p

Figure ground is the ability to find patterns or shapes when hidden within a busy background without getting confused by surrounding images. This skill keeps children from getting lost in the details, for example when looking at pictures in books or reading. Children with poor figure ground become easily confused with too much print on the page, affecting their concentration and attention.

Ask the child to look at the sound spellings, which are overlapping. Ask the child to first find and count all the **y** sound spellings (refer to the sound not the letter name), then the **z** etc. Ask the child to write down how many of each sound spelling they found.

Break this task into a number of shorter tasks over a number of lessons if necessary.

Activity 17 Busy sound spellings Set 7

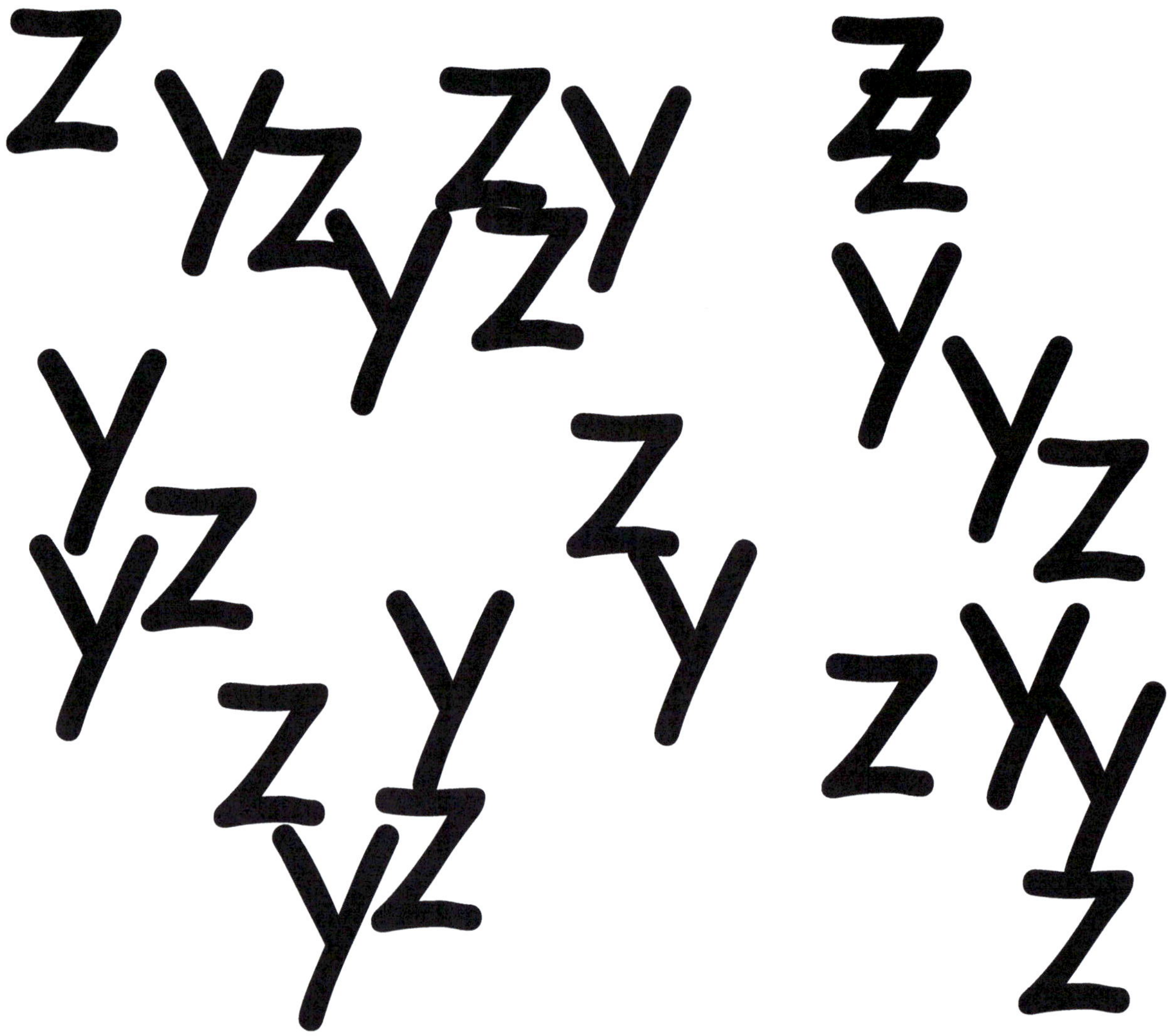

Spatial relations is the ability to perceive the position of objects in relation to ourselves and to each other. This skill helps children to understand relationships between symbols and letters. Children with poor spatial relations may find it difficult to write letters in the correct orientation, write consistently starting at the margin and write letters of the same size.

In the first part, ask the child to copy the sound spellings on the line underneath in exactly the same places as they appear above.
In the second part, ask the child to copy the words on the line underneath in exactly the same places, saying the matching sound as they write each sound spellings.
Break this task into a number of shorter tasks over a number of lessons if necessary.

Activity 18 Where am I? Set 7

y z

z y

yes zip

yet zap

Visual sequential memory is the ability to remember sequences of figures, symbols and shapes. Children with poor visual sequencing struggle to remember a sequence of letters and follow visual patterns. They may have difficulties writing a sequence of letters to form a word and a sequence of words to form a sentence.

Ask the child to look at the sound spellings in the yellow box for at least five seconds, covering the white box underneath. Then cover the yellow box so that the sound spellings cannot be seen and reveal the sequence of sound spellings in the white box below. Ask the child to remember the missing sound spelling and write it in the space.

Break this task into a number of shorter tasks over a number of lessons if necessary.

Activity 19 Remembering lots of sound spellings Set 7

y	z
___	z

z	y
z	___

y x
_ x

s z
s _

y z x
_ z x

s y z
s y _

Tracking is the ability to follow a sequence of symbols. The eyes need to focus on the symbols in order and not look randomly at the symbols on the page. This is an important skill for reading and writing where letters and words are written from left to right and the reader is required to work down a page from the top to the bottom.

Choose a target sound spelling for the child to find. Ask the child to look at the sound spellings, tracking from left to right and down the page.
When they find the target sound spelling the child indicates or puts a ring around it. Repeat with a different sound spelling.

Break this task into a number of shorter tasks over a number of lessons if necessary.

Activity 20 Tracking sound spellings Set 7

y z j y s z y j z s
j z s y j z y s y j

s y j z y z j y s z y j z
s z s y j z y s y j z j y
j y s z y j z j y s z y j

j z y z j y s z y j z s z s y j z s z
y j z s z y j y z j y s z y s z y j z
s z y j y z s z y j z s z j y s z y j

j z s z y j y z j y s z y s z y j z s
z y j y z s z y j z s z y z j y s z y
j z s z j z s z j y s z y j y j y z j

Having introduced the sounds and their corresponding sound spellings it is important that the child is given the opportunity to practise forming the sound spellings. As discussed in the introductory chapter, the child should be provided with lots of sensory and kinaesthetic experiences of forming the sound spellings in a variety of media as well as writing on conventional paper.

In this activity the child can practise forming the sound spellings by copying over the grey sound spellings which act as a guide. Encourage the child to say the sound at the same time as writing the sound spelling. The child can then practise writing the sound spellings within the boxes underneath which focuses the child on the spatial relationship between the sound spelling as it forms and the surrounding visual environment.

Activity 21 Writing sound spellings Set 7

y y y y y

y y y y y y y

y						

z z z z z

z z z z z z z

Blending is the ability to push sounds together to make a word and is a key skill in reading. Blending is a dynamic activity where the child actively pushes the sounds together and listens to the word forming.

Activity 22 'A place to read' prepares the child for blending sounds themselves as part of the process of learning to read. You will model the dynamic blending technique for the child who will then tell you what word they can hear forming. Refer to the full explanation of the 'A place to read' activity in the 'Working through the programme' section.

Segmenting, the ability to split words up into their component sounds in sequence, is a key skill in spelling. The child needs to isolate each sound and match a sound spelling to successfully spell a word.

Activity 28 'A place to listen' activity prepares the child for segmenting words as part of the process of learning to spell. Refer to the full explanation of the 'A place to listen' activity in the 'Working through the programme' section.

Below is a list of words to use for both activities. There are very few meaningful words which can be generated from the sounds studied in set 7. Use words from previous sets if required.

Activity 22 A place to read Set 7
Activity 28 A place to listen

yam yap yes yet

zag zap zig zip

This set of cards is made up of words containing the target sounds for set 7 Copy onto card and cut out. Practise dynamic blending for reading, as described in the 'Working through the programme' section, using these cards. Notice that the letters get gradually darker as the child works through the word, a visual signal that they are pushing together the sounds and preparing them to listen to the word forming. Model this process for the child if necessary.

Activity 23 Dynamic blending Set 7

yam	yes
yet	zag
zap	zig
zip	

Print out onto card and cut out.
Stack them with the biggest (the complete word) on the bottom and in decreasing size so that the smallest is on the top.
Make sure the left-hand edge of the cards are flush. Staple the cards together on the left-hand side.
When the child runs a finger over the cards the sound spellings flip up. Ask the child to say the sounds and match to the flips.

Flippies

Set 7

y	y	e	y	e	t
z	z	i	z	i	p
z	z	a	z	a	p

Read the clue on the left for the child.
Use the clue to work out what the answer word is.
Encourage the child to think about the sounds in the word and write a sound spelling for each sound in the boxes on the right, one by one.
The first one is done as an example for you.
Explain that they may not need to use all the boxes and so some are shaded in.
Break this task into a number of shorter tasks over a number of lessons if necessary.

Activity 30 Sound boxes Set 7

Clue	Sound boxes		
Dogs bark and ________.	y	a	p
Mum said that I ________ go to the party.			
My coat has no buttons but has a ________.			
Sam cannot go home ________ but can go later.			
The opposite of no.			

Support the child to read the words on the left one by one.
For each word support the child to work out what sounds are in the word and count them.
Then support the child to cross out any boxes that are not needed.
In each of the boxes in the middle, have the child write the sound spelling to match each sound.
In the last column the child writes how many sounds there are in the word.
Break this task into a number of shorter tasks over a number of lessons if necessary.

Activity 31 How many sounds? Set 7

Word	Sound spellings					How many sounds?
zap	z	a	p			3
yam						
yes						
am						
zip						
on						
yet						
zig						
zag						

During this activity the child will get the chance to slide sounds in and out of words, i.e. practise phoneme manipulation. Sounds will be swapped, added or taken away. Print the sound spellings on card and cut out.

Build a starting word from the prompt list, demonstrating dynamic blending as you move the sound spelling cards into place.

Repeat the word, running your finger along the cards so that it corresponds with the sounds within the word.

Ask the child to change the word to the next word on the prompt list. As you say the new word run your finger under the cards so that it corresponds with the sounds within the word and gives the child the chance to hear and see what is different.

The child can then swap the appropriate sound spelling cards.

Activity 33 Sound swap Set 7

Sound swap y z

List 1	List 2
yam	peg
yap	leg
zap	let
zip	yet
zig	yes
zag	

a	e	i
y	m	p
z	g	l
t	s	

Support the child to read the word in the first column. Then, referring to the second column, ask the child what sound they are going to take away.
Then ask the child to think about what word would be made if the sound in the second column was taken out of the word, in this case from the beginning of it.
Remind the child to think about the sounds, blend dynamically and listen to the word forming.
Have the child write out the new word on the line at the end, sounding out the word as they write each sound spelling.

Break this task into a number of shorter tasks over a number of lessons if necessary.

Activity 34 Read – Delete – Spell Set 6 & 7

Read	Read without this sound	Spell the new word
win	'w'	____________
yam	'y'	____________
Jan	'J'	____________
jam	'j'	____________
fox	'f'	____________

Support the child to read the word in the first column. Then, referring to the second column, ask the child to think about what word would be made if the sound in the second column was added in front of the word. Remind the child to think about the sounds, blend dynamically and listen to the word forming.
Have the child write out the new word on the line at the end, sounding out the word as they write each sound spelling.

Break this task into a number of shorter tasks over a number of lessons if necessary.

Activity 35 Read – Add – Spell Set 6 & 7

Read	Read with this sound at the beginning this sound at the beginning	Spell the new word
am	'j'	jam
in	'w'	__________
ox	'f'	__________
am	'y'	__________
ox	'b'	__________

This set of cards is made up of words containing the target sounds for set 7. Copy onto card and cut out. Practise dynamic blending for reading, as described in the 'Working through the programme' section, using this card. Model this process for the child if necessary.

Activity 37 Reading words with target sounds Set 7

yam	yap
yes	yet
zag	zap
zig	zip

This set of cards is made up of the high frequency words containing the target sounds for set 7. Copy onto card and cut out.
Practise dynamic blending for reading, as described in the 'Working through the programme' section, using this card. Model this process for the child if necessary.

Activity 38 Reading high frequency words Set 7

yes	

Starting at 'yes' have the child read each of the words as quickly as possible tracking along the line one by one until they get to 'zig'.
Support the child to read the words by giving information about sounds and supporting dynamic blending but do not supply the whole word.
Time how long it takes to read all the words and record the time at the bottom of the page.
Repeat at a later point, e.g. at the end of the lesson or the following day, and see if the child can beat their *own* previous time.

Activity 39 Reading race — Set 7

yes zip yet zap zig

1 _____ minutes ___ seconds
2 _____ minutes ___ seconds
3 _____ minutes ___ seconds

Visual discrimination is the ability to see differences between objects that are similar. Good visual discrimination helps keep us from getting confused when looking at shapes and forms in the environment. Children with poor visual discrimination may find it difficult to recognise letters, may confuse letters such as b and d and may find it difficult to identify mathematical symbols.

Ask the child to look at the word in the pink box then track along the row looking at the other words. The child indicates or puts a ring around the word that is the same as the one in the pink box.

Break this task into a number of shorter tasks over a number of lessons if necessary.

Activity 40 Spot the word Set 7

yet	yet	yes	get
zip	zig	zag	zip
yam	yam	jam	him
bad	dad	bad	bid
did	bib	bid	did

Visual memory is the ability to remember and identify a shape or picture that we have previously seen. Children with poor visual memory may struggle to remember pictures, figures, shapes, letters and numbers and may have difficulties with reading, writing and number work.

Ask the child to look at the word in the yellow box for at least five seconds, covering the white box underneath. Then cover the yellow box so that the letter cannot be seen and reveal the choice of words in the white box below. Ask the child to select the matching word from the white box.

Break this task into a number of shorter tasks over a number of lessons if necessary.

Activity 41 Remembering words Set 7

yes
yep yes

zap
zap zag

zip

zig zip

yam

jam yam

yet

yes yet yep

zag

zip zig zag

Form constancy is the ability to generalise forms and figures and identify them even if they are slightly different from that usually seen. This skill helps us distinguish differences in size, shape, and orientation or position. Children with poor form constancy may frequently reverse letters and numbers.

Ask the child to look at the word in the orange box then track along the row looking at the other words. The child indicates or puts a ring around the word that is the same as the one in the orange box.

Break this task into a number of shorter tasks over a number of lessons if necessary.

Activity 42 Which is the word? Set 7

yam	jam	yam	jab
yes	yet	yes	yap
zip	zip	zig	zap
yet	vet	yet	wet
zap	zap	zip	zag

Visual closure is the ability to identify an object, shape or symbol from a visually incomplete or disorganised presentation and to see where different parts of a whole fit together, i.e. to recognise something when seeing only part of it. This skill helps us understand things quickly because our visual system doesn't have to process every detail to recognise what we're seeing.

Ask the child to look at the large word and then at the choice of smaller words underneath. The child indicates or puts a ring around the word that is the same as the big word.

Break this task into a number of shorter tasks over a number of lessons if necessary.

Activity 43 Word splits — Set 7

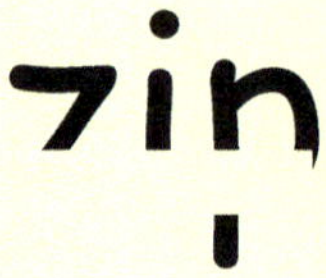

zap zip

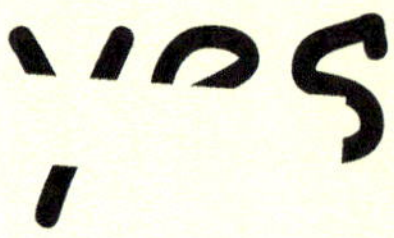

yes yet

yap yap

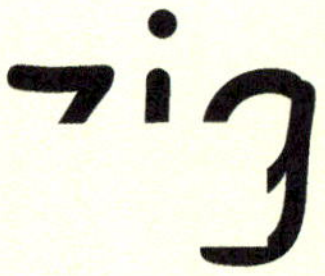

zip zig

Figure ground is the ability to find patterns or shapes when hidden within a busy background without getting confused by surrounding images. This skill keeps children from getting lost in the details, for example when looking at pictures in books or reading. Children with poor figure ground become easily confused with too much print on the page, affecting their concentration and attention.

Ask the child to look at the words, which are overlapping. Ask the child to first find all the words. Some words are written more than once. How many of each word are there?

Break this task into a number of shorter tasks over a number of lessons if necessary.

Activity 44 Busy words — Set 7

yap

zip yet

zig

zap yes zip yet

yet

zig zip yap

zap zag

yes

zip zap yap

yes

Visual sequential memory is the ability to remember sequences of figures, symbols and shapes. Children with poor visual sequencing struggle to remember a sequence of letters and follow visual patterns. They may have difficulties writing a sequence of letters to form a word and a sequence of words to form a sentence.

Ask the child to look at the words in the yellow box for at least five seconds, covering the white box underneath. Then cover the yellow box so that the words cannot be seen and reveal the sequence of words in the white box below. Ask the child to remember the missing word and write it in the space.

Break this task into a number of shorter tasks over a number of lessons if necessary.

Activity 45 Remembering lots of words — Set 7

yes zap
____ zap

zip yam
zip ____

zig zag	
____ zag	

yet yes	
yet ____	

yes	zip	yep
____	zip	yep

zag	zap	zig
zag	____	zig

Tracking is the ability to follow a sequence of letters, figures or symbols. The eyes need to focus on the symbols in order and not look randomly at the symbols on the page. This is an important skill for reading and writing where letters and words are written from left to right and the reader is required to work down a page from the top to the bottom.

Ask the child to look at the symbols and sound spellings and track from left to right. When the child finds a group of sound spellings then they indicate or put a circle around them all. The child then reads the word.

Break this task into a number of shorter tasks over a number of lessons if necessary.

Activity 46 Hidden words Set 7

◁↘↘yes→↔⇦▷▷zag⇦↙▽zip⇨→↘↗▽⇨
⇦yet⇦▷↙▽↘zig⇦▷↙⇨yam⇨↓⇦yep⇨↔

⇦↖⇦↗↙zig▷⇦⇨zag←↙▷↔zip↗▽⇦↘▽⇨
⇨↖←▷↕yes⇦▷↕▽↕↔yet▷↖←↕↗yap⇨⇦↕

ωσyamχϖνμασδφγyesηφκλπψθσμδσχπωyet
ρλαφπλωμεzipδμδφυ

γηκεzipδωκδσzapπωρωαyetφπλφωνyapλδφυτ
zipωφκρεyesεωφψ

Prior to working with the child, read through the instructions in the 'Working through the programme' section.

Activity 47 Word build Set 7

y	a	p	
y	e	s	
z	a	p	
z	i	p	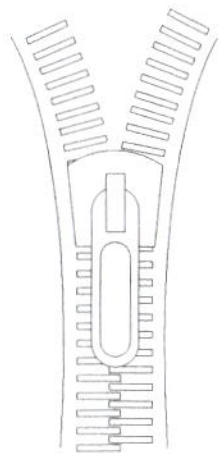

Support the child to look at the picture and work out what the word is.
Then support the child to work out the initial sound in the word and match a sound spelling in the gap provided.
The 'Place to listen' technique should be used to support this.
Read through the 'Place to listen' instructions in the 'Working through the programme' section of this book prior to working with the child.
Ask the child to read the completed word using the dynamic blending technique.

Activity 48 Finish the word 1 Set 6 & 7

_____ a m 

_____ e t 

_____ e s 

_____ u g 

_____ i p 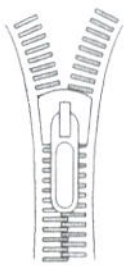

_____ e b 

_____ i x 

Support the child to look at the picture and work out what the word is.
Then support the child to work out the middle sound in the word and match a sound spelling in the gap provided.
The 'Place to listen' technique should be used to support this.
Read through the 'Place to listen' instructions in the 'Working through the programme' section of this book prior to working with the child.
Ask the child to read the completed word using the dynamic blending technique.

Activity 49 Finish the word 2 Set 6 & 7

z ____ p 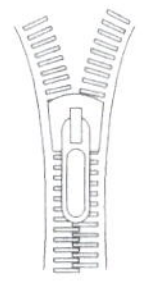

b ____ x 

z ____ p 

y ____ s 

f ____ x 

w ____ t 

y ____ p 

Support the child to look at the picture and work out what the word is.
Then support the child to work out the final sound in the word and match a sound spelling in the gap provided.
The 'Place to listen' technique should be used to support this.
Read through the 'Place to listen' instructions in the 'Working through the programme' section of this book prior to working with the child.
Ask the child to read the completed word using the dynamic blending technique.

Activity 50 Finish the word 3 — Set 6 & 7

y e ____

v a ____

w e ____

z i ____

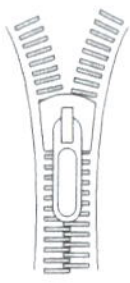

z a ____

j a ____

f o ____

Read the instructions in the introduction of this book to guide you on how to work through this spelling practise sheet with the child.

Activity 52 Spelling challenge — Set 7

yes	y e s	y e s	___ ___ ___	__________
yet	y e t	y e t	___ ___ ___	__________
zig	z i g	z i g	___ ___ ___	__________
zag	z a g	z a g	___ ___ ___	__________
zip	z i p	z i p	___ ___ ___	__________

Support the child to read the sentences. Have the child look at the pictures and find the picture that matches the sentence.
Have the child draw a line from the sentence to the matching picture.
Break this task into a number of shorter tasks over a number of lessons if necessary.

Activity 53 Read the sentence and match to a picture — Set 7

A sad fox; get the vet!

Yam jam - yuk!

Max did the zip on the bag.

The sun had yet to set.

The cat can not sit in the box.

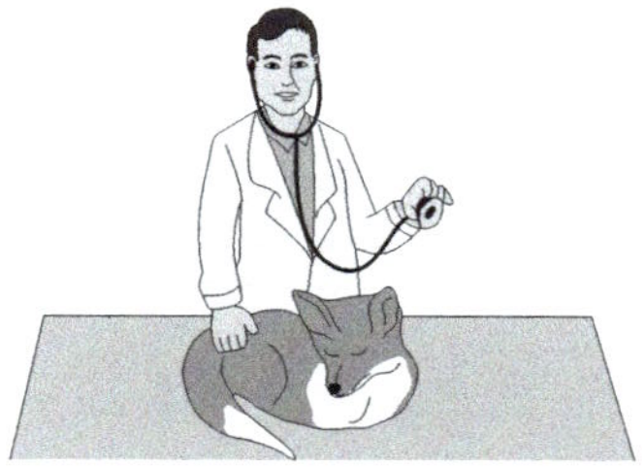

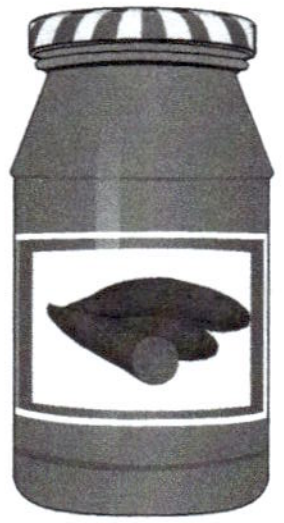

Support the child to read the sentence.
For each sentence, support the child to spot the spelling mistake.
Have the child underline or highlight the mistake and then write out the sentence correcting the mistake.
Encourage the child to say the sounds in each word at the same time as writing the sound spellings.
Break this task into a number of shorter tasks over a number of lessons if necessary.

Activity 54 Oops! Correct the spelling Set 7

1. Yam jam - zuk!

---

2. Max did the sip on the bag.

---

3. A dig can yap at the man.

---

4. The zun had yet to set.

---

5. The cat can not sit in the fox.

Support the child to read the sentences.
There is a missing word with a choice of two words to fill the gap.
For each sentence support the child to identify the missing word which makes sense in the sentence.
Have the child write the word on the line within the sentence.
Break this task into a number of shorter tasks over a number of lessons if necessary.

Activity 55 Spot the spelling Set 7

1. ___________, Max can run.
   Yet Yes

2. The bag had a big, red ___________.
   zip zap

3. Mum put yam in the pot; ___________!
   yuk yet

4. Did the mad rat get ___________?
   wet yet

5. Jon put a bug in the ___________.
   jug jog

6. Dad did not get in the ___________.
   van vet

Support the child to read each sentence.
Ask the child to re-read the sentence, several times if necessary, and try to remember it.
Cover the sentence and ask the child to recall it verbally from memory.
Once they can do this, ask the child to write out the sentence from memory.
The child might find it helpful to say the sounds as they write and say individual words once written.
When the sentence is complete, the child reads out their sentence and then compares it to the original.
Alternatively, using the text to speech function on a laptop or similar software, the child could type the sentence with the computer reading back each word and then the completed sentence.

Activity 56 Writing challenge — Set 7

Yes, Sam can get a hat.

Zip up a big bag.

Can Ben win a fun box?

Yam jam, yuk!

Answers Set 7: y z

Page 385
Activity 12 Spot the sound spelling

y 11

z 12

Page 390
Activity 17 Busy sound spellings

y 12

z 13

Page 399
Activity 30 Sound boxes

can
zip
yet
yes

Page 400
Activity 31 How many sounds?

yam	3	yes	3
am	2	zip	3
on	2	yet	3
zig	3	zag	3

Page 403
Activity 34 Read – Delete – Spell

in	am
an	am
ox	

Page 404
Activity 35 Read – Add – Spell

win
fox
yam
box

Page 413
Activity 44 Busy words

yes 3	yet 3
zap 3	zig 2
yap 3	zag 1
zip 4	

Page 418
Activity 48 Finish the word 1

yam	wet
yes	jug
zip	web
fix	

Page 419
Activity 49 Finish the word 2

zip	box
zap	yes
fix	wet
yap	

Page 420
Activity 50 Finish the word 3

yes	van
wet	zip
zap	jam
fox	

Page 423
Activity 54 Oops! Correct the spelling

yuk
zip
dog
sun
box

Page 424
Activity 55 Spot the spelling

Yes
zip
yuk
wet
jug
van

9781138488373